THE
ALEISTER
CROWLEY
COLLECTION

SIRIUS

SIRIUS

This edition published in 2024 by Sirius Publishing, a division of
Arcturus Publishing Limited,
26/27 Bickels Yard, 151–153 Bermondsey Street,
London SE1 3HA

ISBN: 978-1-3988-3617-4
AD011747UK

Printed in China

CONTENTS

THE BOOK OF THE LAW

INTRODUCTION

Born in 1875, Edward Alexander Crowley was an English occultist, writer, philosopher, and painter who also founded his own religious movement called Thelema. Guided by the esoteric occult and obsessed with spiritual psychology, Crowley created a belief system he thought was truly aligned with the reality of life, death, and human impulses. Despite being born to strict puritan parents, Crowley veered away from the Church at an early age when he went away to boarding school and discovered opportunities to fulfil his artistic and sexual desires.

In October 1895, Crowley adopted the name Aleister and began studying philosophy at the University of Cambridge. Soon after, his love of literature and poetry led him to change his course of study to English Literature – among his favourite writers were Percy Bysshe Shelley and Sir Richard Francis Burton. He took up mountaineering, a much-loved pastime which mirrored his love of the romantic ideas about adventure and would see him gain much recognition among fellow Alpine explorers. It was also at Cambridge that he discovered occultism and served his curiosity by reading books on the subject including A.E Waite's *The Book of Black Magic and of Pacts*. Crowley, himself, began practising magic at university and started a club encouraging his fellow students to join in. One night, Crowley held a gathering to curse a professor he disliked – the next morning, the professor is said to have fallen down a flight of stairs and broken his ankle.

In life, Crowley was a controversial figure whose libertine lifestyle and mysticism were considered too dark for Victorian and early twentieth-century Britain. At home and abroad, he was denounced for his beliefs by a Western society hugely guided by Christianity and a fear of the unknown. Crowley's commitment to exploring the esoteric and his pursuit of power and pleasure often resulted in unorthodox approaches that elicited disgust while also awarding him the notoriety he so desired.

Despite the opprobrium, there were many who felt drawn to the occult and Satanism. In fact, a great number of people found inspiration in Crowley's contribution to the new religious movement which had been growing since the late nineteenth century. Based on Eastern religions, the movement resulted in new schools of thought rooted in transcendentalism and the esoteric. Today, he is revered by many followers of the occult who see him much like a figurehead who

endured reproachment and yet produced valuable writings on the counterculture, and went on to inspire many twentieth-century artists such as David Bowie and Black Sabbath.

This collection seeks to show examples of why his work was particularly affecting. The three books included here include a work of poetry, one of fiction, and his most important magickal work. The fascinating part of the selection is how often the different mediums bleed into one. It is as though Crowley cannot help but infuse his writing with his magickal beliefs or his poetry with his fiction writing. So the poetry prose work *Clouds Without Water*, a title taken from a biblical verse, has him create the character of a puritanical clergyman, Rev. C. Verey, who introduces the work and then adds copious, increasingly outraged, notes to the end of the poem. This shows how well Crowley understood the bluster of "respectable" men of his time and his mockery is clear to see. He regularly added wit to his "wickedness".

He uses this verse from the Bible (Jude 1: 12-13) to gain his title: 'Clouds they are without water; carried about of winds; trees whose fruit withereth, without fruit, twice dead, plucked up by the roots; raging waves of the sea, foaming out their own shame; wandering stars, to whom is reserved the blackness of darkness forever.' The pious cleric that he uses to denounce the work is also following a literary technique he may have picked up from his travels in India. Classic works were often presented by so-called pious narrators who claim to be scandalised by what they have unleashed into the world and wish to be absolved from any guilt or sin in putting it forward for public consumption. The hypocrisy in such an approach is clear and it must have amused Crowley immensely to use it for himself in a ridiculing way.

The three works included here do not run in chronological order since the one that was written first of the three (*The Book of the Law*) appears last here. This work has great significance for followers of Thelema, the religion that Crowley founded. It is not too far a stretch to say that this is the main holy book of the belief system. It covers the key tenets of the religion and Crowley's intentions for the belief system he constructed. Crowley believed the text had been narrated to him by a non-human, spirit-like entity called Aiwass. Since its publication in 1909, many editions of the book have been published due to the various interpretations of the work.

The novel that we have selected for publication in this title is *Moonchild*. This is because the plot runs not dissimilarly to Crowley's own attempt to birth a 'moonchild'. There are other biographical similarities – the southern Italian setting brings to mind Crowley's Abbey of Thelema in Sicily. Several of his friends and enemies appear as thinly veiled characters and it is clear that he identifies himself with the character of Cyril Grey. This is not unusual for Crowley's writings as his novel *Diary of a Drug Fiend* shows. Crowley, being a drug fiend himself, was able to insert in several details drawn from his own life, making him a master of blurring the lines between reality and fiction.

His life could have been – and indeed has been – the subject for books and films. An accomplished mountaineer and explorer, he followed his interest in the occult with equal viguor, becoming the most notorious figure in British occult circles in his lifetime. That his name continues to attract and revile is testament to the importance of his legacy.

By the end of his life, Crowley had penned a vast array of poems, journals, novels, and mystical guides which he believed would guide humanity towards "paganism in a purer form". Despite being born into a wealthy family, he died in poverty in 1947 at the age of 72 from what many believe was heroin addiction. An enjoyable legend, gleefully told by those wanting to augment his reputation for magickal prowess, says that he cursed the doctor attending him in his final days due to his refusal to give him any more drugs. The doctor died in the bath the day after Crowley's death, with 'natural causes' recorded as the cause of death. Much like the legends surrounding the opening of ancient Egyptian tombs, this also, alas, relies more on the desire to believe than it does on evidence. However, there is no doubt that his legacy is alive and well in the public imagination, as much as it is in the work of occultists who continue to ponder his magickal writings.

Do what thou wilt shall be the whole of the Law.
Love is the law, love under will.
There is no law beyond Do what thou wilt.

The Law of Thelema

CLOUDS WITHOUT WATER

CLOUDS WITHOUT WATER

Clouds they are without water, carried about of winds; trees whose fruit withereth, without fruit, twice dead, plucked up by the roots; raging waves of the sea, foaming out their own shame; wandering stars, to whom is reserved the blackness of darkness for ever.

Jude 1:12-13.

CLOUDS WITHOUT WATER

PREFACE

BY THE REV D. C. VEREY

"Receiving in themselves that recompense of their error which was meet."

So wrote the great apostle nearly two thousand years ago; and surely in these latter days, when Satan seems visibly loosed upon earth, the words have a special and dreadful significance even for us who – thanks be to God for His unspeakable mercy! – are washed in the blood of the Lamb and freed from the chains of death – and of hell.

Surely this terrible history is a true Sign of the Times. We walk in the last days, and all the abominations spoken of by the apostle are freely practised in our midst. Nay! they are even the boast and the defence of that spectre of evil, Socialism.

The awful drama which the unhappy wretch who penned these horrible utterances has to unfold is alas! too common. Its study may be useful to us as showing the logical outcome of Atheism and Free Love.

For the former, death; for the latter, the death-in-life of a frightful, loathsome, shameful disease.

"Receiving in themselves that recompense of their error which was meet".

It may seem almost incredible to many of us, perhaps safely established in our comfortable cures, among a simple and God-fearing people, that any man should have been found to pen the disgusting blasphemies, the revolting obscenities, which defile these pages.

Nor can it be denied that a certain power of expression, even at times a certain felicity of phrasing – always, indeed, a profound dramatic feeling – is to be found in these poems. Alas! that we should be compelled to write the words! That an art essentially spiritual, an art dignified by the great names of Gascoigne Mackie, Christina Rossetti, Alfred Tennyson, George Herbert, should here be prostituted to such "ignoble use". Truly the corruption of the best is the lowest – *corruptio optimi pessima*. Nor can one gleam of Hope, even in the infinite mercy of our loving Father, tinge with gold the leprous gloom of our outlook.

These clouds without water have no silver lining.

The unhappy man need not have feared that the poor servants of God would claim him as repentant, though surely we would all have shed the last drop of our blood to bring him to the grace of God. Alas! it was not to be.

The devilish precautions of this human fiend excluded all such possibilities. He died as he had lived, no doubt. Alas! no doubt.

Where is now that spotted soul? There is but one appalling answer to the question. In the "place prepared for the devil and his angels"; for "he that believeth not is condemned *already*".

Not even in that modern evasion, the plea of insanity, can we find any hope. Nothing is clearer than that these wretched victims of Satan were in full possession of their faculties to the last moment.

Surely the maniacal violence of their unhallowed lust and hate is no ground for pity but for reprobation. When our blessed Lord was on earth He made no excuses for those who were possessed of devils. He took this simply as a fact – and He healed them.

It is only the shocking atheism and materialism of modern science that, in an insane endeavour to whittle away the miracles of our blessed Saviour, has sought to include "possession" in the category of disease.

Our Lord had no doubts as to the reality of demoniacal possession; why should we, His humble servants, truckle to the Christless cant of an atheistical profession?

The facts of this shocking case are familiar enough in the drawing-rooms of the West End.

Both the characters in the story were persons of considerable education and position.

On this account, and because a statement of the truth (however guarded) would have compromised persons of high rank, and was in any case too disgusting to publish in the press, the tragedy has not – one is glad to say in these days of yellow prurience – become matter for public comment.

But the wife of the man, driven to drink and prostitution by the inhuman cruelty of his mistress – this modern worse than Lucrezia Borgia or Mdme de Brinvilliers – and the fiancé of the girl betrayed and ruined by her machinations, still haunt the purlieus of the Strand, the one an unfortunate of the lowest order, the other a loafer and parasite upon the ghouls that traffic in human flesh and shame.

Thus we see evil reproducing itself, spreading like an incurable cancer throughout society from one germ of infidelity and unhallowed lust.

I may perhaps be blamed for publishing, even in this limited measure, such filthy and blasphemous orgies of human speech (save the mark) but I am firmly resolved (and I believe that I have the blessing of God on my work) to awake my fellow-workers in the great vineyard to the facts of modern existence.

Unblushing, the old Serpent rears its crest to the sky; unashamed, the Beast and the Scarlet Woman chant the blasphemous litanies of their fornication.

Surely the cup of their abominations is nigh full!

Surely we who await the Advent of our blessed Lord are emboldened to trust that this frenzy of wickedness is a sure sign of the last days; that He will shortly come – whose fan is in His

hand, wherewith He shall thoroughly purge His floor – and take us His saints – however failing and humble we may be – to be with Him in His glory for ever and ever, while those who have rejected Him burn in eternal torment, with wailing and gnashing of teeth, in that Lake of Fire and Brimstone from which – thank God! He in His infinite mercy hath delivered us.

But until that happy day we are bound to work on silently and strenuously in His service.

May the perusal of these atrocious words enlighten us as to the very present influence of Satan in this world – naked and unashamed.

May it show us the full horror of the Enemy with whom we are bound to fight; may it reveal his dispositions, so that under our great Captain we may again and again win the Victory.

It is my prayerful hope that He who turns evil to good may indeed use to His glory even this terrible and wicked book.

It has cost me much to read it; to meditate on it has been a terrible shame and trial; to issue it, much against my own poor human judgment, in obedience to His will, has been a still harder task; were it permitted me to ask a recompense, I would ask none but that of His divine blessing upon my fellow-labourers in His great field.

C. V.

CLOUDS WITHOUT WATER

THE MANUSCRIPT

I
Dieu libre et libertin, sacrifice et hommage;
De ma virginité recevez les louanges!
Votre empire triomphe sur mon pucelage,
Paradis de la boue, empire de la fange!
Dieu libre et libertin, sacrifice et hommage.

II
Chez vous les crimes infâmes ne sont que des blagues;
Chez vous, mon Dieu, les dieux ne sont que des idées.
Frappez votre esclave! Ah! le sang qui coule en vagues
La comblera de joie, éventrée et pâmée. Chez vous les crimes infâmes ne sont que des blagues.

III
Satyre se moquant des femmes légitimes,
La mort est une blague, et l'amour trop comique.
Vous êtes un dieu! pour vous les seules choses intimes,
Dieu qui m'a baisé tant! sont les choses cosmiques.
Satyre se moquant des femmes légitimes!

IV
Dieu qui m'a baisé tant! Baisez-moi donc encore!
Vous m'avez rendu mas chère virginité.
C'est pourquoi follement sous vous, ah! je me tords
Eros inconnu, masque illisible et doré!
Dieu qui m'a baisé tant! Baisez-moi donc encore!

V
Vous qui vous dressez sur l'abîme de l'enfer,
Vous dont les plumes gravissent le haut des cieux,
A moi la bouche d'or, a moi le v.. de fer!
A l'âme, au corps! je suis la déesse des dieux –
Et je me dresse sur l'abîme de l'enfer.

A

Quean of the
Quality being the
Quatorzains of a
Quietist

A TERZAIN

King of myself, I labour to espouse
An equal soul. Alas! how frail I find
The golden light within the gilded house.
Helpless and passionate, and weak of mind!
Lechers and lepers! – as all ivy cling,
Emasculate the healthy bole they haunt.
Eternity is pregnant; I shall sing
Now – by my power – a spirit grave and gaunt
Brilliant and selfish, hard and hot, to flaunt
Reared like a flame across the lampless west,
Until by love or laughter we enchaunt,
Compel ye to Kithairon's thorny crest –
Evoe! Iacche! consummatum est.

CLOUDS WITHOUT WATER

1
THE AUGUR

1

Look! Look! upon the tripod through the smoke
Of slain things kindled, and fine frankincense.
Look – deep beyond the phantoms these evoke
Are sightless halls where spirit stifles sense.
There do I open the old book of Fate
Wherein They[1] pictured my delight and me
Flushed with the dawn of rapture laureate
And leaping with the laughter of ecstacy.
Mine eyes grow aged with that hieroglyph
Of doom that I have sought: the fatal end.
That which is written is written, even if
Great Zeus himself – great Zeus! – were to befriend.
Even in the spring of the first floral kiss:
"No happy end the gods have given for this".

2

Save death alone! I see no happy end,
No happy end for this divine beginning.
Child! let us front a fate too ill to mend,
Take joy in suffering for the sake of sinning.
Ay! from your lips I pluck the purple seed
Of that pomegranate sleek Persephone
Tasted in hell; the irrevocable deed
I do, and it is done. Naught else could be
For us, the chosen of so severe a god
To act so high a tragedy, the elect
To suffer so, and so rejoice, the rod
And scourge of our own shame, the gilt and decked
Oxen that go to our own sacrifice
At our own consecrated shrine of vice.

3

Over the desert ocean of distress
We reach pale eager hands that quiver and bleed
With life of these our hearts that surge and stress
In agony of the meditated deed.
For in the little coppice by the gate
Wherein I drew you shy and sly, and kissed
Your lips, your hushed "I love you" smooth and straight
Sweeping to wrap us in the glittering mist
Of hell that holds us – even there I heard
The lacerating laugh of fate ring out,
The dog-faced god[2] pronounce the mantic word,
And saw the avengers gather round about
Our love. The Moirae neither break nor bend;
The Erinyes hunt us to no happy end.

4

Our love is like a glittering sabre bloodied
With lives of men; upsoared the sudden sun;
The choral heaven woke; the aethyr flooded
All space with joy that you and I were one.
But in the dark and splendid dens of death
Arose an echo of that jewelled song:
There swept a savour of polluted breath
From the lost souls, the unsubstantial throng
That tasted once a shadow of our glory
And turn them in the evil house to adore
The godhead of our sin, the tragic story
We have set ourselves to write, the sombre score
Our daggers carve with poesy sublime
Upon the roof tree of despair and crime!

5

As we read Love and Death in either's eyes,
We see the cool mild splendour of the dawn
Damned by some tragic throw of murderous dice
To slash like lightning over lea and lawn
Jagged and horrible across the curtain
Of heaven, writing ruin, ruin – we see
Our certain joy marred with a doubly certain
Soul-shattering anguish. – Bah! To you and me
Such loathing, such despair are little things.
We are afloat on the flood-tide of lust –
A lust more spiritual than life, that stings
Till death and hell dissolve i' the aftergust.
So? But the Gods avert their faces, bend
Their holy brows, and see – no happy end.

6

Thus shall men write upon our cenotaphs:
"Traitor and lecher! murderess and whore!"
The rat-faced god that lurks in heaven laughs;
There is rejoicing on the immortal shore.
The angels deem us hurled from the above,
Burnt out of bliss, blasted from sense and thought,
Barred from the beauties of celestial love
And branded with the annihilating Naught.
O! pallid triumph! empty victory!
When we sit smiling on the infernal thrones
Starred with our utmost gems of infamy,
Builded with tears, and cushioned with the groans
Of these the victims of our joys immense –
Child![3] I aspire to that bad eminence!

7

Hell hath no queen! But, o thou red mouth curving
In kisses that bring blood, shall I be alone?
What of the accomplice of these deeds unswerving?
Will not your dead hot kisses match mine own?
As here your ardours brand me bone and marrow
Biting like fire and poison in my veins,
Shall you not there still ply your nameless harrow.
Mingle a cup from those our common pains
To intoxicate us with an extreme pleasure
Keener than life's, more dolorous than death's
Till these infernal blisses pass the measure
Of heaven's imagined by the tremulous breaths
Of silly saints and silly sinners, swaying
From scraps of blasphemy to scraps of praying?

8

You love me? trite and idle word to darken
(With all its glow) the splendour of our sun!
No soul of heaven or hell may hearken
The unbearable device that we have done.
Nor may Justine[4] nor Borgia understand
Nor Messalina nor Maria guess
The infernal chorus swelling darkly grand
That echoed us our everlasting "Yes!"
Nor shall the Gods perceive to damn or praise
The deed that shakes their essence into dust,
Disrupts their dreams, divides their dreary days.
Supreme, abominable, rides our lust
Armed in the panoply of brazen youth
And strength, since, if we are Hell's, Hell's worm is Truth.

9

We are still young enough to take delight
In wickedness for wickedness' sole sake.
Eve did not fall because she knew aright
The fruit an apple, but the snake a snake.
Nor shall we sink among the foolish throng
That seek an end, but rise among the few
Who do the strong thing because they are strong
And care not why they do, so that they do.
Therefore we wear our dread iniquity
Even as an aureole therefore we attain
Measureless heights of nameless ecstasy,
Measureless depths of unimagined pain
Mingled in one initiating kiss
That those dissolve in the athanor of this.

10

We tread on earth in our divine disdain
And crush its blood out into purple wine,
Staining our feet with hot and amorous stain,
The foam involving all the sensual shrine
Of love whose godhead dwells upon your mouth
Wherein the kisses clustering overflow
With brimming ardour of the new sin's growth
Till round us all the poisonous blossoms blow,
And all the cruel things and hideous forms
Of night awake and revel in our revel,
While in us rage the devastating storms
Whose dam is Luxury and their sire the devil...
It is well seen, however things intend,
The Gods have given for this – no happy end.

CLOUDS WITHOUT WATER

11

Crown me with poppy and hibiscus! crown
These brows with nightshade, monkshood and vervain!
Let us anoint us with the unguents brown
That waft our wizard bodies to the plain
Where in the circle of unholy stones
The unconsecrated Sabbath[5] is at height;
Where the grim goat rattling his skulls and bones
Makes music that dissolves the dusk of night
Into a ruddy fervour from the abyss
Such as I see (when cunning can surprise
Our Argus foe and give us leave to kiss)
Within your deep, your damned, your darling eyes.
Ay! to the Sabbath where the crowned worm
Exults, with twisted yard and slime-cold sperm.

12

There gods descend; there devils rise. We dance,
Dance to the madness of the waning moon,
Write centuries of murder in a glance,
Chiliads of rape in one unearthly tune.
There is the sacrament of sin unveiled
And there the abortion of Demeter eaten,
The potion of black Dione distilled,
The measure of Pan by whirling women beaten.
These are but symbols, and our souls the truth;
These sacraments, and we the gods of them;
The sabbath incense curls to us to soothe
Our spleen, engarlands us, a diadem
For that unutterable deed that hurled
Us, flaming thunderbolts! against the world.

13

There needs not ask the obscure oracle
Whereto these dire imaginations tend.
We read this sigil[6] in the dust of Hell:
"The Gods have given for this no happy end."
What end should we desire, who grasp the gain
We have despoiled from everlasting time,
Who gather sunshine from the iciest rain
And turn the dullest prose to rhythm and rime?
Think you we cannot warm our hands and laugh
Even at the fire that scatheth adamant?
Think you we shall not knead the utmost chaff
Into a bread worth Heaven's high sacrament
And from the bitter dregs of Hell's own wine
Distil a liquor utterly divine?

14

Behold! I have said. The destiny obscure
Of this our deed obscure we shall not skry.
We know "no happy end!" – but we endure,
Abiding as the Pole Star in the sky.
You mix your life in mine – then soul in soul
We shoot forth, meteors, travelling on and on
Far beyond Space to some dark-glimmering goal
Where never sun or star hath risen or shone;
Where we shall be the evil light beyond time,
Beyond space, beyond thought, supreme in deathless pang;
Nor shall a sound invade that hall of crime,
Only the champing of the insatiate fang
Of the undying worm our love, fast wed
Unto – no happy end. Behold! I have said.

2
THE ALCHEMIST

1

Love is sore wounded by the dragon shame,
O maiden o'mine! its life in jets of blood
Languidly ebbs. I see the gathering flame
Aspire – expire. I see the evil flood
Of time roll even and steady over it,
Bearing our God to the accurst ravines;
Bearing our God to the abysmal pit
Whence never a God may rise. The wolfish queens[7]
Of earth have set their faces stern and sour
Against us; we are bidden to cease – to cease!
Ha! how eternity laughs down their hour,
Dragoons their malice with its dominant peace.
We are forbidden to love – as one who tries
At noontide to forbid the sun to rise.

2

There is an alchemy to heal the hurt
Done to our love by shame the dragon of ill
With his allies the fear, that wars begirt
With clouds, and that sad sceptic in the will
That sneaks within our citadel, that steals
The keys and opens stealthily the gates
When we are sleeping, when the dawn conceals
Its earliest glimmer and our blood abates
Awhile its tide! O mystic maiden o' mine,
Did I not warn you of the insulting foes?
Blind worms that writhe for envy, pious swine[8]
That gnash their teeth to espy the gold and rose
Out flaming like the dawn when kiss for kiss
Passed and for ever sealed our bale and bliss.

3

Behold! the elixir for the weeping wound!
Is it that wine that Avallaunius poured
From the Red Cup when fair Titania swooned
Before the wrath of her insulted lord?
Is it the purple essence that distilled
From Jesu's side beneath the invoking spear?
Or that pale vase that Proserpina filled
From wells of her sad garden, cold and clear
And something overbitter and oversweet?
Or in the rout of Dionysus did
Some Bassarid prophesy in her holy heat
On such a draught as I for you have hid
In this the Graal of mine enchaunted shrine
To pour for you, o mystic maiden o' mine?

4

Lola. The name is like the amorous call
Of some bright-bosomed bird in bowers of blue.
'Tis like the great moon-crested waterfall
With hammering hearst. 'Tis like the rain of dew
That quires to the angel stars. 'Tis like a bell
Rung by an holy anchoret to summon
Out of the labyrinths of heaven and hell
Some grave, majestic, and deep-breasted woman
To bring her naked body shining, shining
With flowers of heaven or flames of Phlegethon
Into his hermit cell, her love entwining
Into his life with spells that murmur on
Black words! For one thing be you sure the same
My wine is as the music of your name!

5

Maiden. Believe me, mystic maiden o' mine,
That title shall assure the throne of heaven
To you – the more so that your love divine
That maidenhood to me hath freely given?
Nor have I touched the ark with hands unholy,
Nor with unsaintly kisses soiled the shrine:
Nepenthe, amaranth, vervain, myrrh and moly
Are deathless blooms about our chaste design.
Not you resisting, but myself refraining,
Gives us the eternal spring, the elixir rare,
That mage and sage have sought, and uncomplaining
Never attained. We found it early where
The Gods find children.[9] Maiden o' mine, be sure
My wine shall be as pure as you are pure!

6

Sweet. O my sweet, if all the heavenly portion
Of nectar were in one blue ocean poured
Their fine quintessence were a vile abortion
Bitter and flat, foul, stagnant and abhorred
Should one compare it with the tiniest tithe
Of one soft glance your eyes on me might shed,
One gesture of your body limber and lithe,
One smile – the sudden white, the abiding red!
Then – should one slander you in idiot verse
By speaking of the subtle seven-fold sweetness
Your lips can answer me, all fate to amerce
In one mad kiss in all its mad completeness?
O Gods and Muses! give me grace for this
To match my wine for sweet with Lola's kiss.

7

Mine. 'Tis impossible, but so it is,
My mouth is Lola's and my Lola's mine
When in the trance, the death we call a kiss,
Earth is done down, and the immanent divine
Exists! Impossible! no mortal yet
Suffered such bliss from the all-envious gods;
Whence we may guess we are immortal, set
From the beginning over the periods
Of ages, set on thrones of jasper and pearl,
Wreathed with the lilies of Eternity,
While on our brow the starry clusters curl
Like flashes from the sunkissed jewelry,
Dew on the flowers our garlands. Ay! you are mine,
And mine as you are shall I pour the wine.

8

Now I have told you all the ingredients
That go to make the elixir for our shame.
Already make the fumes their spired ascents;
The bubbles burst in tiny jets of flame.
And you and I are half-intoxicated
(I hid the heart of madness in my verse)
Therewith, like Maenads ready to be mated
Before the Lord of bassara and thyrse.
Yea! we are lifted up! Crested Kithairon
Shakes his black mane of pines, and roars for prey.
Heave all his bristling flanks of barbèd iron!
Flesh they red hunger on the bleeding day,
O fangèd night! till from thy mother maw
We wrench the lion child of wonder and awe!

9

This wine is sovereign against all complaints.
This is the wine the great king-angels use
To inspire the souls of sinners and of saints
Unto the deeds that win the world or lose.
One drop of this raised Attis from the dead;
One drop of this, and slain Osiris stirs;
One drop of this; before young Horus fled
Thine hosts, Typhon! – this wine is mine and hers
Ye Gods that gave it! not in trickling gouts,
But from the very fountain whence 'tis drawn
Gushing in crystal jets and ruby spouts
From the authentic throne and shrine of dawn.
Drink it? Ay, so! and bathe therein – and swim
Out to the wide world's everlasting rim!

10

To drink one drop thereof is to be drunk.
The firm feet stagger, and the world spins round;
The fair speech stammers – nature's God hath sunk
Into some trivial place of the profound.
But he who is drunk thereon is wholly sane,
Being wholly mad; he moves with space-wide wings
Sees not a world – engulphed in the inane!
Nor needs a voice for speech, because he sings.
What then of them who are most drunk together
As you and I are, mystic maiden o' mine,
Beyond Dionysus and his tedious tether,
Beyond Kithairon and his topmost pine?
Why, even now I am drunk who scribble amiss
These lines, not thinking – save of your last kiss!

11[10]

So Lola! Lola! Lola! Lola! peals,
And Lola! Lola! Lola! Lola! echoes back,
Till Lola! Lola! Lola! Lola! reels
The world in a dance of woven white and black
Shimmering with clear gold greys as hell resounds
With Lola! Lola! Lola! and heaven responds
With Lola! Lola! Lola! Lola! – swounds
All light to clustered dazzling diamonds,
And Lola! Lola! Lola! Lola! rings
Ever and again on these inchaunted ears,
And Lola! Lola! Lola! Lola! swings
My soul across to those inchaunted spheres
Where Lola is God and priest and wafer and wine –
O Lola! Lola! mystic maiden o' mine!

12

I think the hurt is healed, for (by the law
That forms our being) you must suffer as I,
Hunger as I, rejoice as I, withdraw
Into the same far transcendental sky
Of this initiated rapture. Hurt
Of shame for me is past, beholding Gods
Only a little part of me, and dirt
Such as men fling and women paste, no odds.
Moreover, by the subtle and austere
Vintage we drain, albeit we drain the lees,
There is no headache for the morning drear,
No fluctuant in our tideless ecstasies –
Whereby, o maiden o' mine, the runic rime
Tells me we have ree'd the riddle of old Time.

13

Never, o never shall I call you bride!
Never, o never shall I draw you down
Unto my kisses by the dim bedside
Bathing my body in the choral crown,
Your comet hair! Nor smooth our shimmering skins
Each to the other and mount the sacred stair
Even from the lesser to the greater sins
Up to the throne where sits the royal and rare
Vision of Pan. O never shall I raise
This oriflamme,[11] and lead the hope forlorn
Up to the ruining bloody breach, to daze
Death's self with pangs too blissful to be borne.
No! dear my maid. A maiden as you be
You may be all your lily life, for me.

14

Alas! the appointed term is sternly set
Inviolable to this our colloquy.
For though you be afar, my Lola, yet
You have been with me, whispering to me.
I bow my head to write, and on the nape
O' th' neck I feel your lips. I raise my head
To dream – our mouth achieves its luscious rape –
I fall back – you are on me – I am dead.
Could it be better? For I surely know
That you will follow me adown the deep
When I lay pen and paper by, and go
Into the ardent avenues of sleep:–
There also will we drink the appeasing wine,
Lola, my Lola, mystic maiden o' mine!

CLOUDS WITHOUT WATER

3
HERMIT

1

Lonely, o life, art thou when circumstance
Occult or open keeps us twain apart!
Lamenting through the dreary day there dance
Anaemic thoughts; the bruised and bloodless heart
Beats as if tired of life, as I am tired
Who all these days have never seen your face,
Nor touched the body that my soul desired,
Nor have inhaled the perfume of the place
That you make sweet – black dogs of doubt and fear
Howl at my heels while care plies whip and spur,
Driving me down to the dull damned dead sphere
Where is no sight or sound or scent of Her
Our Lady Dian, but where hag and witch
Hecat bestrides her broom – the bestial bitch!

2

Like to a country in the interdict
Whose folk lack all the grace of eucharist,
My heart is; all the pangs its foes inflict
Are naught to this unutterable mist
Of absence. Where's the daily sacrament,
The glad devouring of your body and blood,
Sweet soul of Christ, my Lola? I am rent
Even as the demons from the face of God
When they would peer into beatitude.
I am barred from the incalculable bliss,
The unutterable chrism, the soul's food,
Of you, your gaze, your word, your touch, your kiss
O Gods, Fates, Fiends – whoever plays the Pope!
Lift up your curse – leave me not without hope!

3

My soul is like the savage upland plains
Of utmost wretchedness in Tartary.
No strength of sun, no fertilizing rains!
Only a bitter wind, intense and dry,
Cuts over them. Hardly the memory stands
Of one who travels there; his pain forgets
The golden bliss of all those other lands
Where he was happy. So the blizzard frets
Its sterile death across my soul, and chills
All hope of life even from the rare sad seeds
It blows from sunnier vales and happier hills,
Though at the best they be but worthless weeds.
I stand – I scan the infinite horizon
Of hopeless hope – yet I must travel on.

4

When for an hour we met (to call it meeting
Barred by the bleak ice of society
From even the lover's glance, the lover's greeting.
The intonation that means ecstasy!)
One ray of saddest gladness lit the dusk:
This – that I saw you pale and suffering,
A goddess armed with myrrh instead of musk,[12]
With lips too cold to pray, too dry to sing.
For by that sigh I knew the adorable
Truth, that you wept in secret over me.
Your silence was the dumb despair of hell;
Who read it right read love. Strange cruelty,
That who would die for you, sweet murderess,
Should find his comfort in your bitterness!

5

For there you sat, you smiled, you chatted on,
Myself alone perceiving the keen cold
Sword at your heart, the speechless malison
That trembled on your tongue, the while it trolled
Its senseless clamour of necessary wit,
And woke the senseless necessary laughter,
The senseless necessary reply to it,
The long sad silly commonplace thereafter.
Suppose we had risen, as quick as thought, and stood
And caught and kissed – what could the storm have done
Worse than this sickening fog of solitude?
Who can do worse than take away the sun?
They better had take care, I think. One day
We shall go mad, and take ourselves away.

6

Yet we may hope; for this, and not from fear,
We kept our counsel; we may hope anon
To turn the corner of the evil year
And find a brave new springtide coming on.
Meanwhile by stealth I may invoke your shade
And clasp you to me, though it be a dream
Or little more, a vision from the Maid[13]
That rules by Phlegethon's sepulchral stream.
Nay! it is more: by magic art compel
(My soul!) my maiden's body to appear
Visible, tangible, enjoyable
Even to the senses of the amorous seer,
Whose demon ministers through the gulphs and glooms
Convey his mistress on their meteor plumes.

7¹⁴

More, I will visit you, forlorn who lie
Crying for lack of me; your very flesh
Shall tingle with the touch of me as I
Wrap you about with the ensorcelled mesh
Of my fine body of fire: oh! you shall feel
My kisses on your mouth like living coals,
And piercing like an arrow of barbed steel
The arcane caress that shall unite our souls.
Till, when I see you next, I shall have doubt
Whether your pallor be from love distressed
Or from the exhaustion of the age-long bout
Of love you had of me upon your breast
Held hard all night, with mouths that never ceased
To engorge love's single sacramental feast.

8

One writes, and all is easy. Drop the pen,
And Paradise is blotted out! The earth,
Fair as it seemed, becomes a hideous den,
And all life's promises of little worth.
Like to a mother whose one child is dead,
I wander, aching for the sight, the sound.
The touch – familiar, now inhibited.
The child is under ground – is under ground –
The child is under ground – who comforts her?
The bastard fool her priest? The useless clod
Her husband? The accursed murderer
Her God? – if so be that she hath a God.
Foul curses from my life's envenomed flood
Break in a vomit of black foam and blood.

9

As one entranced by dint of cannabis,[15]
Whose sense of time is changed past recognition,
Whether he suffer woe or taste of bliss,
He loses both his reason and volition.
He says one word – what countless ages pass!
He walks across the room – a voyage as far
As the astronomer's who turns his glass
On faintest star-webs past the farthest star
And travels thither in the spirit. So
It seems impossible to me that ever
The sands of our ill luck should run so low
That splendidly success should match endeavour;
Yet it must be, and very soon must be:
For I believe in you, and you in me.

10

To-morrow is the day when Christ our Lord
Rose from the dead; therefore, the shops are shut.
Men may get drunk, or syphilized, or bored,
Robbed, murdered, or regenerated, – but!
But they must not get letters, be amused,
Or do a thing they want to do till Monday;
Whence comes the universally-diffused
And steady popularity of Sunday.
And yet I grumble! any other day
I might receive a message from my Lola:
"The siege is raised. Meet me as usual!" Nay!
For me the sofa and Verlaine or Zola,[16]
Till Christ's affair is over, and the town
Runs a young resurrection of its own.

11

Were you a shop-girl and myself a clerk,
Things might be better – we could surely meet
With due umbrellas in the dripping Park
And decorously spoon upon a seat.
This is the penalty one pays for rank
And fortune! Ah, my Lola, I am dying
And mad – or would God play me such a prank
As to dictate such verse while you are crying?
Let me too weep, weep on! weep out my soul,
Weep till the world of sense was wept away
And, dead, I reached you at the glimmering goal
Whither you had outrun me! Weep, I say,
Weep! It is better. Thus one earns a chrism –
Who ever gained one by cheap cynicism?

12

Wherefore I duly invoke the God
Of Tears that he may mingle yours and mine,
Water therewith Life's unresponsive sod,
And raise therefrom some sickly growth of vine
Whose grape shall yield a bitter draught of woe
Fit for the assuaging of a deadlier thirst
Than Attis knew or Abelard:[17] even so
I suffer; than some lovely nun accurst
Who beats her breast upon the convent bars,
Even so you suffer: let its draught restore
All lovers (that invoke the sad cold stars)
Unto good luck: then you and I once more
(Though still we were forbidden word and kiss)
Might find a certain happiness in this.

13

For truth it is, my maiden, we have had
Already more than our fair share of pleasure.
The good god Dionysus ivy-clad
Hath poured us out a draught of brimming measure.
Let us then rather give the lustiest praise
Our throats can sound than pray for further favour;
Even though our sorrow, eating up our days,
Devour us also. Gods enjoy the savour
Of Man's thanksgivings; from their holy place
Beholding mortals, they are wroth to see
Tears; they rejoice to see a proud glad face
Master of itself and of eternity.
Let us, reflecting on how dear we love,
Shew laughter and courage to the gods above!

14

Now then the fickle song hath changed and shifted
Round from the dirge to the primordial paean.
Lola! my Lola! let our voices lifted
Proclaim to all the Masters of the Aeon:
We love each other! let them meditate
Awhile on that glad cry, and you will see
How they consult, and smile, and hint to fate
That none can mar so holy a destiny.
We love each other! loud and glad; let heaven
And all the gods be deafened! Sing, O sing!
We love each other! through the storm-cloud riven
Let the wild anthem of our triumph ring!
Hark! the glad chorus as we drag the stars
In chains behind our mad colossal cars![18]

4
THE THAUMATURGE

1

Then the Lord answered me out of the wind,[19]
Out of the whirlwind did He answer me;
Gird up thy loins now like a man, and find
If thou canst answer like a man to Me!
Who art thou darkening counsel by thy word,
And in thine ignorance accusing Them
Who, ere thy prayer was formulated, heard
And crowned it with its passion's diadem?
Who is the Son of Man, that We should mind him?
Or visit the vain virgin of his pleasance?
Yet ever as we went We stood behind him
And compassed her with Our continual presence?
From the black whirlwind the most high God sayeth:
Why did ye doubt, o ye of little faith?

2

I answer Thee out of the utmost dust.
I am a worm, I abase myself, I cry
Against myself that I am found unjust
More than all they that dwell beneath the sky.
I do repent, I do lament, o Thou
Who hast watched over us and cared for us,
Beating i' the dust this consecrated brow,
And answer Thee in broken murmur thus,
That I am altogether base and vile,
That Thou art altogether good and great,
That Thou hast given the guerdon grace for guile
Even while I lifted up myself to Fate
And cursed Thee. And from me who scorned to pray
Thou hast rolled the sad sepulchral stone away.

3

On this wise: that by uttermost good Fortune
I met you walking out in London city,
Even when from Heaven I did not dare importune
Hardly to pass your house! The Gods took pity
They whirled us in a chariot of fire
About the highest heavens for many an age!
So Regent's Park may seem to hot desire;
So the archangel gets a cabman's wage;
So all the aeons that pass still leave one time
To take one's lunch at the appointed hour –
This is the difference between prose and rime
And this the great gulf fixed for leaf and flower.
The British public grunts and growls and grovels,
Swilling its hogwash of neurotic novels.

4

We knew enough to wake to choral rapture
All answering Nature: I will swear the sun
Came out; you saw the moulting trees recapture
Their plumage, and the green destroy the dun.
Nothing could jar; the British workman took
A kindly interest in our kind caresses;
The loafing nursemaid and the musing cook
Agreed with us entirely. Love impresses
Its seal upon the world; is skilled to wake
The sympathy of everything that lives.
Kindliness, flows, not venom, from the snake;
The trodden worm dies duly – but forgives
The cabman asked four shillings for the job,
And almost boggled at my glad ten bob![20]

5

Oh! it was rapture and madness once again
To turn our tears to kisses brimming over
The mouths that never were too wide and fain
For lover to hold intercourse with lover.
Ah! we were owls of dusk to doubt the light,
Bats to mistrust the Wolf's tail's[21] holy warning:
"Sorrow endureth maybe for a night,
But joy must surely cometh in the morning".
Joy, ay! what joy poured straight from the high treasure,
The inexhaustible treasure of delight
The gods have poured us, pouring overmeasure
Because we love with all our life and might.
Believe me, it is better than all prayers
To show the gods our love surpasses theirs!

6

Nay, even thus you could not credit Fate,
Even in my arms close cuddled as you lay
With hard-shut eyes and lips inebriate
With their own kisses all this happy day.
Nay, but blaspheming you put hope aside,
Bade me forget you, swore yourself a liar,
Smiled through the words because you knew you lied
Knew that – what waters can put out our fire?
So we amused ourselves with cunning brisk
Careful arrangements to forget each other.
You cut that love-curl from your neck at risk
Of comment – at the slightest – from your mother.
You gave it me – God forget me, dear girl,
When I forget to treasure up that curl!

7

Your loveliness should help me to forget you;
Your murmurous "I love you" like soft bees
Humming should help; although my kisses fret you,
They are intended but to give you ease,
And help you to forget me; then, the fixed
Ardent intentness of my cat-green eyes
Flecked with red fire is like a potion mixed
Straight out of Lethe, or divination lies.
If there be truth in augury, your lips
Fastened to mine should be a certain spell
To put your memory of me in eclipse:–
In short, if all be true that sages tell,
Two days of absence with roast beef and beer
Will cure me of you perfectly, my dear!

8

Why did you play with such ungracious folly?
Because our passion is too bitter-sweet?
Because the acute and maddening melancholy
Is stronger than the rapture when we meet?
Because you weep beyond your own control
Like to one wounded bleeding inwardly?
Because you are not the mistress of your soul
Mighty enough to master fate and me?
It cuts me to the heart to see the brine
Not falling from your bad bewitching eyes,
To feel you are weeping in the central shrine
Whose woes the peristyle may not surprise.
I want to treat you as a lover rather;
You make me lecture to you like a father!

9

Write in your heart, dear maid, that Hitherto
The Lord hath helped us. Give him duly praise
(As I have given Him for making you).
Pray not, ask not for wealth and length of days
Or even for wisdom, lest one day you find
That you are saddled with some thousand grooms
(You bear the case of Solomon in mind!)
All in frock-coats and helmeted (with plumes)
– A scarcely pleasant prospect! Just give thanks
O Lord, for what we have received, Amen!
And then if Jordan overflows his banks,
Our vines increase, and one seed turns to ten,
Keep on thanksgiving! Even if things go wrong,
Howls are less pleasant to the ear than song.

10

Keep on thanksgiving! We are tenfold blest
Beyond others, simply having found each other.
Were we to part for ever, breast from breast,
Now, even now, there would not be another
In all the earth that should not envy aright
With plenty cause our short-lived happiness.
No life can hold one half-an-hour's delight
Such as we had – this morning! Why then, bless,
Bless all that lives and moves and hath its being!
Bless all the Gods, without omitting one!
Bless all the company of heaven, agreeing
To veil their fires to our stupendous sun!
Bless all the lesser glories that excite
In the great gladness of our mother light!

11

How purely unexpected was the chance!
When things looked blackest, on a sudden, the sun!
Chance is another word for ignorance;
We do not know how all these things are done.
But what has happened once may happen again,
And "Hitherto the Lord hath helped us", dear!"
"History repeats itself" – which makes it plain
That "Evermore the Lord will help us." Fear
And sorrow are folly; you must sleep o' nights
(Try reading me!) and I can promise you
You will awake to more divine delights
Than ever in the world you guessed or knew.
Stick to it! One fine day you'll find on waking
Me in your arms, and – oh! your body aching!

12

This is an effort of prophetic skill
Not passing range of human calculation.
A woman gets exactly what she will
If she keeps willing it sans divagation.
To have me secretly and altogether
Yours is your will – unless your kisses lied.
Sooner or later we shall slip the tether
And all the world before us deep and wide
Gape like the abyss, through which we fall to find
Strange equilibrium without support,
Strange rapture without sense, and void of mind
Strange ecstasies that mock the name of thought.
Sooner or later, Lola! Circumstance
Bows before those who never miss a chance.

13

This is enough to make a donkey laugh!
I talk like a Dutch uncle; and you listen
Like a man reading his own epitaph.
But, really! Truly! How our glad eyes glisten!
How our hearts romp! Whatever we may say,
Have never a doubt, Lord, that it's all thanksgiving!
If Thou dost thus for people every day,
How very easy Thou must make a living!
We would be like Thee! if we had the power
We would fill all folk with supernal blisses,
Breed life's sweet briar to the full June flower
And on their praises feed our proper kisses.
For as you said "However kind the gods are,
We could be kinder yet I think the odds are".

14[22]

Let me take leave of you as heretofore
With solemn kiss and sacred reverence!
I love you better and I love you more
Daily, and whether you are hither or hence.
I adore you as I adore the holy ones
That do abide exalted in their shrine
Starry beyond mere splendour of stars and suns,
Drunken beyond mere Dionysian wine.
Thus do I hold you; thus I pray you hold
Me as a secret and a blessed chrism
That you have gained to adorn your house of gold
By some strange silent sacred exorcism.
You have said 'I love you' – sacraments are true –
I exchange the salutation. I love you.

5
THE BLACK MASS

1

Lord! on love's altar lies the sacrament.
O willing victim, eager to be slain,
Lusting to feel the knife, the life-veil rent,
Assumption energized by death! O fain
To feel the murderous ardour of the priest
Clutch at his throat, theurgic frenzy fly
About the initiates of the Paschal feast
And know it centred in the dim dead I
Loosed by the pang – even thus you know it is,
Even thus, when I invoke your harsh caress,
Put up my mouth to your immortal kiss,
Confess you for my lady and murderess –
In mine own life-blood I exult to float
Even as your white fangs fasten in my throat.

2

You stand away – to let your long lash curl
About this aching body, fiery rings
Of torture, o my hot enamoured girl
Whose passion rides me like a steed and stings.
Like to a wounded snake infuriated
With pain, you drive your reeking kisses home
Into my flesh, their poisonous frenzy mated
With this delirious anguish, bitter foam
Of storm on some innavigable sea.
Whip, whip me till I burn! Whip on! Whip on!
Is it not madness that you wake in me?
Is not this curse the devil's orison?
Ah, devil! devil! when you grip me and glare
Into mine eyes, and answer all the prayer!

CLOUDS WITHOUT WATER

3

A virgin with the lusts of Messaline,
A goat-soul in the body of a saint,
You writhe on me with cruel and epicene
Phrenzy and agony of acute restraint.
You ache – you burn – you dizzy me with blows –
You call me coward and eunuch, who say No.
Volcanic child! upon your masking snows
I will not raise my rod, that forth may flow
Torrents of blazing lava, that shall hiss
And roar, and ruin all the glad green world.
I like the attack of your seducing kiss,
The lashes of your love about me curled,
Better than slack delight and murmuring sigh –
Flowers by the road to sad satiety.

4

Spit in my face! I love you. Clench your fists
And beat me! Still, I love you. Let your eyes
Like fiery opals or mad amethysts
Curse me! I love you. Let your anger rise
And with your teeth tear bleeding bits of flesh
Out of my body – kill me if you can!
I love you. I will have you fair and fresh,
A maenad maiden maddening for a man.
Ay! you shall weary in the erotic craving!
I'll have you panting – aching to the marrow –
Exhausted, but a maiden (Lesbia raving:
"Catullus brings a song and not a sparrow")
Famished with love, fed full with love, your soul
Still on the threshold of the unenvied goal.

5

The goal of love is gotten not of these
White-blooded fools that haste and marry and tire.
They grasp and break their bubble ecstasies;
We know desire the secret of desire.
We have the wisdom of the saints of old
Who know that what divinely is begun
Glows from dawn's grey to noon's deliberate gold
Darkens to crimson – and day's race is run.
For us the glamour of the dawn suborning,
We escape the enervating heat of noon:
We hear Astarte for Adonis mourning,
And close our lover's calendar at June.
Ah, Lola! but we suffer. Hell's own worm
Aches less than this, and hath an earlier term.

6

You grind your tiny shoes into my face;
You roll upon the furs before the fire,
Smiting and cursing in the devil's race
Whose goal and prize is Unassuaged Desire.
You rub your naked body against mine:
You madden me by blows and bites and kisses;
You make me drunken with your stormy wine;
We swoon, we roll into unguessed abysses
Of torture and of bliss; we wake and yearn,
Doing violence on ourselves – anon we are slain,
Slain and reborn again to ache and burn:
Aeon on aeon thunders through our brain.
– At last you see, my maiden? Kiss me! Kiss!
There is no end – happy or not – to this!

7

There is a respite – we must part anon.
Short are the hours of sweetness: it is well.
Could such a bout of murder carry on
We should drink poison and awake in hell;
Or being but mortal, or nearly mortal, yield
Exhausted spirit to the clamant flesh;
The book of common love should be unsealed,
And we be caught within the common mesh
That catches common folk. O God! bite hard!
Smite down rebellious flesh with hideous pain!
Bite hard! Smite hard! By bruises scarred and marred
Love this exultant face! Again! Again!
O Lola! Lola! Lola! Kiss me, Kiss!
Nay – nay! Kiss not! I cannot bear the bliss.

8

You are a devil gloating on the pain
You suffer and I suffer; you laugh shrill
Over the pangs of those pale fools, the twain
Whom we deceive, whom we shall surely kill
Whispering a word of this. Ah! joy it is
That false to faith is all the honied pressing;
A traitor triumphs in each stolen kiss,
Caligula and Cressida caressing.
You love yourself for stealing me away
From the proud lovely wife; you love me more
That in my arms a prostitute you lay,
And to your troth-plight lover played the whore
When mouth to mouth we clung, and breath for breath
Exchanged the royal accolade of death.

CLOUDS WITHOUT WATER

9

I love you for your cruelty to them;
I love you for your cruelty to me;
I see their blood glittering a diadem
Upon your dazzling brows; my blood I see
Sucked deep into your body, curling round
Like fire in every artery and vein
Massed in your heart, colossal and profound.
I am mad for you to brand me with the stain
Of your own vice. Our souls, a murdering crew
Of itching Mullahs, wallow, dervish-drunk.
Love surges at the pang! Our poisonous dew
Of sweat and kisses blinds us. A mad monk
Kissing fanatically the cross that had
Devoured his vitals is not half as mad!

10

Ay! rub yourself, you big lascivious cat,
On the electric soft, the wanton fur!
Call upon Hera! You've a furious gnat
Worth any gadfly ever sent from her!
Call upon Aphrodite! she will send
No sparrows from her prudish Paphian home!
Call upon Artemis! She will not bend
To lift you from your seas of bitter foam!
Nay! wrap yourself and rub yourself in silk!
Drink of my blood, engorge my fruitless sperm!
For you were suckled on the poisonous milk
That betrays virgins to the deathless worm.
Are we not glad thereof? Kiss, Lola, kiss,
Comrade of mine in the uttermost abyss!

11

Follow Iacchus from the Indian vales!
Set him with song upon the milk-white ass!
Follow Iacchus while the sunset pales!
Revel it on the flower-enamelled grass
While the moon lasts; then plunge in trackless woods!
Slay beasts unheard-of and blaspheming kings![23]
Mingle in madness with strange sisterhoods!
Dare black Aornos with Daedalian wings!
All words! words! there's a hunger to express
The infinite pangs, the infinite mighty blisses
Stored in the house of rapture and distress
Whose key is one of our blood-tainted kisses
Whose fume arises from the accursed sod
Where we lie burning and blaspheming God.

12

So in this agony of enforcèd silence
The sober song breaks to a phrenzied scream;
The shattering brain admits the mad god's violence,
And wild things course as in an evil dream:
Devils and dancers, druid rites and dread,
Horrible symbols scarred across the sky,
Invisible terrors of the quick and dead,
Impossible phantoms in mad revelry
Conjoined in spinthriae of bestial form,
Human-faced toads, and serpent-headed women,
All lashed and slashed by the all-wandering storm
Caricature of all things holy and human –
– Such are the discords that absolve the strain
As this wild threnody dissolves the brain.

13

Forgive me, o my holy and happy maid,
Lola, sweet Lola, for the imagination
Of all things monstrous that your soul dismayed
Reads on the palimpsest of my elation.
Simple and sweet and chaste our love is ever,
And these its wild and mystic characters
That rage and storm in impotent endeavour
To unveil our glory to our worshippers.
Lola, dear Lola, mystic maiden o' mine,
Let us not mingle with the ribald rout
That throng our temple. Close, Palladian shrine,
With our reverberate glory rayed about!
Abide within – with me! Let silence sever
This velvet 'now' from that unclothed 'for ever'!

14

Though I adorn my thought with angel tresses
Or pluck its pallium from the demon-kings,
My spirit rests at ease in your caresses,
And cares not for the song, so that it sings.
Life is but one caress, one song of gladness,
One infinite pulse of love in tune with you;
One infinite pulse, upsoaring into madness,
Down sinking to content. O far and few
The stars that follow our lofty pilgrimage
Into the abyss of silence and delight
Beyond the glamour of the world, the age,
The illusions of the light and of the night.
Wherefore accept these meteor flames that dance
Pale coruscations to our brilliance!

CLOUDS WITHOUT WATER

6
THE ADEPT

1

Even as the holy Ra[24] that travelleth
Within his bark upon the firmament,
Looking with fire-keen eyes on life and death
In simple state and cardinal content:
Even as the holy hawk[25] that towers sublime
Into the great abyss, with icy gaze
Fronting the calm immensities of time
And making space to shudder; so I praise
With infinite contempt the joyous world
That I have figured in this brain of mine.
The sails of this life's argosy are furled;
The anchor drops in those abodes divine.
Master of self and God, freewill and Fate.
I am alone – at last – to meditate.

2

Wrapped in the wool of wizardry I sit;[26]
Mantled in mystery; the little things
That I have made through weariness of wit,
Stars, cells, and whorls, all wonder in their wings!
These Gods and men, these laws, these hieroglyphs
And sigils of my fancy seem to spire
In worship up mine everlasting cliffs
I built between my will and my desire.
They reach me not: I made a monstrous crowd,
Innumerable monuments of thought,
But none is equal; this high head is bowed
In vain to the wise God it would have wrought,
Had not – Who sitteth on the Holy Throne
Thereby must make himself to be alone.

3

See! to be God is to be lost to God.
That which I cling to is my proper essence;
Nor is there aught at any period
That may endure the horror of my presence.
I conjure up dim gods; how frail and thin!
How fast they slip from this appalling level!
This is the wage of the fellatrix[27] Sin
Drunk on the icy death-sperm of the Devil.
I were a maniac did I contemplate
The outward glory and the inward terror,
Sick with the hideous light myself create
From the dark certainty of gloom and error.
For I am that I am – behold! this 'I'
Hath nothing constant it may measure by.

4[28]

Should I take pleasure in the fond perfume
That curls about my altars? in the throats
That chant my glory in the decent gloom
Of lofty ministers? Shall the blood of goats
And bulls and men send up a fragrant steam
To me, who am? Shall shriek of pythoness
Or wail of augur move this dreadful dream
To some less melancholy consciousness?
I have created men, who made them gods
Of their own excrements, and worshipped them.
I cannot match these calculating clods
Who twist themselves a faecal diadem
From all the thorny thoughts that plague them most;
Break wind, and call upon the Holy Ghost.

5

Yet I abide; for who is Pan is all.
He hath no refuge in deceitful death.
What soul is immanent may never fall;
What soul is Breath can never fail of breath.
The pity and the terror and the yearning
 Of this my silence and my solitude
Are broken by the blazing and the burning
 Of this dread majesty, this million-hued
Brilliance that coruscates its jetted fire
 Into the infinite aether; this austere
 And noble countenance set fast in dire
And royal wrath, this awful face of fear
Before whose glance the ashen world grows grey,
 Crashes, and chaos crumbles all away.

6

As when the living eyes of man behold
The embalmed seductions of a queen of Khem
Wrapped with much spice and linen and red gold
 And guardian gods on every side of them;
 Yet inasmuch as life is life, they shrink,
 Shrivel and waste to ashes as men gaze:
So doth the world grow giddy at the brink
 Of these unfathomable eyes, that blaze
Swifter and deadlier than storms or snakes.
 Then – o what wonder, as I strain afar
The basilisk[29] flame! – what breathless wonder wakes
 That I behold unsinged a silver star!
 O joy! O terror! O! – O can it be
There is a thing that is, apart from me?

7

I travelled; so the star. We neared; we saw
Each other, knew each other; in your face
Mine equal self with majesty and awe
Abode; and thus we stayed for a great space.
What was the manner of our countenance?
I saw you seated, as a great lost God
With blasphemy exulting in your glance
And horror at your lips; my soul was shod
With glory, and your body bathed in glory,
So that from out the uttermost abyss
The very darkness churned itself to hoary
And phosphor foam of agony and bliss.
The authentic seal of our majestic might
Stamped on the light in light the light of light.

8

So presently, most solemnly and slowly,
Our fingers touched and caught; our lips reached forth
And with conscious purpose smote their holy
Lives into one, and loosed their common wrath.
Unto the ends of our dead universe
Their frenzy rolled; henceforth no prince or power
Should lift the sterile strength of that one curse
Even to bring one thought to birth one hour.
For now we knew; "it is a lonely thing
To sit supreme upon the single throne;"
But being come thus far, goes glittering:
"It is a lovely thing to be alone!"
Silence! Beware to speak the fatal word
That might inweave our two-ply with a third!

9

Wherefore again in sexless sanctity
The mighty lingam[30] rears its stilled sublime;
The mighty yoni[31] spreads its chastity
Against the assaulting gods of space and time.
Rather be Phaedra[32] than Semiramis!
I will deny you, though you doom to dare
To abdicate, and risk the spirit kiss
In the embraces of the wanton air.
Why should we cast our crowns to gods unborn?
Why yield our bleeding garlands till the hour
When to ourselves we seem a shame and scorn
And seek some craft to span a statelier power?
Not for a while evoke that sombre spell!
The present still exceeds the possible.

10

That is his truth that seems to sink supine
Into your bosom's bliss, the scented snare,
Killed by your kisses shuddering in his spine
And blinded in the bowers of your hair!
This is his truth, who seems to writhe and sob
Beneath the earthquake pangs of your caress,
Whose heart burns out in one volcanic throb,
Whose life is eaten up of nothingness.
This is his truth, and yours, that seem to be
Mere beauteous bodies gripped in epicene
And sterile passion, all unchastity
In being chaste, all chaste in our obscene
And sexless mouthings, that repugnant roll
Their bestial billows on the snow-pure soul.

11

This is our truth, that only Nothing is,[33]
And Nothing is an universe of Bliss;
That loves denote supernal ecstasies,
And saintship lurks in the colossal kiss.
Loves are the letters of the holy word
That contradicts the curse "Let Being be!"
Since all things, even one thing, are absurd;
And no thing is the utmost ecstasy.
Kisses induct the soft and solemn tune
That Israfel shall blow on Doomisday[34] –
Your silky eyes are blue as that pale moon
(For ere it dies it sickens into grey)
That witches see, whose eager violence
Aborts the gods of cosmic permanence.

12

The uninstructed and blaspheming man
Looks on the world and sees it void and base.
Let him endure its horror as he can!
There is no help for his unhappy case.
The love-taught magus, the hermaphrodite,
Knows how to woo the Mother,[35] and awake her;
Beholding, in the very self-same sight,
The self-illumined image of the Maker.
I love, and you are wise; our spirits dance
A merry measure to the music moving
In waves through that mirific brilliance.
Will you first tire of wit, or I of loving?
Tire? O thou sea of love, thy ripples run
Into themselves, to my serener sun!

13

For you I built this faery dome of words
And crowned it with the cross of my desire.
I circled it with songs of blessed birds
And cradled all in the celestial fire.
The stars enfold it; the eternal sun
And moon give light; nor clouds nor rain intrude;
Only the dews of Dionysus run
In this intoxicating solitude.
I have begemmed its marble flame of spires
With jewels from the bliss of God, and set
Chryselephantine columns curled like fires
Below each misty opal minaret.
Is there no window to the east? Behold
The eyes of Love, your love, the essential gold!

14

For me therein shall you erect a statue
Even as you know me with the mystic eyes
Hungrily, hungrily a-gazing at you,
Afeast upon our strange sad ecstasies.
Make me the aching mouth parched-up with blisses
The lips curled back, the breath desiring you,
The whole face fragrant with your full free kisses,
The soul thereof exhaling scented dew
Born in the utmost world where we in truth
Abide like Bacchus with a Bassarid
Drunk with our art, love, beauty, force and youth;
But place that head upon a pyramid
Of snaky lightnings, lest – but that shall be
Always a secret between you and me.

15

Or, an you will, evoke me as the Sphinx
With lion's claws, bull's breast, and eagle's wings!
You are my riddle, and the answer sinks
Below the deep essential base of things,
Rises above the utmost brim of thought
And bubbles over as impatient song.
Yet "We are one" is all, and all is naught;
And this one "one", and "all", and "naught"
The whole content of our imagining, [shall throng
The great arcanum in the adytum[36] hid
From men, and though we carve or kiss or sing,
The Sphinx is dumb, and blind the Pyramid.
– Now our affairs are ordered perfectly.
Give me your mouth, your mouth, and let us die!

7
THE VAMPIRE

1

Let me away! Then is it not enough
That you have won me to your wickedness?
That we have touched the strange and sexless love
Whose heart is death? That you and I express
The poison of a thousand evil flowers
And drain that cup of bitterness, my Lola?
That you have killed my safe and sunny hours –
A Venus to seduce Savonarola![37]
Why have you taken this most monstrous shape,
Imperious malison and hate flung after?
You clutch me like a gross lascivious ape,
And like a gloating devil's rings the laughter.
O sweet my maid, bethink yourself awhile!
Recall the glad kiss and the gentle smile!

2

Where are you? Who am I? O who am I?
Why do I lie and let you? I was strong –
I was so strong I might have bid you die
With one swift arrow from my quiver, song.
Now you are over me; you hold me here;
You grip my flesh till bleeding bruises start;
You threaten me with – can I name the fear?
I always knew you never had a heart.
God! who am I? My Lola, speak to me!
Tell me you love me; tell me – I am dazed
With something terrible and strange I see
Even in the mouth that kissed, the lips that praised.
You leer above me like a brooding fiend
Waiting to leap upon a babe unweaned.

3

Kiss me at least! We always were good friends –
Kiss me for old times' sake – Kiss me just once!
I know this ends – as every sweet thing ends!
But – say you are not angry! Ere you pounce,
Forgive me! You could make me glad to die,
I think, if you would only kill me kindly.
Just one swift razor-stroke – cut low! – and I
Would pass the portal happily and blindly.
Yes! I would like to think the fountain sprang
Straight from my throat and slaked your aching thirst,
Shot to your hot red heart one red hot pang,
Then left you cool and smiling as at first.
I give you freely my heart's agony.
But oh! oh! speak to me! do speak to me!

4

God! do not wait then! kill me now; have done!
Why do you watch me mute and immobile,
Sitting like death between me and the sun,
A sphinx with eyes of jade and jaws of steel?
Let me rise up to kneel to you and pray!
I hate this hell of agony supine.
You killed her yesterday; kill me to-day;
Let me not hang like Christ! Now snap my spine!
Surely you know the trick – when from your lips
I see a thin chill stream of stark black blood
Trickling, the stream of hate that glows and grips
My lesser life within its sickening flood.
Be pitiful, and end your cruelty!
Suck out the life of me, that I may die!

CLOUDS WITHOUT WATER

5

O brooding vampire,[38] why art thou arisen?
Why art thou so unquiet in the tomb?
Why has thy corpse burst brilliant out of prison?
Whence get the lips their blood, the cheeks their bloom?
Is there no garlic I may wear against thee?
No succour in the consecrated Host?
Nay, if thou slay not it is thou restraint thee.
I am the virgin, thou the Holy Ghost.
There is no comfort nor defence nor peace
From thee (and all thy malice) in the world:
Thou sittest through the aching centuries
Like the old serpent in his horror curled
Ready to strike home – and yet not striking
Till thou hast lipped the victim to thy liking!

6

Am I not beautiful? Your lithe mouth twitches
As if already you were glutted on
This fair firm flesh that fears you and yet itches
– You know it – for some master malison.
Perhaps you mean to let me go? Ah sweet!
How seven times sweet if you will let me go –
Oh! Oh! I want to worship at your feet.
Why do you stab me with a smiling "No"?
Say "no" at least – to see you sitting there
So dumb is madness – why then, let me go!
I will – and you sit quiet – did you dare?
To everything the answer still is "No!"
You coward! Coward! Coward! let me rise! –
I cannot bear the hunger in your eyes.

7

You are afraid of me – I see it now.
You know that if you loose me, never again
Will I be such a fool. I wonder how
I ever took this destiny of pain.
Loose me! You dare not. Take your eyes away!
You dare not. O you laugh! You trust your power
There you are wrong – but had you turned to-day
I would have murdered you within the hour.
Yes! you do well – you know the dreadful weight
Pale silence sheds, not Atlas could uplift.
You know the spell to conquer love and hate,
To win the world and win it at a gift.
You are afraid of that then – had you spoken
You fear the spell upon me had been broken!

8

Even that taunt has left you smiling still,
And silent still – and that is ten times worse.
Where is my will, my adamantine will?
Curse God and die? I can nor die nor curse.
Ah, but I can. The agony extends –
I am wrapt up all in an equal hell.
There is a point at which emotion ends.
I am come through to peace, though pain yet swell
Its paean in my every vein and nerve.
Try me, o God, convulse me to the marrow!
I am its element; I shall not swerve.
I am Apollo too; I loose one arrow
Swift enough, straight enough to conquer you.
O Sphinx! Gaze on! I can be silent too.

9

Now then the pressure and the pain increase,
And ever nearer grows the exulting rose
Your face; and like a Malay with his kriss[39]
That runs amok[40] your passion gleams and grows.
It shakes me to the soul: by that you are stilled;
You hold yourself together, like a man
Stabbed to the heart, who, knowing he is killed,
Lets his whole life out in his yataghan,[41]
And strikes one masterstroke. So now you breathe
Close on my face; you strip me of defence;
You sing in obscure words whose crowns enwreathe
My forehead with their viewless violence,
So that I lie, as at the appointed term,
Awaiting the foul kisses of the worm.

10

You close on me; by God, you breed in me!
My flesh corrupt is tingling with the kiss
Of myriads, like the innumerable sea
In waves of life that feeds its boundless bliss
On the eroded earth. These are your thoughts,
Your living thoughts that throng my stagnant veins!
Your jackals howl among the holy courts;
Your monster brood of devils in my brains
Laughs; oh! they feast on my decaying blood;
They gnaw the last sweet morsel from my bones. –
As on the parched-up earth there flames the flood
Of the monsoon, black dust and barren stones
Leap into green, so I whose epitaph
Your passion writes, awake to live – to laugh!

11

Even to the end of all must I resist.
New deaths, new births, each minute boiling over.
I can go on for ever, an you list –
Now, now! O no! I will not. O my love!
Spare me! Enough! Take pity! Mutely moans
Your mouth in little sobs and calls and cries
And catches of the breath, whose bliss atones
In once for all the long-drawn agonies.
Now that the pain swings over into pleasure,
Now that the union which is death is done,
The wine of bliss rolls out in brimming measure.
The moon is dead – all glory to the Sun!
Now, now! Oh no! Oh no! I penetrate –
I pierce. Enough. God! God! how Thou art great!

12

Then closer, closer. No! – then stop – think well
What is this wonder we awake. Now think
We are cast down to the abyss of hell
Or tremble upon heaven's dizzy brink –
Which? All's the same. Go on. No – what is this?
Why dally? To the hilt! Ah mine, ah mine!
Kiss me – I cannot kiss you – kiss me! Kiss!
Oh! God! Oh God! Forgive me; I am thine. –
Horses and chariots that champ and clang!
The roar of blazing cressets that environ
The form that fuses in the perfect pang.
A blast of air thorough the molten iron[42] –
One scream of light. Creating silence drops
Into that silence when creation – stops.

CLOUDS WITHOUT WATER

13
So – é finita la commedia.[43]
"And if the King like not the comedy"
(Twine in your hair the fallen gardenia!)
"Why then, belike he likes it not, pardie!"
What will the "King" – the British Public – say
When they perceive their sorrow was my fun,
Their Hecuba my mocking Brinvilliers?[44]
I neither know nor care. What we have done
We have done. Admit, though, you are rare and rich!
This palely-wandering knight has found a flame
Both merciless and beautiful, you witch![45]
You play the game, and frankly, as a game!
This is the hour of prattle – tell me true!
I have never met another such. Have you?

14
Yet all the comedy was tragedy.
I truly felt all that I farced to feel.
Because the wheel revolves, forsooth, shall we
Deny a top and bottom to the wheel?
I am the centre too, and stand apart.
I am the All, who made the All, in All[46]
Who am, being Naught. I am the bloodbright Heart.
Wreathed with the Snake, and chaos is their pall[47]
Thou art as I; this mystery is ours.
These blood-bought bastards[48] of futility
Can never know us, fair and free-born flowers.
So they may say – they will – of you and me:
"These poets never know green cheese from chalk:
"This is the sort of nonsense lovers talk."

8
THE INITIATION

1

Lola! now look me straight between the eyes.
Our fate is come upon us. Tell me now
Love still shall arbitrate our destinies,
And joy inform the swart Plutonic brow.
Behold! the doom foreseen, the doom embraced,
Fastens its fang; the gods of death and birth
Make friends to slay us, Pilate interlaced
With Herod in obscene and murderous mirth.
Lola! come close! confront them! Let us read
The book once sealed, now open to our gaze!
Avenge our love and vindicate our breed
With courage to the ending of the days.
Since fall we must, o arm ourselves aright,
Fall fighting in the forefront of the fight!

2

First; let us face the foemen, number them,
Measure their arms! Who smiteth us? We wove
In grove and garden many a diadem
Dewy with all the purity of love.
The Hermes of the orchard lets the string
Slip from his finger, and the arrow speeds
Striking our love beneath the flamy wing
So that the heart of heaven breaks and bleeds.
That poisoned shaft fed with corrupting germs
Hath stricken us to earth: the wound corrodes,
Breeding within us all its noisome worms,
All the black larvae of the accurst abodes:–
The virgin of our reed-shrill ecstasies
Raped by the stinking satyr of disease!

3[49]

I who have loved you – shall I love you now,
Your teeth dropt out, your fair flesh fallen away,
The Crown of Venus on your itching brow,
The coppery flush, the leprous scurf of grey?
The god that rots the living flesh of man
Fills up your mouth – one ulcer – with his groans
And all our blessings choke and turn to ban
The beast that gnaws the marrow of our bones.
Caught in corrupt caresses of disease,
Shall we dispute us with his fervour, fain
To woo with sores your turbid arteries
And kiss black ulcers in your spotted brain?
We married close, my Lola, with a kiss:–
Now for the lifelong lover, Syphilis!

4

Yea! but we love. We win. The body's curse
Is bitter, but he hath not won the whole.
There's more than life in this brave universe.
Death cannot touch the secret of the soul!
Nor shall we shrink, although this further pang
Strike through the liver with its fiery dart,
The hope – the horrid hope – whose gleaming fang
Now stirs, a serpent's, underneath your heart!
For lo! not vainly we invoked the god
That looseneth the girdle of a maid;
Even now draws nigh the dreadful period
That maketh all the mother-world afraid.
With rotten fruit your belly is grown big
– Thanks to the bastard god that cursed the fig![50]

5

Your swollen neck[51] is grown a swollen breast
Gushing with poisoned milk; your breath is caught
In quick sharp gasps; you get nor sleep nor rest,
The monster moving in you in his sport.
Surely a monster! some unnatural thing,
Some Minotaur of shame, no egg of pride
To hatch the miniature of love and spring
In your own image, subtly glorified.
White swan you were! not Zeus but Cerberus
Hath ravished you; you brood on harpy eggs –
Sweet sister! is the wine too sour for us
We have drunk deep – nay! nay! but to the dregs!
And all their bitterness is braver brew
Than the dull syrup of the pious crew.

6[52]

Still we can laugh at burgesses and churls
In our excess of agony and lust.
We pity these poor prudes, insipid girls
And tepid boys, these creatures of the dust.
We pity all these meal-mouthed montebanks
That prate of Jesus, ethics, faith and reason,
These jerry-built dyspeptics, stuccoed cranks,
Their lives one dreary plain, one moist dull season
Like their grey land. O costive crapulence!
They ache and strain within the water-closet
Of church and State, their shocked bleat of offence:
"This poet's life was such a failure". Was it?
Fools! our worst boredom was a loftier thrill
Than all you ever felt – or ever will.

7

If we are weary, it is flesh that faints.
We cannot bear such worlds of happiness.
Even in this torture that consumes and taints,
We writhe in bliss, one terrible caress
Of the great Gods of Hells. Ah! surely, dear,
Our way is wise, transcending human woe:
We are most happy and of great good cheer.
What do we know? It matters not. We know.
This is enough, that we have slain the Sphinx,
Worked out her wizardry, dissolved her doom;
And though her wine be death to him that drinks
We shall carouse for ever in the tomb.
We drank bull's blood;[53] and all our pangs immense
Are better than eupeptic innocence.

8

Ah! if flesh fails, may we not also fail?
May not the vulture liars gather round
Our death-beds, and drone out their dismal tale
With drawl and whine, the Galilean sound
Of snuffle and twang? May not their stinking souls
Interpret our last sighs as penitence
When we close up the coruscating scrolls
Of our life's joy, seal up the jar of sense
To broach the starry flagon – splendid spilth?
These creeping cravens shall be circumvented;
They shall not belch their flatulence and filth
On us, or tell the world that we repented.
Come, as we strained it, let us break the tether
In the last luxury – to die together!

9

Let Death steal softly through the gate of sleep
On tiptoe! win away the maiden life
On velvet pinions to his azure steep;
At ease, at peace, to woo her for a wife!
His white horse waiting quietly without
Let him push gently the delicious door
And take us. We have lived. How should we doubt
Or fear? we have lived well. For ever more
We must be well. The cypress[54] cannot daunt,
Nor the acacia[55] thrill; we are content
To wonder in the shadowy groves, to haunt
The dark delight of our own element;
Or – could we send a messenger – to tell
Our brothers of the happiness of Hell!

10

Are not the poppy-fields[56] one snowy flame?
Come, let us wander hand in hand therein,
Straining with joyous juice our lips of shame,
Draining their bitter draught of sterile sin!
Are not the eyes of sleep already dull,
The lashes drooping over their desire?
Are not the gods awaiting to annul
With Lethe the last flicker of the fire?
Ay, let us kiss, my darling; let us twitch
For the last time the flesh against the flesh,
Before the coming of the lovely witch
That shall excite our sleepy souls afresh,
Anointing us with subtle drugs and suave,
Fit for the grave, for love beyond the grave!

11

For the last time, my Lola! Still the name
Fills me with music, echoing afar
Faint, like the rapture of some ghostly flame
Rejoicing in some lone secreted star
Beyond the visible heaven. Come to me!
Come closer! Is not this as close as death?
Are we not one to all eternity
Jewelled with joy? Mix me your subtle breath
Into the words well-known and never worn,
Into the kiss well-kissed and never tired,
Into the love well-loved and not forlorn,
The love beyond all that ever was desired?
Ay! all the cloudy must of life is strained
To clearer liquor that our souls attained.

12

How the yahoos[57] will rage and rave about
Our sloughs! "Appalling double suicide!
'Orrible detiles!" In the world without
We never yet consented to abide.
What should we care, within this cave of bliss,
This ocean of content, wherein we dive
And play like dolphins, for the horrid hiss
Of blow-flies? Nay, they never were alive!
O the sweet sleep that fastens on these brows!
O the enchauntment of this dreamy god,
My mystic sister, my mellific spouse,
That shepherds us with his hermetic rod
Into the flowery folds of love and sleep
Where we have strayed – O never yet so deep!

CLOUDS WITHOUT WATER

13

Lola, dear Lola, how the stillness grows!
How drowsy is the world, that folds her wings
Over us, folding like a sunset rose
Her crimson raptures to the night of things!
How all the voices and the visions fail
As we pass through into the silent hall
Beyond the vapours and beyond the veil,
Beyond the Nothing as beyond the All!
Ah! then, our voice must also fail in this;
Our symbols are but shadows in the sun;
Love's self springs from the shadow of the kiss;
Our bliss! O, that was hardly half begun!
We fight the Fate as we have fought the foemen.
The poison takes us. – Χαίρετε νιχωμεν.[58]

14

Farewell! O passionate world of changeful hours!
Come, Lola, let us sleep! Elysian groves
Await us and the beatific bowers
Where Love is ours at last – as we were Love's.
Come, with our mouths still kissing, with our limbs
Still twined, relax the ecstasy! pass by
To the abyss of night where no star swims!
On to the end beyond the prophecy!
Ah Lola mine "No happy end is this" –
I love you – ah! you love me – you love me!
For we have passed beyond imagined bliss
Into the kingdom of reality,
Where we are crowned with flowers – yet closer creep!
Sleep, Lola, now! I love you – sleep – ah, sleep!

NOTES

THE AUGUR

1. **They**. – The Fates or Moirae.
2. **The dog-faced god**. – Anubis, the Threshold-Guardian of the 'Gods' of Egypt. Mantic means prophetic.
3. **Child**. – The unhappy girl was at this time but 17 years old.
4. **Justine**. – The virtuous but victimized heroine of the infamous novel of the Marquis de Sade.
5. **Sabbath**. – Consult Payne Knight: 'Essays on the worship of Priapus', Eliphas Levi: 'Dogme et rituel de la haute Magie' and others.
6. **Sigil**. – Sign-manual.

THE ALCHEMIST

7. **Wolfish queens**. – Thus these wicked wretches dare to speak of their kind and godly relations.
8. **Blind Worms – pious swine**. – The poor servants of God! Ah, well! we have our comfort in Him; like Our Blessed Lord, we can forgive. It is for our loving Lord to set His foot upon the necks of our enemies, and to cast them out into the blackness of darkness for ever.
9. This is quite unintelligible to me.
10. I think this is what is called Echolalia, a sure sign of 'degeneracy'; or, as I prefer to think, a wickedness which has gone, dreadful as it sounds to write, beyond the Infinite Mercy of God. "I will send them strong delusion."
11. **Oriflamme**. – How obscene is all this symbolism!

THE HERMIT

12. **Myrrh – Musk.** – The Perfumes of Sorrow and of Lust. Many prostitutes scent themselves strongly with musk, the better to allure their unhappy victims.
13. **Maid**. – Proserpine, or Hecate. I think the latter, as Proserpine became wife of Hades.
14. This disgusting sonnet seems to refer to the wicked magical practice of travelling by the astral double.

15.   **Cannabis**. – Indian hemp, a drug producing maniacal intoxication.
16.   **Verlaine! Zola!** – These are the vampires that suck out the virtue from our young people, the foreign corrupters of our purer manners!
17.   **Attis – Abelard**. – 'Thirst' here clearly means unhallowed lust, since Attis and Abelard were both mutilated persons.
18.   What mad megalomania!

THE THAUMATURGE

19.   Horrible blasphemy of this adaptation of Job to their vile purposes!
20.   **Ten bob**. – Vulgarity must always go with wickedness. Christ is not only a saving but a refining influence.
21.   **Wolf's tail.** – The Zodiacal Light, seen before dawn.
22.   I suppose that such mixture of ribaldry, blasphemy, vulgarity, and obscenity, as this series of sonnets has never been known. But worse is to follow!

THE BLACK MASS

23.   A reference to the Bacchae of Euripides.

THE ADEPT

24.   **Ra**. – The 'Sun-God'
25.   **Horus**. – The hawk, also a 'Sun-God'   z
26.   Apollonius of Tyana, the notorious pseudo-Christ, used to cover himself in wool in order to meditate.
27.   **Fellatrix**. – Only a Latin dictionary can unveil the loathsome horror of this filthy word.
28.   Impossible to comment on this shocking 'sin against the Holy Ghost' to compare the very Spirit or Breath of God to – Oh, Lord, how long?
29.   **Basilisk**. – a fabulous creature that slew all that it looked upon.
30.   **Lingam**. – The Hindu God(!) – the male organ of generation.
31.   **Yoni** – Its feminine equivalent. That the poor Hindus should worship these shameful things! And we? Oh how poor and inadequate is all our missionary effort! Let us send out more, and yet more, to our perishing brothers!
32.   Phaedra was repulsed by her son Hippolytus; Semiramis received the willing embraces of her son Ninus.

33. **Only Nothing is**. – There is much metaphysical nonsense culled from German Atheistic philosophy, in these poems. A wicked philosopher is far more dangerous than a mere voluptuary.

34. **Doomisday**. – An affected archaism for the day of Judgement. How can the writer dare to speak of this great day, on which he shall be damned for ever? "For he that believeth not is condemned already."

35. **Mother**. – Nature. How true would be these striking words, if only for "the love-taught magus, the hermaphrodite" with all its superstition, blasphemy, and obscenity, one were to write "The Christ-saved sinner, brought into the light"!

36. **The arcanum in the adytum**. – More classical affectation for "the secret thing in the holy place".

THE VAMPIRE

37. **Savonarola**. – An ascetic Florentine doctor.

38. For a good modern account of vampires and their habits, consult Mr Bram Stoker's Dracula

39. **Kriss**. – The Malayan dagger.

40. **Runs amok**. – Maddened by drink, these wretches run wildly through the streets, slaying all they meet until they themselves are slain. Only the gospel of Christ can save such.

41. **Yataghan**. – The Afghan sword.

42. The writer is evidently thinking of the "Bessemer converter".

43. "The comedy is finished".

44. A reference to Hamlet and the Players.

45. Reference to Keats' Belle Dame sans Merci.

46. Quoted from Arnold's Song Celestial.

47. Quoted from a magical Coptic papyrus.

48. **Blood-bought bastards** – Christians! O Saviour! what didst Thou come to save?

THE INITIATION

49. This shocking sonnet awakes pity and disgust in equal proportions. If even then they had only turned to the "Great Physician!" But no! "God hardened Pharaoh's heart".

50. Alas! no doubt that the reference is to our blessed Lord and Master. The barren fig-tree has been no doubt a stumbling-block to many weak souls. But the fig tree has here a deeper signification in its reference to certain loathsome forms of disease, and it is a symbol of lust. See Rosenbaum's "Plague of Lust"

51. **Swollen neck**. – A superstition of the ancients was that the neck swelled on the bridal night, and virginity was tested by the proportion of the skull and the neck. See Beverland "Draped Virginity".

52. Poor, poor deluded victims of Satan! If they only knew the holy joy of even the least of Jesu's lambs!

53. **Bull's blood**. – Supposed to be a poison by the ancients. Thus Themistocles is said to have died.

54. **Cypress** – Symbol of death.

55. **Acacia** – Symbol of resurrection.

56. **The poppy-fields**. – They killed themselves with laudanum.

57. **Yahoos**. – See Swift's Voyage to Laputa. It is to be feared that the mad Dean intended to satirize mankind, the race for which the Lord of Glory died!

58. Χαίρετε, νιχωμεν. Rejoice, we conquer. It is very extraordinary how Satan's blindness and fury possess them to the very end. Even as they died, maybe one fervent cry of repentance to the dear Saviour of all men would have been heard, and the gates of Paradise swung open as Satan, cheated of his prey, sank yelling into the Pit. But alas! there is no such word: nothing but a pagan Epicureanism even in the jaws of death.

A PRAYER

Merciful and loving Father, almighty God, grant unto us Thy humble servants and ministers a double portion of Thy Spirit that our eyes may be opened to the wickedness of them that love Thee not, that by Thy grace our ministrations may be used to bring them out of darkness into Light, by the virtue of our crucified Lord, risen and ascended, Thine only-begotten Son, in Whose name we ask this Thy blessing. For Jesus Christ's sake, Amen.

MOONCHILD

PROLOGUE

AUTHOR'S NOTE

This book was written in 1917, during such leisure as my efforts to bring America into the War on our side allowed me. Hence my illusions on the subject, and the sad showing of Simon Iff at the end. Need I add that, as the book itself demonstrates beyond all doubt, all persons and incidents are purely the figment of a disordered imagination?

London, 1929.

—Aleister Crowley

CHAPTER I

A CHINESE GOD

LONDON, in England, the capital city of the British Empire, is situated upon the banks of the Thames. It is not likely that these facts were unfamiliar to James Abbott McNeill Whistler, a Scottish gentleman born in America and resident in Paris but it is certain that he did not appreciate them. For he settled quietly down to discover a fact which no one had previously observed; namely, that it was very beautiful at night. The man was steeped in Highland fantasy, and he revealed London as Wrapt in a soft haze of mystic beauty, a fairy tale of delicacy and wistfulness.

It is here that the Fates showed partiality; for London should rather have been painted by Goya. The city is monstrous and misshapen; its mystery is not a brooding, but a conspiracy. And these truths are evident above all to one who recognises that London's heart is Charing Cross.

For the old Cross, which is, even technically, the centre of the city, is so in sober moral geography. The Strand roars toward Fleet Street, and so to Ludgate Hill, crowned by St. Paul's Cathedral; Whitehall sweeps down to Westminster Abbey and the Houses of Parliament. Trafalgar Square, which guards it at the third angle, saves it to some extent from the modern banalities of Piccadilly and Pall Mall, mere Georgian sham stucco, not even rivals to the historic grandeur of the great religious monuments, for Trafalgar really did make history; but it is to be observed that Nelson, on his monument, is careful to turn his gaze upon the Thames. For here is the true life of the city, the aorta of that great heart of which London and Westminster are the ventricles. Charing Cross Station, moreover, is the only true Metropolitan terminus. Euston, St. Pancras, and King's Cross merely convey one to the provinces, even, perhaps, to savage Scotland, as nude and barren today as in the time of Dr. Johnson; Victoria and Paddington seem to serve the vices of Brighton and Bournemouth in winter, Maidenhead and Henley in summer. Liverpool Street and Fenchurch Street are mere suburban sewers; Waterloo is the funereal antechamber to Woking; Great Central is a "notion" imported, name and all, from Broadway, by an enterprising kind of railway Barnum, named Yerkes; nobody ever goes there, except to golf at Sandy Lodge. If there are any other terminals in London, I forget them; clear proof of their insignificance.

But Charing Cross dates from before the Norman Conquest. Here Caesar scorned the advances of Boadicea, who had come to the station to meet him; and here St. Augustin uttered his famous mot, "*Non Angli, sed angeli*".

Stay: there is no need to exaggerate. Honestly, Charing Cross is the true link with Europe, and therefore with history. It understands its dignity and its destiny; the station officials never forget the story of King Alfred and the cakes, and are too wrapped in the cares of – who knows what? – to pay any attention to the necessities of would-be travellers. The speed of the trains is adjusted to that of the Roman Legions: three miles per hour. And they are always late, in honour of the immortal Fabius, "*qui cunctando restituit rem*".

This terminus is swathed in immemorial gloom; it was in one of the waiting-rooms that James Thomson conceived the idea for his City of Dreadful Night; but it is still the heart of London, throbbing with a clear longing towards Paris. A man who goes to Paris from Victoria will never reach Paris! He will find only the city of the *demi-mondaine* and the tourist.

It was not by appreciation of these facts, it was not even by instinct, that Lavinia King chose to arrive at Charing Cross. She was, in her peculiar, esoteric style, the most famous dancer in the world; and she was about to poise upon one exquisite toe in London, execute one blithe pirouette, and leap to Petersburg. No: her reason for alighting at Charing Cross was utterly unconnected with any one of the facts hitherto discussed; had you asked her, she would have replied with her unusual smile, insured for seventy-five thousand dollars, that it was convenient for the Savoy Hotel.

So, on that October night, when London almost shouted its pity and terror at the poet, she only opened the windows of her suite because it was unseasonably hot. It was nothing to her that they gave on to the historic Temple Gardens; nothing that London's favourite bridge for suicides loomed dark beside the lighted span of the railway.

She was merely bored with her friend and constant companion, Lisa la Giuffria, who had been celebrating her birthday for twenty-three hours without cessation as Big Ben tolled eleven.

Lisa was having her fortune told for the eighth time that day by a lady so stout and so iron-clad in corsets that any reliable authority on high explosives might have been tempted to hurl her into Temple Gardens, lest a worse thing come unto him, and so intoxicated that she was certainly worth her weight in grape-juice to any Temperance lecturer.

The name of this lady was Amy Brough, and she told the cards with resistless reiteration. "You'll certainly have thirteen birthday presents," she said, for the hundred and thirteenth time, "and that means a death in the family. Then there's a letter about a journey; and there's something about a dark man connected with a large building. He is very tall, and I think there's a journey coming to you – something about a letter. Yes; nine and three's twelve, and one's thirteen; you'll certainly have thirteen presents." "I've only had twelve," complained Lisa, who was tired, bored, and peevish. "Oh, forget it!" snapped Lavinia King from the window, "you've got an hour to go, anyhow!" "I see something about a large building," insisted Amy Brough, "I think it means Hasty News." "That's extraordinary!" cried Lisa, suddenly awake. "That's what Bunyip said my dream last night meant! That's absolutely wonderful! And to think there are people who don't believe in clairvoyance!"

From the depths of an armchair came a sigh of infinite sadness "Gimme a peach!" Harsh and hollow, the voice issued cavernously from a lantern-jawed American with blue cheeks. He was

incongruously clad in a Greek dress, with sandals. It is difficult to find a philosophical reason for disliking the combination of this costume with a pronounced Chicago accent. But one does. He was Lavinia's brother; he wore the costume as an advertisement; it was part of the family game. As he himself would explain in confidence, it made people think he was a fool, which enabled him to pick their pockets while they were preoccupied with this amiable delusion.

"Who said peaches?" observed a second sleeper, a young Jewish artist of uncannily clever powers of observation.

Lavinia King went from the window to the table. Four enormous silver bowls occupied it. Three contained the finest flowers to be bought in London, the tribute of the natives to her talent; the fourth was brimmed with peaches at four shillings a peach. She threw one apiece to her brother and the Knight of the Silver Point.

"I can't make out this Jack of Clubs," went on Amy Brough, "it's something about a large building!"

Blaustein, the artist, buried his face and his heavy curved spectacles in his peach.

"Yes, dearie," went on Amy, with a hiccough, "there's a journey about a letter. And nine and one's ten, and three's thirteen. You'll get another present, dearie, as sure as I'm sitting here."

"I really will?" asked Lisa, yawning.

"If I never take my hand off this table again!"

"Oh, cut it out!" cried Lavinia. "I'm going to bed!"

"If you go to bed on my birthday I'll never speak to you again!"

"Oh, can't we do something?" said Blaustein, who never did anything, anyhow, but draw.

"Sing something!" said Lavinia's brother, throwing away the peach-stone, and settling himself again to sleep. Big Ben struck the half hour. Big Ben is far too big to take any notice of anything terrestrial. A change of dynasty is nothing in his young life!

"Come in, for the land's sake!" cried Lavinia King. Her quick ear had caught a light knock upon the door.

She had hoped for something exciting, but it was only her private tame pianist, a cadaverous individual with the manners of an undertaker gone mad, the morals of a stool-pigeon, and imagining himself a bishop.

"I had to wish you many happy returns," he said to Lisa, when he had greeted the company in general, "and I wanted to introduce my friend, Cyril Grey."

Every one was amazed. They only then perceived that a second man had entered the room without being heard or seen. This individual was tall and thin, almost, as the pianist; but he had the peculiar quality of failing to attract attention. When they saw him, he acted in the most conventional way possible; a smile, and a bow, and a formal handshake, and the right word of greeting. But the moment that introductions were over, he apparently vanished! The conversation became general; Amy Brough went to sleep; Blaustein took his leave; Arnold King followed; the pianist rose for the same purpose and looked round for his friend. Only then did anyone observe that he was seated on the floor with crossed legs, perfectly indifferent to the company.

The effect of the discovery was hypnotic. From being nothing in the room, he became everything. Even Lavinia King, who had wearied of the world at thirty, and was now forty-three, saw that here was something new to her. She looked at that impassive face. The jaw was square, the planes of the face curiously flat. The mouth was small, a poppy-petal of vermilion, intensely sensuous. The nose was small and rounded, but fine, and the life of the face seemed concentrated in the nostrils. The eyes were tiny and oblique, with strange brows of defiance. A small tuft of irrepressible hair upon the forehead started up like a lone pine-tree on the slope of a mountain; for with this exception, the man was entirely bald; or, rather, clean-shaven, for the scalp was grey. The skull was extraordinarily narrow and long.

Again she looked at the eyes. They were parallel, focussed on infinity. The pupils were pin-points. It was clear to her that he saw nothing in the room. Her dancer's vanity came to her rescue; she moved in front of the still figure, and made a mock obeisance. She might have done the same to a stone image.

To her astonishment, she found the hand of Lisa on her shoulder. A look, half shocked, half pious, was in her friend's eyes. She found herself rudely pushed aside. Turning, she saw Lisa squatting on the floor opposite the visitor, with her eyes fixed upon his. He remained apparently quite unconscious of what was going on.

Lavinia King was flooded with a sudden causeless anger. She plucked her pianist by the arm, and drew him to the window-seat.

Rumour accused Lavinia of too close intimacy with the musician: and rumour does not always lie. She took advantage of the situation to caress him. Monet-Knott, for that was his name, took her action as a matter of course. Her passion satisfied alike his purse and his vanity; and, being without temperament – he was the curate type of ladies' man – he suited the dancer, who would have found a more masterful lover in her way. This creature could not even excite the jealousy of the wealthy automobile manufacturer who financed her.

But this night she could not concentrate her thoughts upon him; they wandered continually to the man on the floor. "Who is he?" she whispered, rather fiercely, "what did you say his name was?" "Cyril Grey," answered Monet-Knott, indifferently; "he's probably the greatest man in England, in his art." "And what's his art?" "Nobody knows," was the surprising reply, "he won't show anything. He's the one big mystery of London."

"I never heard such nonsense," retorted the dancer, angrily; "anyhow, I'm from Missouri!" The pianist stared. "I mean you've got to show me," she explained; "he looks to me like One Big Bluff!" Monet-Knott shrugged his shoulders; he did not care to pursue that topic.

Suddenly Big Ben struck midnight. It woke the room to normality. Cyril Grey unwound himself, like a snake after six months' sleep; but in a moment he was a normal suave gentleman, all smiles and bows again. He thanked Miss King for a very pleasant evening; he only tore himself away from a consideration of the lateness of the hour –

"Do come again!" said Lavinia sarcastically, "one doesn't often enjoy so delightful a conversation."

"My birthday's over," moaned Lisa from the floor, "and I haven't got my thirteenth present."

Amy Brough half woke up. "It's something to do with a large building," she began and broke off suddenly, abashed, she knew not why.

"I'm always in at tea-time," said Lisa suddenly to Cyril. He simpered over her hand. Before they realised it, he had bowed himself out of the room.

The three women looked at each other. Suddenly Lavinia King began to laugh. It was a harsh, unnatural performance: and for some reason her friend took it amiss. She went tempestuously into her bedroom, and banged the door behind her.

Lavinia, almost equally cross, went into the opposite room and called her maid. In half-an-hour she was asleep. In the morning she went in to see her friend. She found her lying on the bed, still dressed, her eyes red and haggard. She had not slept all night. Amy Brough on the contrary, was still asleep in the armchair. When she was roused, she only muttered: "something about a journey in a letter." Then she suddenly shook herself and went off without a word to her place of business in Bond Street. For she was the representative of one of the great Paris dressmaking houses.

Lavinia King never knew how it was managed; she never realised even that it had been managed; but that afternoon she found herself inextricably bound to her motor millionaire.

So Lisa was alone in the apartment. She sat upon the couch, with great eyes, black and lively, staring into eternity. Her black hair coiled upon her head, plait over plait; her dark skin glowed; her full mouth moved continually.

She was not surprised when the door opened without warning. Cyril Grey closed it behind him, with swift stealth. She was fascinated; she could not rise to greet him. He came over to her, caught her throat in both his hands, bent back her head, and, taking her lips in his teeth, bit them, bit them almost through. It was a single deliberate act: instantly he released her, sat down upon the couch by her, and made some trivial remark about the weather. She gazed at him in horror and amazement. He took no notice; he poured out a flood of small-talk – theatres, politics, literature, the latest news of art –

Ultimately she recovered herself enough to order tea when the maid knocked.

After tea – another ordeal of small-talk – she had made up her mind. Or, more accurately, she had become conscious of herself. She knew that she belonged to this man, body and soul. Every trace of shame departed; it was burnt out by the fire that consumed her. She gave him a thousand opportunities; she fought to turn his words to serious things. He baffled her with his shallow smile and ready tongue, that twisted all topics to triviality. By six o'clock she was morally on her knees before him; she was imploring him to stay to dinner with her. He refused. He was engaged to dine with a Miss Badger in Cheyne Walk; possibly he might telephone later, if he got away early. She begged him to excuse himself; he answered – serious for the first time – that he never broke his word.

At last he rose to go. She clung to him. He pretended mere embarrassment. She became a tigress; he pretended innocence, with that silly shallow smile.

He looked at his watch. Suddenly his manner changed, like a flash. "I'll telephone later, if I can," he said, with a sort of silky ferocity, and flung her from him violently on to the sofa.

He was gone. She lay upon the cushions, and sobbed her heart out.

The whole evening was a nightmare for her – and also for Lavinia King.

The pianist, who had looked in with the idea of dinner, was thrown out with objurgations. Why had he brought that cad, that brute, that fool? Amy Brough was caught by her fat wrists, and sat down to the cards; but the first time that she said "large building", was bundled bodily out of the apartment. Finally, Lavinia was astounded to have Lisa tell her that she would not come to see her dance – her only appearance that season in London! It was incredible. But when she had gone, thoroughly huffed, Lisa threw on her wraps to follow her; then changed her mind before she had gone halfway down the corridor.

Her evening was a tempest of indecisions. When Big Ben sounded eleven she was lying on the floor, collapsed. A moment later the telephone rang. It was Cyril Grey – of course – of course – how could it be any other?

"When are you likely to be in?" he was asking. She could imagine the faint hateful smile, as if she had known it all her life. "Never!" she answered, "I'm going to Paris the first train tomorrow." "Then I'd better come up now." The voice was nonchalant as death – or she would have hung up the receiver. "You can't come now; I'm undressed!" "Then when may I come?" It was terrible, this antimony of persistence with a stifled yawn! Her soul failed her. "When you will," she murmured. The receiver dropped from her hand; but she caught one word – the word "taxi".

In the morning, she awoke, almost a corpse. He had come, and he had gone – he had not spoken a single word, not even given a token that he would come again. She told her maid to pack for Paris: but she could not go. Instead, she fell ill. Hysteria became neurasthenia; yet she knew that a single word would cure her.

But no word came. Incidentally she heard that Cyril Grey was playing golf at Hoylake; she had a mad impulse to go to find him; another to kill herself.

But Lavinia King, perceiving after many days that something was wrong – after many days, for her thoughts rarely strayed beyond the contemplation of her own talents and amusements – carried her off to Paris. She needed her, anyhow, to play hostess.

But three days after their arrival Lisa received a postcard. It bore nothing but an address and a question-mark. No signature; she had never seen the handwriting; but she knew. She snatched up her hat, and her furs, and ran downstairs. Her car was at the door; in ten minutes she was knocking at the door of Cyril's studio.

He opened.

His arms were ready to receive her; but she was on the floor, kissing his feet.

"My Chinese God! My Chinese God!" she cried. "May I be permitted," observed Cyril, earnestly, "to present my friend and master, Mr. Simon Iff?"

Lisa looked up. She was in the presence of a man, very old, but very alert and active. She scrambled to her feet in confusion.

"I am not really the master," said the old man, cordially, "for our host is a Chinese God, as it appears. I am merely a student of Chinese Philosophy."

CHAPTER II
A PHILOSOPHICAL DISQUISITION

UPON THE NATURE OF THE SOUL

"THERE is little difference – barring our Occidental subtlety – between Chinese philosophy and English," observed Cyril Grey. "The Chinese bury a man alive in an ant heap; the English introduce him to a woman."

Lisa la Giuffria was startled into normality by the words. They were not spoken in jest.

And she began to take stock of her surroundings. Cyril Grey himself was radically changed. In fashionable London he had worn a claret-coloured suit, an enormous grey butterfly tie hiding a soft silk collar. In bohemian Paris his costume was diabolically clerical in its formality. A frock coat, tightly buttoned to the body, fell to the knees; its cut was as severe as it was distinguished; the trousers were of sober grey. A big black four-in-hand tie was fastened about a tall uncompromising collar by a cabochon sapphire so dark as to be hardly noticeable. A rimless monocle was fixed in his right eye. His manner had changed to parallel his dress. The supercilious air was gone; the smile was gone. He might have been a diplomatist at the crisis of an empire: he looked even more like a duellist.

The studio in which she stood was situated on the Boulevard Arago, below the Santé prison. It was reached from the road through an archway, which opened upon an oblong patch of garden. Across this, a row of studios nestled; and behind these again were other gardens, one to each studio, whose gates gave on to a tiny pathway. It was not only private – it was rural. One might have been ten miles from the city limits.

The studio itself was severely elegant – *simplex munditiis*; its walls were concealed by dull tapestries. In the centre of the room stood a square carved ebony table, matched by a sideboard in the west and a writing-desk in the east.

Four chairs with high Gothic backs stood about the table; in the north was a divan, covered with the pelt of a Polar bear. The floor was also furred, but with black bears from the Himalayas. On the table stood a Burmese dragon of dark green bronze. The smoke of incense issued from its mouth.

But Simon Iff was the strangest object in that strange room. She had heard of him, of course; he was known for his writings on mysticism and had long borne the reputation of a crank. But in the last few years he had chosen to use his abilities in ways intelligible to the average man; it was he who had saved Professor Briggs, and, incidentally, England when that genius had been accused of and condemned to death for murder, but was too preoccupied with the theory of his new flying-machine to notice that his fellows were about to hang him. And it was he who had solved a dozen other mysteries of crime, with apparently no other resource than pure capacity to analyse the minds of men. People had consequently begun to revise their opinions of him; they even began to read his books. But the man himself remained unspeakably mysterious. He had a habit of disappearing for long periods, and it was rumoured that he had the secret of the Elixir of Life. For although he was known to be over eighty years of age, his brightness and activity would have done credit to a man of forty; and the vitality of his whole being, the fire of his eyes, the quick conciseness of his mind, bore witness to an interior energy almost more than human.

He was a small man, dressed carelessly in a blue serge suit with a narrow dark red tie. His iron-grey hair was curly and irrepressible; his complexion, although wrinkled, was clear and healthy; his small mouth was a moving wreath of smiles; and his whole being radiated an intense and contagious happiness.

His greeting to Lisa had been more than cordial; at Cyril's remark he took her friendlily by the arm, and sat her down on the divan. "I'm sure you smoke," he said, "never mind Cyril! Try one of these; they come from the Khedive's own man."

He extracted an immense cigar-case from his pocket. One side was full of long Partagas, the other of cigarettes. "These are musk-scented the dark ones; the yellowish kind are ambergris; and the thin white ones are scented with attar of roses." Lisa hesitated; then she chose the ambergris. The old man laughed happily. "Just the right choice: the Middle Way! Now I know we are going to be friends." He lit her cigarette, and his own cigar. "I know what is in your mind, my dear young lady: you are thinking that two's company and three's none; and I agree; but we are going to put that right by asking Brother Cyril to study his Qabalah for a little; for before leaving him in the ant-heap – he has really a shocking turn of mind – I want a little chat with you. You see, you are one of Us now, my dear."

"I don't understand," uttered the girl, rather angrily, as Cyril obediently went to his desk, pulled a large square volume out of it, and became immediately engrossed.

"Brother Cyril has told me of your three interviews with him, and I am perfectly prepared to give a description of your mind. You are in rude health, and yet you are hysterical; you are fascinated and subdued by all things weird and unusual, though to the world you hold yourself so high, proud, and passionate. You need love, it is true; so much you know yourself; and you

know also that no common love attracts you; you need the sensational, the bizarre, the unique. But perhaps you do not understand what is at the root of that passion. I will tell you. You have an inexpressible hunger of the soul; you despise earth and its delusions; and you aspire unconsciously to a higher life than anything this planet can offer.

"I will tell you something that may convince you of my right to speak. You were born on October the eleventh; so Brother Cyril told me. But he did not tell me the hour; you never told him; it was a little before sunrise."

Lisa was taken aback; the mystic had guessed right.

"The Order to which I belong," pursued Simon Iff, "does not believe anything; it knows, or it doubts, as the case may be; and it seeks ever to increase human knowledge by the method of science, that is to say by observation and experiment. Therefore you must not expect me to satisfy your real craving by answering your questions as to the existence of the Soul; but I will tell you what I know, and can prove; further, what hypotheses seem worthy of consideration; lastly what experiments ought to be tried. For it is in this last matter that you can aid us; and with this in mind I have come up from St. Jean de Luz to see you."

Lisa's eyes danced with pleasure. "Do you know," she cried, "you are the first man that ever understood me?"

"Let me see whether I do understand you fully. I know very little of your life. You are half Italian, evidently; the other half probably Irish."

"Quite right."

"You come of peasant stock, but you were brought up in refined surroundings, and your nature developed on the best lines possible without check. You married early."

"Yes; but there was trouble. I divorced my husband, and married again two years later."

"That was the Marquis la Giuffria?"

"Yes."

"Well, then, you left him, although he was a good husband, and devoted to you, to throw in your lot with Lavinia King."

"I have lived with her for five years, almost to a month."

"Then why? I used to know her pretty well myself. She was, even in those days, heartless, and mercenary; she was a sponger, the worst type of courtesan; and she was an intolerable *poseuse*. Every word of hers must have disgusted you. Yet you stick to her closer than a brother."

"That's all true! But she's a sublime genius, the greatest artist the world has ever seen."

"She has a genius," distinguished Simon Iff. "Her dancing is a species of angelic possession, if I may coin a phrase. She comes off the stage from an interpretation of the subtlest and most spiritual music of Chopin or Tschaikowsky; and forthwith proceeds to scold, to wheedle, or to blackmail. Can you explain that reasonably by talking of 'two sides to her character'? It is nonsense to do so. The only analogy is that of a noble thinker and his stupid, dishonest, and immoral secretary. The dictation is taken down correctly, and given to the world. The last person to be enlightened by it is the secretary himself! So, I take it, is the case with all genius; only in many cases the man is in

more or less conscious harmony with his genius, and strives eternally to make himself a worthier instrument for his master's touch. The clever man, so-called, the man of talent, shuts out his genius by setting up his conscious will as a positive entity. The true man of genius deliberately subordinates himself, reduces himself to a negative, and allows his genius to play through him as It will. We all know how stupid we are when we try to do things. Seek to make any other muscle work as consistently as your heart does without your silly interference – you cannot keep it up for forty-eight hours. (I forget what the record is, but it's not much over twenty-four.) All this, which is truth ascertained and certain, lies at the base of the Taoistic doctrine of non-action; the plan of a doing everything by seeming to do nothing. Yield yourself utterly to the Will of Heaven, and you become the omnipotent instrument of that Will. Most systems of mysticism have a similar doctrine; but that it is true in action is only properly expressed by the Chinese. Nothing that any man can do will improve that genius; but the genius needs his mind, and he can broaden that mind, fertilise it with knowledge of all kinds, improve its powers of expression; supply the genius, in short, with an orchestra instead of a tin whistle. All our little great men, our one-poem poets, our one-picture painters, have merely failed to perfect themselves as instruments. The Genius who wrote *The Ancient Mariner* is no less sublime than he who wrote *The Tempest* ; but Coleridge had some incapacity to catch and express the thoughts of his genius – was ever such wooden stuff as his conscious work? – while Shakespeare had the knack of acquiring the knowledge necessary to the expression of every conceivable harmony, and his technique was sufficiently fluent to transcribe with ease. Thus we have two equal angels, one with a good secretary, the other with a bad one. I think this is the only explanation of genius – in the extreme case of Lavinia King it stands out as the one thing thinkable."

Lisa la Giuffria listened with constantly growing surprise and enthusiasm.

"I don't say," went on the mystic, "that the genius and his artist are not inseparably connected. It may be a little more closely than the horse and his rider. But there is at least a distinction to be drawn. And here is a point for you to consider: the genius appears to have all knowledge, all illumination, and to be limited merely by the powers of his medium's mind. Even this is not always a bar: how often do we see a writer gasp at his own work? 'I never knew that,' he cries, amazed, although only a minute previously he has written it down in plain English. In short, the genius appears to be a being of another plane, a soul of light and immortality! I know that much of this may be explained by supposing what I have called the genius to be a bodily substance in which the consciousness of the whole race (in his particular time) may become active under certain stimuli. There is much to be said for this view; language itself confirms it; for the words 'to know', *gnosis*, are merely sub-echoes of the first cries implying generation in the physical sense; for the root *GAN* means 'to know' only in the second place; its original sense is 'to beget.' Similarly 'spirit' only means 'breath'; 'divine' and most other words of identical purport imply no more than 'shining'. So it is one of the limitations of our minds that we are fettered by language to the crude ideas of our savage ancestors; and we ought to be free to investigate whether there may not be something in the evolution of language besides a monkey-trick of metaphysical abstractions; whether, in short, men have not been right to sophisticate primitive

ideas; whether the growth of language is not evidence of a true growth of knowledge; whether, when all is said and done, there may not be some valid evidence for the existence of a soul."

"The soul!" exclaimed Lisa, joyfully. "Oh, I believe in the soul!"

"Very improper!" rejoined the mystic; "Belief is the enemy of knowledge. Skeat tells us that Soul probably comes from *SU*, to beget."

"I wish you would speak simply to me, you lift me up, and throw me down again all the time."

"Only because you try to build without foundations. Now I am going to try to show you some good reasons for thinking that the soul exists, and is omniscient and immortal, other than that about genius which we have discussed already. I am not going to bore you with the arguments of Socrates, for, although, as a member of the Hemlock Club, which he founded, I perhaps ought not to say so, the *Phaedo* is a tissue of the silliest sophistry.

"But I am going to tell you one curious fact in medicine. In certain cases of dementia, where the mind has long been gone, and where subsequent examination has shown the brain to be definitely degenerated, there sometimes occur moments of complete lucidity, where the man is in possession of his full powers. If the mind depended absolutely on the physical condition of the brain, this would be difficult to explain.

"Science, too, is beginning to discover that in various abnormal circumstances, totally different personalities may chase each other through a single body. Do you know what is the great difficulty with regard to spiritualism? It is that of proving the identity of the dead man. In practice, since we have lost the sense of smell on which dogs, for instance, principally rely, we judge that a man is himself either by anthropometric methods, which have nothing to do with the mind or the personality, or by the sound of the voice, or by the handwriting, or by the contents of the mind. In the case of a dead man, only the last method is available. And here we are tossed on a dilemma. Either the 'spirit' says something which he is known to have known during his life, or something else. In the first case, somebody else must have known it, and may conceivably have informed the medium; in the second case, it is rather disproof than proof of the identity!

"Various plans have been proposed to avoid this difficulty; notably the device of the sealed letter to be opened a year after death. Any medium divulging the contents before that date receives the felicitations of her critics. So far no one has succeeded, though success would mean many thousands of pounds in the medium's pocket; but even if it happened, proof of survival would still be lacking. Clairvoyance, telepathy, guesswork – there are plenty of alternative explanations.

"Then there is the elaborate method of cross-correspondences: I won't bore you with that; Brother Cyril will have plenty of time to talk to you at Naples."

Lisa sat up with a shock. Despite her interest in the subject, her brain had tired. The last words galvanised her.

"I shall explain after lunch," continued the mystic, lighting a third Partaga; "meanwhile, I have wandered slightly from the subject, as you were too polite to remark. I was going to show

you how a soul with a weak hold on its tenant could be expelled by another; how, indeed, half-a-dozen personalities could take turns to live in one body. That they are real, independent souls is shown by the fact that not only do the contents of the mind differ – which might conceivably be a fake – but their handwritings, their voices, and that in ways which are quite beyond anything we know in the way of conscious simulation, or even possible simulation.

"These personalities are constant quantities; they depart and return unchanged. It is then sure that they do not exist merely by manifestation; they need no body for existence."

"You are coming back to the theory of possession, like the Gadarene swine," cried Lisa, delighted, she could hardly say why. Cyril Grey interrupted the conversation for the first time. He swung round in his armchair, and deliberately cleared his throat while he refixed his eyeglass.

"In these days," he observed, "when devils enter into swine, they do not rush violently down a steep place. They call themselves moral reformers, and vote the Prohibition ticket." He shut up with a snap, swung his chair round again, and returned to the study of his big square book.

"I hope you realise," remarked Simon Iff, "what you have let yourself in for."

Lisa blushed laughingly. "You have set me at my ease. I should certainly never know how to talk to him."

"Always talk," observed Cyril Grey, without looking up. "Words! Words! Words! It's an awful thing to be Hamlet when Ophelia takes after Polonius. She wants to know how to talk to me! And I want to teach her to be silent – even as the friend of Catullus turned his uncle into a statue of Harpocrates."

"Oh yes! I know Harpocrates, the Egyptian God of Silence," gushed the Irish-Italian girl.

Simon Iff gave her a significant glance, and she was wise enough to take it. There are subjects which it is better to drop.

"You know, Mr. Iff," said Lisa, to lighten the sudden tension, "I've been most fearfully interested in all you have said, and I think I have understood quite a part of it; but I don't see the practical application. Do you want me to get messages from the Mighty Dead?"

"Just at present," said the mystic, "I want you to digest what you have heard, and the *déjeuner* which Brother Cyril is about to offer us. After that we shall feel better able to cope with the problems of the Fourth Dimension."

"Dear me! And poor little Lisa has to do all that before she learns the reason of your leaving St. Jean de Luz?"

"All that, and the whole story of the Homunculus!"

"Whatever is that?"

"After lunch."

But as it turned out, it was a very long while before lunch. The bell of the studio rang brusquely.

Cyril Grey went to the door; and once again Lisa had the impression of a duellist. No: it was a sentinel that stood there. Her vivid power of visualisation put a spear in his hand.

It was his own studio, but he announced his visitors as if he had been a butler. "Akbar

Pasha and Countess Helena Mottich." Simon Iff sprang to the door. It was not his studio, but he welcomed the visitors with both hands outstretched.

"Since you have crossed our threshold," he cried, "I am sure you will stay to *déjeuner*." The visitors murmured a polite acceptance. Cyril Grey was frowning formidably. It was evident that he knew and detested his guests; that he feared their coming; that he suspected – who could say what? He acquiesced instantly in his master's words; yet if silence ever spoke, this was the moment when it beggared curses.

He had not given his hand to his guests. Simon Iff did so: but he did it in such a way that each of them was obliged to take a hand at the same moment as the other.

Lisa had risen from the divan. She could see that some intricacy was on foot, but could form no notion of its nature.

When the newcomers were seated, Lisa found that she was expected to regale them with the news of Paris. It was rather a relief to her to get away from the mystic's theories. The others left everything to her. She rattled off some details of Lavinia King's latest success. Then suddenly noticed that Cyril Grey had laid the table. For his eager cynical voice broke into the conversation. "I was there," he said, "I liked the first number: the Dying Grampus Phantasy in B flat was extraordinarily realistic. I didn't care so much for the 'Misadventures of a pat of butter' Sonata. But the Tschaikowsky symphony was best: that was Atmosphere; it put me right back among the old familiar scenes; I thought I was somewhere on the South-Eastern Railway waiting for a train."

Lisa flamed indignation. "She's the most wonderful dancer in the world." "Yes, she is that," said her lover, with affected heavy sadness. "Wonderful! My father used to say, too, that she used even to dance well when she was forty."

The nostrils of la Giuffria dilated. She understood that it was a monster that had carried her away; and she made ready for a last battle.

But Simon Iff announced the meal. "Pray you, be seated!" he said. "Unfortunately, today is a fast-day with us; we have but some salt fish with our bread and wine."

Lisa wondered what kind of a fast-day it might be: it was certainly not Friday. The Pasha made a wry face. "Ah!" said Iff, as if he had just remembered it, "but we have some Caviar." The Pasha refused coldly. "I do not really want *déjeuner*" he said. "I only came to ask whether you would care for a seance with the Countess."

"Delighted! Delighted!" cried Iff, and again Lisa understood that he was on the alert; that he sensed some deadly yet invisible peril; that he loathed the visitors, and yet would be careful to do every thing that they suggested. Already she had a sort of intuition of the nature of "the way of the Tao".

CHAPTER III

TELEKINESIS

BEING THE ART OF MOVING

OBJECTS AT A DISTANCE

T HE Countess Mottich was far more famous than most Prime Ministers or Imperial Chancellors. For, to the great bewilderment of many alleged men of science, she had the power of inducing small objects to move without apparent physical contact. Her first experiments had been with a purblind old person named Oudouwitz, who was in love with her in his senile way. Few people swallowed the published results of his experiments with her. If convinced they would have been very much startled. For she was supposed to be able to stop clocks at will, to open and close doors without approaching them – and other feats of the same general type. But she had sobered down since leaving the Professor – which she had done, just as soon as she had acquired enough money to get married to the man she wanted. Her power had left her instantly, strange to say; and many were the theories propounded connecting these circumstances. But her husband had displeased her; she had flown off in a rage – and her power had returned! But most of her sensational feats were relegated to the bad mad old days of wild and headstrong youth; at present she merely undertook to raise light small objects, such as tiny celluloid spheres, from the table, without touching them.

So Cyril explained, when Lisa asked "What does she do?"

(The Countess was supposed to know no English. She spoke it as well as anyone in the room, of course.)

"She moves things," he said; "manages to get hold of a couple of hairs when we're tired of looking at foolishness for hours together, twists them in her fingers, and, miracle of miracles! the ball rises in the air. This is everywhere considered by all rightly disposed people to be certain proof of the immortality of the soul."

"But doesn't she challenge you? Ask you to search her, and all that?"

"Oh yes! You've got the same chance as a deaf man has to detect a mistake in a Casals recital. If she can't get a hair, she'll pull a thread from her silk stockings or her dress; if you get people that are really too clever for her, then 'the force is very weak this afternoon,' though she keeps you longer than ever in the hope of tiring your attention, and perhaps to pay you out for baffling her!"

Grey said all this with an air of the most hideous boredom. It was evident that he hated the whole business. He was restless and anxious, too, with another part of his brain; Lisa could see that, but she dared not question him. So she went on the old track.

"Doesn't she get messages from the dead?"

"It's not done much now. It's too easy to fake, and the monied fools lost interest, as a class. This new game tickles the vanity of some of the sham scientific people, like Lombroso; they think they'll make a reputation like Newton out of it. They don't know enough science to criticise the business on sensible lines. Oh, really, I prefer your fat friend with the large building and the letter about a journey!"

"You mean that the whole thing is absolute fraud?"

"Can't say. Hard to prove a negative, or to affirm a universal proposition. But the onus of proof is on the spiritualists, and there are only two cases worth considering, Mrs. Piper, who never did anything very striking, anyhow, and Eusapia Palladino."

"She was exposed in America some time ago," said the girl, "but I think it was only in the Hearst newspapers."

"Hearst is the American Northcliffe," explained Cyril for the benefit of the Pasha. "And so is Northcliffe," he added musingly and unblushingly!

"I'm afraid I don't know who Northcliffe is," said Akbar.

"Northcliffe was Harmsworth." Cyril's voice was caressing, like one soothing a fractious child.

"But who was Harmsworth?" asked the Turk.

The young magician spoke in a hollow tone: "Nobody."

"Nobody?" cried Akbar. "I don't understand!"

Cyril shook his head solemnly and sadly. "There ain't no such person."

Akbar Pasha looked at Grey as if he were a ghost. It was a horrible trick of the boy's. He would invite confidence by a sensible, even possibly a bright, remark; then, in an explanatory way, he would lead his interlocutor, with exquisite skill, through quaking sands of various forms of insanity, only to drop them at the end into the bog of dementia. The dialogue suddenly realised itself as a nightmare. To Cyril it was probably the one genuine pleasure of conversation. He went on, in a brisk professional manner, with a suave persuasive smile: "I am trying to affirm the metaphysical dogma enunciated by Schelling in his philosophy of the relative, emphasising in particular the lemma that the acceptation of the objective as real involves the conception of the individual as a tabula rasa, thus correlating Occidental theories of the Absolute with the Buddhist doctrine of Sakyaditthi! But confer in rebuttal the Vagasaneyi-Samhita-Upanishad!" He turned brusquely to Lisa with the finality of one who has explained everything to the satisfaction of everybody. "Yes, you do right to speak in defence of Eusapia Palladino; we will investigate her when we reach Naples."

"You seem determined that I should go to Naples."

"Nothing to do with me: the master's orders. He'll explain, by-and-by. Now let's prove that this lady, whose locks are bushy and black as a raven's, has no hairs concealed upon her person!"

"I hate you when you're cynical and sarcastic."

"Love me, love my dog!" –

Simon Iff arrested his attention with an imperious gesture.

"Come into the garden, Maud," said Cyril suddenly; "For the black bat, Night, hath flown." He took her by the arm.

"Girl," he said, when they were among the flowers with his long arms about her, and a passionate kiss still flaming through every nerve of both their bodies, "I can't explain now, but you're in the most deadly danger from these people. And we simply can't get rid of them. Trust us, and wait! Till they're gone, keep away from them: make any excuse you like, if it's necessary; sham a hysterical attack and bolt if the worst comes to the worst – but don't let either of them manage to scratch you! It might be your death."

His evident earnestness did more than convince her. It reassured her on her whole position. She realised that he loved her, that his manner was merely an ornament, an affectation like his shaved head and his strange dress. And her own love for him, freed from all doubt, rushed out as does the sun from behind the crest of some cold pyramid of rock and ice, in mountain lands.

When they returned to the studio, they found that the simple preparations for the seance had been completed. The medium was already seated at the table, with the two men one on either side of her. Before her, between her hands, were some small spheres of celluloid, a couple of pencil-ends, and various other small objects. These had been "examined" with the utmost care, as who should examine the tail of a dog to find out whether he would bite. The history of spiritualism is that of blocking up every crack in a room with putty, and then leaving the door wide open.

It may well be doubted whether even the most tedious writer could describe a seance with success. People generally have an idea that there is something exciting and mysterious about it. In reality, people who boast of their ability to enjoy their third consecutive sleepless night have been known to pray to their Maker for sudden death at least two hours before the occurrence of the first "phenomenon". To be asked to keep the attention unceasingly on things of not the slightest intrinsic interest or importance is absolutely maddening to anyone above the mental level of a limpet.

"Observe how advantageously we are placed," whispered Cyril to Lisa as they took seats on the divan, toward which the table had been drawn. "For all we know, one or both those men are in collusion with Mottich. I'd stake my life Simple Simon isn't; but I wouldn't expect my own twin brother to take my word for it, in a matter like this. Then the curtains have been drawn; why? To help the force along. Yet it is supposed to be kinetic force; and we cannot even imagine how light could interfere with it. Otherwise, it is that the light 'distresses the medium in her peculiar state'. Just as the policeman's bull's-eye distresses the burglar in his peculiar state! Now look here! These arguments about 'evidential' phenomena always resolve themselves into questions of the conditions prevailing at the time; but the jest is that it always turns out that the argument is about conjuring tricks, not about 'forces' at all."

"Won't she mind us talking?"

"Mediums alway's encourage the sitters to talk. The moment she sees us getting interested in what we are saying, she takes the opportunity to do the dangerous, delicate part of the trick; then she calls our attention, says we must watch her very carefully to see that the control is good and no cheating possible, because she feels the force coming very strong. Everybody disguises himself as a cat at a mousehole – which you can keep up, after long training, for about three minutes; then the attention slackens slightly again, and she pulls off the dear old miracle. Listen!"

Simon Iff was engaged in a violent controversy with the Pasha as to the disposition of the six legs at their end of the table. On the accurate solution of this problem, knotty in more than one sense, depended the question as to whether the medium could have kicked the table and made one of the balls jump. If it were proved that it was impossible, the question would properly arise as to whether a ball had jumped, anyhow.

"Isn't it the dullest thing on earth?" droned Cyril. But, even without what he had said in the garden, she would have known that he was lying. For all his nonchalance, he was watching very acutely; for all his bored, faded voice, she could feel every tone tingling with suppressed excitement. It was certainly not the seance that interested him; but what was it?

The medium began to moan. She complained of cold; she began to twist her body about; she dropped her head suddenly on the table in collapse. Nobody took any particular notice; it was all part of the performance. "Give me your hands!" she said to Lisa, "I feel you are so sympathetic." As a matter of fact, the girl's natural warmth of heart had stirred her for a moment. She reached her hands out. But Simon Iff rose from the table and caught them. "You may have a hair or a loose thread," he said sharply. "Lights up, please, Cyril!"

The old mystic proceeded to make a careful examination of Lisa's hands. But Cyril watching him, divined an ulterior purpose. "I say," he drawled, "I'm afraid I was in the garden when you examined the Countess. Oughtn't I to look at her hands if this is to be evidential?" Simon Iff's smile showed him that he was on the right track. He took the medium's hands, and inspected them minutely. Of course he found no hairs; he was not looking for them. "Do you know," he said, "I think we ought to file off these nails. There's such a lot of room for hairs and things."

The Pasha immediately protested. "I don't think we ought to interfere with a lady's manicuring," he said indignantly. "Surely we can trust our eyes!"

Cyril Grey had beaten links in the Open Championship; but he only murmured: "I'm so sorry, Pasha; I can't trust mine. I'm threatened with tobacco amblyopia."

The imbecility of the remark, as intended, came near to upset the Turk's temper.

"I've always agreed with Berkeley," he went on, completely changing the plane of the conversation, while maintaining its original subject, "that our eyes bear no witness to anything external. I am afraid I'm only wasting your time, because I don't believe anything I see, in any case."

The Turk was intensely irritated at the magician's insolence. Whenever Cyril was among strangers, or in any danger, he invariably donned the bomb-proof armour of British aristocracy. He had been on the *Titanic*; a second and a half before she took the last plunge, he had turned to his neighbour, and asked casually, "Do you think there is any danger?"

Half an hour later he had been dragged into a boat, and, on recovering consciousness, took occasion to remark that the last time he had been spilt out of a boat was in Byron's Pool – "above Cambridge, England, you know" – and proceeded to relate the entire story of his adventure. He passed from one story to another, quite indifferent to the tumult on the boat, and ended by transporting the minds of the others far from the ice of the Atlantic to the sunny joys of the May Week at Cambridge. He had got everybody worked up as to what would happen after "First shot just before Ditton, and missed by half a blade; Jesus washed us off, and went away like the devil! Third were coming up like steam, with Hall behind them, and old T. J. cursing them to blazes from his gee; it was L for leather all up the Long Reach; then, thank goodness, Hall bumped Third just under the Railway Bridge: Cox yelled, and there was Jesus –" But they never heard what happened to the first boat of that excellent college, for Grey suddenly fainted, and they found that he was bleeding slowly to death from a deep wound over the heart.

This was the man who was frightened out of his life at the possibility of a chance scratch from an exquisitely clean and polished finger-nail.

The Turk could do nothing but bow. "Well, if you insist, Mr. Grey, we can only ask the lady."

He did so, and she professed most willing eagerness. The operation was a short one, and the seance recommenced.

But in a few minutes the Countess herself wearied. "I know I shall get nothing; it's no use; I do wish Baby were here; she could do what you want in a minute."

The Pasha nodded gleefully. "That's always the way we begin," he explained to Simple Simon. "Now I'll have to hypnotise her and she'll wake up in her other personality."

"Very, very interesting," agreed Simon; "curiously enough, we were just discussing double personalities with Madame la Giuffria when you honoured us with your visit. She has never seen anything of the kind."

"You'll be charmed, Marquise," the old Turk assured Lisa; "it's the most wonderful thing you ever saw." He began to make passes over the medium's forehead; she made a series of convulsive movements, which gradually died away, and were succeeded by deep sleep. Cyril took Lisa to one side. "This is really great magic! This is the old original confidence trick. Pretend to be asleep yourself, so that all the others may go to sleep in reality. It is described at no length whatever by Frazer in his book on sympathetic magic. For that most learned doctor, *vir praeclarus et optimus*, omits the single essential of his subject. It is not enough to pretend that your wax image is the person you want to bewitch; you must make a real connexion. That is the whole art of magic, to be able to do that; and it is the one point that Frazer omits."

The Countess was now heaving horribly, and emitting a series of complicated snorts. The Pasha explained that this was "normal", that she was "waking up into the new personality". Almost before he finished, she had slid off her chair on to the floor, where she uttered an intense and prolonged wail. The men removed the table, that her extrication might become more simple. They found her on her back, smiling and crowing, opening and closing her hands. When she saw the men she began to cry with fright. Then her first articulation was "Mum – Mum – Mum – Mum – Mum."

"She wants her mother," explained Akbar. "I didn't know a lady was to be present; but as we are so happy, would you mind pretending to be her mother? It would help immensely."

Lisa had quite forgotten Cyril's warning, and would have accepted. She was quite willing to enter into the spirit of the performance, whether it was a serious affair, a swindle, or merely an idiotic game; but Simon Iff interfered.

"Madame is not accustomed to seances," he said; and Cyril darted a look at her which compelled her obedience, though she had no idea in the world why she should, or why she shouldn't, do any given thing. She was like one in a strange country; the only thing to do is to conform to the customs as well as one can; and to trust one's guide.

"Baby" continued to yell. The Pasha, prepared for the event, whipped a bottle of milk out of his pocket, and she began to suck at it contentedly.

"What ridiculous fellows those old alchemists were!" said Cyril to his beloved. "How could they have gone on fooling with their athanors and cucurbites and alembics, and their Red Dragon, and their Caput Mortuum, and their Lunar Water? They really had no notion of the Dignity of Scientific Research."

There was no need to press home the bitterness of his speech; Lisa was already conscious of a sense of shame at assisting at such degrading imbecilities.

"Baby" relinquished the bottle, and began to crawl after one of the celluloid balls, which had rolled off the table when they moved it. She found it in a corner, sat up, and began to play with it.

All of a sudden something happened which shocked Lisa into a disgusted exclamation.

"It is all part of the assumption of baby-hood," said Cyril, coldly "and a bad one; for there is no reason why obsession by a baby's soul or mind should interfere with adult reflexes. The real reason is that this woman comes from the lowest sewers of Buda-Pesth. She was a common prostitute at the age of nine, and only took up this game as a better speculation. It is part of her pleasure to abuse the licence we allow her by such bestialities: it is a mark of her black envy; she does not understand that her foulness does not so much as soil our shoe-leather."

Despite her years of practice in the art of not understanding English, "Baby" winced momentarily. For her dearest thought was the social prestige which she enjoyed. It was terrible to see that the Real Thing was not under the slightest illusion. She did not mind a thousand "exposures" as a fraud; but she did want to keep up the bluff of being a Countess. She was past thirty-five; it was high time she found an old fool to marry her. She had designs on the Pasha; she had agreed to certain proposals in respect of this very seance with a view to getting him into her power.

He was apologising for her in the conventional way to Simon Iff. She had no consciousness or memory of this state at all, it appeared. "She will grow up in a little while; wait a few moments only."

And so it happened; soon she was prattling to the Pasha, who thoughtfully produced a doll for her to play with. Finally, she came over on her knees to Lisa, and began to cry, and simulate fear, and stammer out a confession of some kind. But Lisa did not wait to hear it; she was hot-tempered, and constitutionally unable to conceal her feelings beyond a certain point. She

dragged her skirts away roughly, and went to the other end of the room. The Pasha deprecated the action, with oriental aplomb; but the medium had already reached the next and final stage. She went to the Pasha, sat on his knee, and began to make the most violent love to him, with wanton kisses and caresses.

"That's the best trick of the lot," explained Cyril; "It goes wonderfully with a great many men. It gets their powers of observation rattled; she can pull off the most obvious 'miracles', and get them to swear that the control was perfect. That's how she fooled Oudouwitz; he was a very old man, and she proved to him that he was not as old as he thought he was. Great Harry Lauder! apart from any deception, a man in such circumstances might be willing to swear away his own reputation in order to assure her a career!"

"It's rather embarrassing," said the Pasha, "especially to a Mohammedan like myself; but one must endure everything in the cause of Science. In a moment now she'll be ready for the sitting."

Indeed, she changed suddenly into Personality Number Three, a very sdecorous young Frenchwoman named Annette, maid to the wife of a Jewish Banker. She went with rather stiff decorum to the table – she had to lay breakfast for her mistress, it appeared – but the moment she got there, she began to tremble violently all over, sank into the chair, and resumed the "Baby" personality, after a struggle. "Det away, bad Annette – naughty, naughty!" was the burden of her inspiring monologue for a few minutes. Then she suddenly became absorbed in the small objects before her – the Pasha had replaced them – and began to play with them, as intently as many children do with toys.

"Now we must have the lights down!" said the Pasha. Cyril complied. "Light is terribly painful and dangerous to her in this state. Once she lost her reason for a month through some one switching on the current unexpectedly. But we shall make a close examination, for all that." He took a thick silk scarf, and bound it over her eyes. Then, with an electric torch, he swept the table. He pulled back her sleeves to the shoulder and fastened them there; and he went over her hands inch by inch, opening the fingers and separating them, searching the nails, proving, in short, to demonstration, that there was no deception.

"You see," whispered Cyril, "we're not preparing for a scientific experiment; we're preparing for a conjuring trick. It's the psychology of trickery. Not my idea; the master's."

However, the attention of Lisa la Giuffria, almost despite herself, was drawn to the restless fingers on the table. They moved and twisted into such uncanny shapes; and there was something in the play of them, their intention towards the frail globe on which they converged, that fascinated her.

The medium drew her fingers swiftly away from the ball; at the same instant it jumped three or four inches into the air. The Turk purred delight. "Quite evidential, don't you think, sir?" he observed to Simon.

"Oh, quite," returned the old man, but in a tone that would have made any one who knew him well continue the conversation with these words "Evidential of WHAT?" But Akbar was fully satisfied. As a matter of form, he turned the torch on again, and made a new examination of the medium's fingers; but no hairs were to be discovered.

From this moment the phenomena became continuous. The articles upon the table hopped, skipped and danced like autumn leaves in a whirlwind. For ten minutes this went on, with constantly increasing energy.

"The fun is fast and furious," cried Lisa.

Cyril adjusted his monocle with immense deliberation. "The epithet of which you appear to be in search," he remarked, "is, possibly, 'chronic'."

Lisa stared at him, while the pencils and balls still pattered on the table like dancing hail.

"Doctor Johnson once remarked that we need not criticise too closely the performance of a whistling cabbage, or whatever it was," he explained wearily, "the wonder being in the fact of the animal being able to do it at all. But I would venture to add that for my part I find wonder amply satisfied by a single exhibition of this kind; to fall into a habit appears to me utterly out of accord with the views of the late John Stuart Mill on Liberty."

Lisa always found herself whirled about like a Dervish by the strange twists which her lover continued to give to his conversation.

Monet-Knott had told her in London of his famous faux pas at Cannon Street Station, when the railway official had passed along the train, shouting "All change! All change!" only to be publicly embraced by Cyril, who pretended to believe that he was a Buddhist Missionary, on the ground that one of the chief doctrines of Buddhism is that change is a principle inherent in all component things!

And unless you knew beforehand what Cyril was thinking, his words gave you no clue. You could never tell whether he were serious or joking. He had fashioned his irony on the model of that hard, cold, cruel, smooth glittering black ice that one finds only in deep gullies of the loftiest mountains; it was said in the clubs that he had found seventy-seven distinct ways of calling a man, to his face, something which only the most brazen fish-wives of Billingsgate care to call by its name, without his suspecting anything beyond a well-turned compliment.

Fortunately his lighter side was equally prominent. It was he who had gone into Lincoln Bennett's – Hatters to his Majesty since helmets ceased to be the wear – had asked with diffidence and embarrassment to see the proprietor on a matter of the utmost importance; and, on being deferentially conducted to a private room, had enquired earnestly: "Do you sell hats?"

The mystery of the man was an endless inquietude to her. She wished to save herself from loving, him, but only because she felt that she could never be sure that she had got him. And that intensified her determination to make him wholly and forever hers.

Another story of Monet-Knott's had frightened her terribly. He had once put himself to a great deal of trouble to obtain a walking-stick to his liking. Ultimately he had found it, with such joy that he had called his friends and neighbours together, and bidden them to a lunch at the Carlton. After the meal, he had walked down Pall Mall with two of his guests – and discovered that he had forgotten the walking-stick. "Careless of me!" had been his only remark; and nothing would persuade him to stir a step towards its recovery.

She preferred to think of that other side of his character which she knew from the *Titanic* episode, and that other of how his men had feared to follow him across a certain snow-slope that

hung above a Himalayan precipice – when he had glissaded on his back, head foremost, to within a yard of the brink. The men had followed him then; and she knew that she too would follow him to the end of the world.

Lost in these meditations, she hardly noticed that the seance was over. The medium had gradually fallen "asleep" again, to wake up in her Number One personality. But as the others rose from the table, Lisa too rose, more or less automatically, with them.

The foot of Akbar Pasha caught in the edge of a bearskin; and he stumbled violently. She shot out an arm to save him; but the young magician was quicker. He caught the Turk's shoulder with his left hand, and steadied him; at the same moment she felt his other hand crushing her wrist, and her arm bent back with such suddenness that she wondered that it did not snap.

The next moment she saw that Cyril, with his hand on the Pasha's arm, was begging permission in his silkiest tones to examine a signet-ring of very beautiful design. "Admirable!" he was saying, "but isn't the edge too sharp, Pasha? One could cut oneself if one drew one's hand across it sharply, like this." He made a swift gesture. "You see?" he remarked. A stream of blood was already trickling from his hand. The Turk looked at him with sudden black rage, of which she could not guess the cause. Cyril had expressly told her that a scratch might be death. Yet he had courted it; and now he stood exchanging commonplaces, with his blood dripping upon the floor. Impulsively she seized his hand and bound it with her handkerchief.

The Countess had wrapped her furs about her; but suddenly she felt faint. "I can't bear the sight of blood," she said, and collapsed upon the divan. Simon Iff appeared at her side with a glass of brandy. "I feel better now; do give me my hat, Marquise!" Again Cyril intervened. "Over my dead body!" he cried, feigning to be a jealous lover; and adjusted it with his own hands.

Presently the visitors were at the door. The Turk became voluble over the seance. "Wonderful!" he cried; "one of the most remarkable I was ever present at!"

"So glad, Pasha!" replied Grey, with his hand on the door, "one can't pick a winner every time at this game, can one?"

Lisa La Giuffria saw that (somehow) the courteous phrase cut like a whip of whalebone.

She turned as the door closed. To her surprise she saw that Simon Iff had sunk on the divan, and that he was wiping the sweat from his brows.

Behind her, her lover took a great breath, as one who comes out of deep water.

And then she realised that she had been present not at a seance, but at a battle. She became conscious of the strain upon herself, and she broke into a flood of tears.

Cyril Grey, with a pale smile, was bending upon her face, kissing away the drops even as they issued; and, beneath her, his strong arm bore her whole weight without a tremor.

CHAPTER IV

LUNCH, AFTER ALL

AND A LUMINOUS ACCOUNT
OF THE FOURTH DIMENSION

"I CONFESS to hunger," said Simon Iff, after a few moments. Cyril kissed Lisa on the mouth, and walked with his arm still circling her, to the sideboard. "You are hostess here now, you know," he said quite simply. All his affectations dropped from him at that moment, and Lisa understood that he was just a simple-minded, brave, and honest man, who, walking in the midst of perils, had devised a formidable armament both for attack and defence.

She felt a curious pang of pain simultaneously with a sense of exaltation. For she was no longer merely his mistress; he had accepted her as a friend. It was no longer a purely sexual relation, which is always in the nature of a duel; he might cease to love her, in the crude savage sense; but he would always be a pal – just as if she were a man. And here was the pang: was he sure to return to the mood that her whole body and soul were even at that moment crying out for?

The story of his "Judgment of Paris", as they called it, came into her mind. Some years before, he had had three women in love with him at once. It seemed to each that she was the only one. But they discovered the arrangement – he never took pains to hide such things – and they agreed to confront him. They called at his studio together, and told him that he must choose one of them. He smoked a full pipe before replying; then went to his bedroom and returned with a pair of socks – in need of attention. "Simon, Son of Jonas, lovest thou me? – Yea, Lord, thou knowest that I love thee. Mend my socks," he misquoted somewhat blasphemously, and threw the socks to the one he really loved.

Lisa meant to lay the table in that sense of the word, so to speak. She remembered that the only words spoken by Kundry after her redemption were "*Dienen! Dienen!*"

"Is this your fast?" she cried gaily, discovering the contents of the sideboard. For her gaze fell upon a lobster salad of surprising glory flanked by a bowl of caviar in ice on one side, and one

of those *foie gras* pies – the only kind really worth eating which you have to cut with a spoon dipped in hot water. On an upper shelf was a pyramid of woodcock, prepared for the chafing dish which stood beside them; there was a basket of pears and grapes of more value than a virtuous woman – and we know that her price is above rubies! In the background stood the wines in cohorts. There was hock from the cellars of Prince Metternich; there was Burgundy – a Chambertin that could have given body to a ghost, and hardly lost its potency; there was a Tokay that really was Imperial; there was 1865 brandy made in 1865 – which is as rare as radium in pitchblende.

Simon Iff took it upon himself to explain his apparent lack of hospitality toward the visitors.

"Akbar Pasha came here for blood: a drop of your blood, my dear; Cyril's and mine are not in his power – you saw how contemptuously the boy played up to his trick! So I persisted in offering him salt, and nothing but salt."

"But why should he want my blood? And why should you give him salt?"

"If he accepts salt it limits his powers to injure the house where he accepts it, or its inmates; and it exposes him to a terrible riposte. Why he should want your blood – that is another question, and a very serious one. Unfortunately, it implies that he knows who you are, and what we purpose for you. If he had it, he could influence you to do his will; we only wish that you should be free to do your own. I won't insult you by telling you that you can go scatheless by the simple process of returning to your ordinary life. I've been watching you, and I know you would despise me for suggesting it. I know that you are ignorant of what may lie before you, but that you judge it to be formidable; and that you embrace the adventure with both hands."

"I mustn't contradict the famous expert in psychology!" she laughed back at him. "I ought to deny it indignantly. And I surely am crazy to leap in the dark – only it isn't dark when Love is the lamp."

"Be careful of love!" the old magician warned her. "Love is a Jack o' Lantern, and hovers over bogs and graves; it's but a luminous bubble of poisonous gas. In our Order we say, 'Love is the law, love under will.' Will is the iron signal staff. Fix love on that, and you have a lighthouse, and your ship comes safe to harbour!"

"I may now apologise," remarked Cyril, as they seated themselves at the table, "for leaving you the other night to dine at Miss Badger's. I had given my word to her, and nothing but physical inability would have stopped me from going. I didn't want to go, any more than I wanted to drown myself; and that is a great compliment to you, for she is one of the two nicest women in London; but I would have faced a thousand deaths to get there."

"It is right to be so stern about a trifle?"

"Keeping one's word is no trifle. False in one, false in all. Can't you see how simple it makes life for me, never to have to worry about a decision, always to be able to refer everything to a simple standard, my Will? And can't you see how simple it makes life for you, to know that if I once say a thing, I'll do it?"

"Yes. I do see. But, oh, Cyril, what agony I passed through that evening!"

"That was ignorance," said Simon Iff, "the cause of all suffering. You failed to read him, to be

assured that, just as he was keeping his word to Miss Badger about the dinner, he would keep his to you about the telephone."

"Now, tell me about the Battle. I see that I am in the thick of the fight; but I haven't got a ghost of a notion why!"

I'm sorry, dear child, but this Knowledge is unsuited to your exalted grade," he answered playfully. "We must get up to it slowly by telling you exactly what we want to do, and why. Then you will see why others should try to thwart us. And I deeply regret to have to inform you that our road lies through somewhat hilly country. You will have to listen to a lecture on the Fourth Dimension."

"Whatever in the world is that?"

"I think we had better talk of simpler matters until lunch is over."

They began to discuss their private affairs. There was no reason at all why Lisa should not take up her residence with Cyril from that moment. She had merely to telephone her maid to pack, and come along. She offered to do so when Simon Iff said that he thought they ought to leave Paris without a day's delay. But he said: "I don't think it quite fair on the girl. It's a battle, and no call for her to fight. Besides" – he turned to Cyril – "she would probably be obsessed in twenty-four hours."

"I shouldn't be surprised to learn that they were after her already. Let's try! Call her, Lisa, and say you'll not be back tonight; tell her to await further instructions."

Lisa went to the telephone. Instead of getting her room, she was connected with the manager of the hotel. "I much regret to have to tell you, madame, that your maid was seized with epileptic fits shortly after you left this morning."

Lisa was too stunned to reply. She dropped the receiver. Cyril crossed to her instantly, and told the man that his news had upset Madame; she would telephone again later.

Lisa repeated what the manager had said.

"I thought as much," said Cyril.

"I didn't," said Iff frankly, "and it worries me. I'm not guessing, like you are – and it's no credit to guess right, my young friend, but a deceit of the devil, like winning at roulette. I'm deducing from what I know. Therefore, the fact that I'm wrong proves that there is something I don't know – and it worries me. But, clearly, we must get into a properly protected area without a moment wasted. That is, you must. I'll watch at the front. There must be somebody big behind that clumsy fool Akbar Pasha."

"Yes; I've been guessing," admitted Cyril, with some shame. "Or, perhaps worse, I've let my ego expand, and taken the largest possible view of the importance of our project."

"Well, tell me the project!" said Lisa. "Can't you see I can hardly bear this any more?"

"You're safe within these walls," said Simon, "now that there is no enemy within the gates; and tonight we shall take you under guard to a protected area. Tomorrow the fun will begin in good earnest. Meanwhile, here is the preliminary knowledge with regard to the project. Before you start, you have to take a certain vow; and we cannot allow you to do that in ignorance of all that it implies, down to the tiniest iota."

"I am ready."

"I am going to make everything as simple as I possibly can. You have a good imagination, and I think you should be able to follow.

"See here: I take a pencil and a piece of paper. I make a point. It stays there. It doesn't go in any direction. In mathematics we say: 'It is extended in no dimension.' Now I draw a straight line. That goes in one direction. We say, it is extended in one dimension.

"Now I make another line to cross it at right angles. That is one extension in a second dimension."

"I see, and another line would make a third dimension."

"Don't go too fast. Your third line is no use. If I want to show the position of any point on the paper, I can do it by reference to these two lines only. Make a point, and I'll show you."

She obeyed.

"Now, I draw lines from your point to make right angles with my lines. I say your point is so far east of the central point, and so far north. You see? I determine the position by only two measurements."

"But if I made my point right in the air here?"

"Exactly. We need a third line, but it must be at right angles to the other two; sticking straight up, as you might say. Then we can measure in three directions, and determine the point. It is so far east, so far south, and so high."

"Yes."

"Now I'll go over that again in another way.

"Here is a point, not long nor broad nor thick: no dimension.

"Here is a line, long but neither broad nor thick: one dimension. Here is a surface, long and broad, but not thick: two dimensions.

"Here is a solid, long and broad and thick: three dimensions."

"Now I quite understand. But you said: four dimensions."

"I will say it presently. But just now I am going to hammer at two.

"Observe: I make a triangle. All the sides are equal. Now I draw a line through it from one angle to the middle of the other side. I have two triangles. They are exactly alike, as you see; same size, same shape. But – they point in opposite directions. Now we will cut them out with scissors."

He did so.

"Slide them about, so that one lies exactly to cover the other!"

She tried and failed: then, with a laugh, turned one over, when it easily fitted.

"Ah, you cheated. I said, 'slide them.'"

"I'm sorry."

"On the contrary, you have acted divinely, in the best sense! You took the thing that wouldn't fit out of its world of two into the world of three, put it back, and they all lived happy ever after!

"The next thing is this. Everything that exists – everything material – has these three dimensions. These points and lines and surfaces have all a minute extension in some other dimension, or they would be merely things in our imagination. The surface of water, for instance, is merely the boundary between it and the air.

"Now I am going to tell you why some people have thought that another dimension might exist. Those triangles, so like, yet so unlike, have analogies in the world of what we call real things. For example, there are two kinds of sugar, exactly alike in every way but one. You know how a prism bends a ray of light? Well, if you take a hollow prism, and fill it with a solution of one of these kinds of sugar, the ray bends to the right; use the other kind, and it bends to the left. Chemistry is full of these examples.

"Then we have our hands and feet; however we move about, we can never make them fill exactly the same place. A right hand is always a right hand, however you move it. It only becomes a left hand in a looking-glass – so your mirror should in future afford you a superior sort of reflection! It should remind you that there is a looking-glass world, if you could only get through!"

"Yes, but we can't get through!"

"Don't let us lose our way! Enough to say that there might be such a world. But we must try to find a reason for thinking that there is one. Now the best reason of all is a very deep one; but try to understand it."

Lisa nodded.

"We know that the planets move at certain rates in certain paths, and we know that the laws which govern them are the same as those which made Newton's apple fall. But Newton couldn't explain the law, and he said that he found himself quite unable to imagine a force acting at a distance, as gravitation (so called) appears to do. Science was hard put to it, and had finally to invent a substance called the ether, of which there was no evidence, only it must be there! But this ether had so many contradictory and impossible qualities, that people began to cast about for some other explanation. And it was found that by supposing an extension of the universe (thin but uniform) in a fourth dimension, that the law would hold good.

"I know it's hard to grasp the idea; let me put it to you this way. Take this cube. Here is a point, a corner, where the three bounding lines join. The point is nothing, yet it is part of the lines. To imagine it at all as a reality, we must say that it has a minute extension in these lines.

"Now take a line. It has a similar minute uniform extension in the two surfaces which it bounds. Take the surface; it is similarly part of the one cube.

"Go one step further; imagine that the cube is related to some unknown thing as the surface is to the cube. You can't? True; you can't make a definite image of it; but you can form an idea – and if you train yourself to think of this very hard, presently you will get a little closer to it. I'm not going to bother you much longer with this dry theoretical part; I'll only just tell you that a fourth dimension, besides explaining the difficulties of gravitation, and some others, gives us an idea of how it is that there is only a definite fixed number of kinds of things, from which all others are combined.

"And now we can get down to business. Brother Cyril, who obliged with the cube, will be so good as to produce a wooden cone and a basin of water."

Brother Cyril complied.

"I want you to realise," went on the old man, "that all the talk about the Progress of Science is cheap journalism. Most of the boasted progress is mere commercial adaptation of science, as

who should say that he is Experimenting with Electricity when he rides in an electric train. One hears of Edison and Marconi as 'men of science'; neither of them ever discovered a single fact; they merely exploited facts already known. The real men of Science are in absolute agreement that the advance in our knowledge, great as it has been, leaves us as ignorant of ultimate truth and reality as we were ten thousand years ago. The universe guards its secret: Isis can still boast that no man hath lifted her veil!

"But, suppose our trouble were due to the fact that we only received our impressions in disconnected pieces. A very simple thing might seem the maddest jumble. Ready, Cyril?"

"Quite ready."

"I. A. A. I. U. I. A."

"R. F. G. L. S. L."

"What were we saying?"

Lisa laughed rather excitedly. Her vivid mind told her that these instructions were going to take sudden shape.

"Only your very pretty name, my dear! Now, Cyril, the cone." He took it in his hand, and poised it over a bowl of water.

"We are now going to suppose that this very simple object is going to try its best to explain its nature to the surface of the water, which we will imagine as endowed with powers of observation and reasoning equal to our own. All that the cone can do is to show itself to the water, and it can only impress the water by touching it.

"So it dips its point, thus. The water perceives a point. The cone goes on dipping. The water sees a circle round where the point was. The cone goes on. The circle gets bigger and bigger. Suddenly, as the cone goes completely through, snap!

"Now, what does the water know?

"Nothing about any cone. If it got any idea that the various commotions were caused by a single object, which it would only do if it compared them carefully, noted a regularity of rate of increase in the size of the circle, and so on – in other words, used the scientific method – it would not evolve a theory of a cone, for we must remember that any solid body is to it a thing as wildly inconceivable as a fourth-dimensional body is to us.

"The cone would try again. This time, we dip it obliquely. The water now perceives a totally different set of phenomena; there are no circles, but ellipses. Dip again, first at this angle, then at that. One way we get curious curves called parabolas, the other way equally curious curves called hyperbolas.

"By this time the water would be nearly out of its mind, if it insisted on trying to refer all these absolutely different phenomena to a single cause!

"It might work out a geometry – our own plane geometry, in fact – and it would perhaps get some extraordinary poetic conception of a Creator who manifested in his universe such marvellous and beautiful relations. It would get all sorts of fantastic theories of this Creator's power; what it would never get – until it produced a James Hinton – would be the idea that all this diversity was caused by seeing, disjointedly, different aspects of one single simple thing.

"I purposely took the easiest case. Suppose that instead of a cone we used an irregular body – the series of impressions would seem to the water like absolute madness!

"Now slide your imagination up one dimension! Do you not see at once how parallel is our situation to that of the surface of the water?

"The first impression of the savage about the universe is of a great mysterious jumble of things which come upon him without rhyme or reason, usually to smite him down.

"Long later, man developed the idea of connecting phenomena, at least a few at a time.

"Centuries elapse; he begins to perceive law, at first operating only in a very few matters.

"More centuries; some bold thinker invents a single cause for all these diverse effects, and calls it God. This hypothesis leads to interminable disputes about the nature of God; in fact, they have never been settled. The problem of the origin of evil, alone, has quite baffled Theology.

"Science advances; we now find that all things are subject to law. There is no need of any mysterious creator, in the old sense; we look for causes in the same order of nature as the effects they produce. We no longer propitiate ghosts to keep our fires alight.

"Now, at last, I and a few others are asking whether the whole universe be not illusion, in exactly the same way as a true surface is an illusion.

"Perhaps the universe is a four-dimensional object, or collection of objects, quite sane, and simple, and intelligible, manifesting itself in diversity, regular or irregular, just as the cone did to the water."

"Of course I can't grasp all this; I will ask Cyril to tell me again and again till I do. But what is this fourth-dimensional universe? Can't you give me something to cling to?"

"Just so. Here this long lecture links up with that little chat about the soul!"

"O – o – oh!"

"And the double personality, and all the rest of it!

"It's perfectly simple. I, the fourth-dimensional reality, am going about my business in a perfectly legitimate way. I find myself pushing through to my surface, or let us say, I become conscious of my surface, the material universe, much as the cone did as it went through the water. I make my appearance with a yell. I grow. I die. There are the same phenomena of change which we all perceive around us. My three-dimensional mind thinks all this 'real,' a history; where at most it is a geography, a partial set of infinite aspects. I say infinite, for the cone contains an infinite number of curves. Yet this three-dimensional being is actually a part of me, though such a minute one; and it rather amuses me, now I have discovered a little bit more of myself, to find that mind think that he, or even his yet baser body, is the one and only."

"I'm understanding you with a part of me that I didn't know was there."

"That's the way, child. But I'm going on a little. I want you to consider how nicely this explains the psychology of crowds, for example. We may suppose an Idea to be a real four-dimensional thing. I, when I know myself more fully, shall probably turn out to be a pretty simple kind of a thing, manifesting in perhaps one person only. But we can imagine abstract 'Individuals' who come to the surface in hundreds or thousands of minds at the same time. Liberty, for example. It begins to push through. It is noticed by one or two men only at first; that is like the point of the

cone. Then it spreads gradually – or it breaks out suddenly, just as the circle would, if, instead of a cone, you dropped a spiked shield upon the water. And that is all the lesson for this afternoon, child. Think it over, and see if you have it all clear, and if you can find any other little problems to straighten out. The next lesson will be of a more desperate sort – the kind that leads directly to action."

Cyril broke in on the word. "We have a great deal to do," he said sharply, "even before we leave this house. It's pretty dark – and there's a Thing in the garden."

CHAPTER V

OF THE THING IN THE GARDEN

AND OF THE WAY OF THE TAO

"**O**H, little Brother!" said the old mystic sadly.

"How long will it take you to work through this wretched business?"

"I have omnipotence at my command, and eternity at my disposal," smiled the boy, using Eliphaz Levi's well-known formula.

"I ought to explain," said Simple Simon, turning to Lisa. "This boy is a desperate magician confined within the circle of this forest. His plan is Action; he is all for magick; give him a Wand and a host of Demons to control, and he is happy. For my part, I prefer the Way of the Tao, and to do everything by doing nothing. I know it sounds difficult; one day I will explain. But the practical result is that I lead a placid and contented life, and nothing ever happens; he, on the contrary, makes trouble everywhere, excites the wrath of Turks, and worse, if I am right; he thereby brings about a situation where perfectly competent ladies' maids have epileptic fits, mediums endeavour to procure blood from bewitching damozels – and now there's a Thing in the Garden." His voice had a wail of comic disgust.

"However, this is Cyril's funeral, not mine. He called me in; I must say I approve of his general plan, on the whole, and I dare say much of the opposition is unavoidable. In any case he is the magician; Principal Boy in a Pantomime. I merely hold the sponge; and we have to use his formula throughout, not mine. If it ends in disaster," he added as a cheerful afterthought, "perhaps it will teach him a lesson! A Chinese God, indeed! He would be better as a Chinese coolie, smoking opium at the feet of Chwangtze!"

"He tells me that I stand in my own way, that I love struggle and adventure, and that this is weakness and not strength."

"This girl is in danger: quite unnecessary danger."

"I am going to ask my master to show you his method; you will see plenty of mine in the next few weeks; and I should like you to have a standard of comparison. Maybe you'll want to choose one day!"

"I'm afraid I, too, like danger and excitement!" cried Lisa.

"I'm afraid you do! However, since Brother Cyril asks it, the Way of the Tao shall be trodden so far as this is possible: What would Brother Cyril do?"

"I should take the Magic Sword, make the appropriate symbols, and invoke the Names Divine appurtenant thereto: the Thing, shrivelled and blasted, would go back to those that sent it, screaming in agony, cursing at the gods, ready to turn even on its employers, that they might wail with it in torment."

"One of the best numbers on the programme," said Simon Iff. "Now see the other way!"

"Yes: if your way is better than that!" cried the girl, her eyes gleaming.

"It isn't *my* way," said the mystic, with a sudden inflection of solemnity. His voice rose in a low monotonous chant as he quoted from *The Book of the Heart irt with the Serpent*.

"I, and Me, and Mine were sitting with lutes in the market-place of the great city, the city of the violets and the roses.

"The night fell, and the music of the lutes was stilled.

"The tempest arose, and the music of the lutes was stilled.

"The hour passed, and the music of the lutes was stilled.

"But Thou art Eternity and Space; Thou art Matter and Motion; and Thou art the Negation of all these things. For there is no symbol of Thee."

The listeners were thrilled to the marrow of their bones. But the old man merely gathered a handful of dittany leaves from the chased golden box where they were kept, and led the way to the garden.

It was very dark; nothing could be distinguished but the outlines of the shrubs and the line of the fence beyond.

"Do you see the Thing?" said Iff.

Lisa strained her eyes.

"You mustn't look for anything very definite," said the mystic.

"It seems as if the darkness were somehow different in that corner," said Lisa at last, pointing. "A sort of reddish tinge to the murk."

"Oh dear me! if you will use words like 'murk'! I'm afraid you're all on Cyril's side! Look now!" And he put his hand on her head. With the other he offered her the dittany. "Chew one of these leaves!" he said.

She took one of the silver-grey heaves, with its delicate snow-bloom, between her teeth.

"I can see a sort of shapeless mass, dark-red," she said after a pause.

"Now watch!" cried Iff. He took several steps into the garden, and raised his right hand. "Do what thou wilt shall be the whole of the Law!" he proclaimed in such a voice as once shook Sinai.

Then he threw the rest of the dittany in the direction of the Thing.

"By all the powers of the Pentagram!" shouted Cyril Grey; "he's deliberately making a magical link between it and Lisa." He bit his lip, and cursed himself in silence; he knew he had been startled out of prudence.

Simon Iff had not noticed the outburst. He quoted *The Book of the Law*, "Be strong!" he cried. "Enjoy all things of sense and rapture! There is no god that shall deny thee for this!'"

The Thing became coherent. It contracted slightly. Lisa could now see that it was an animal of the wolf type, couchant. The body was as big as that of a small elephant. It became quite clearly visible. It was a dull fiery red. The head was turned toward her, and she was suddenly shocked to see that it had no eyes.

The old man advanced towards it. He had abandoned his prophetic attitude. His whole gait expressed indifference – no, forgetfulness. He was merely a quiet old gentleman taking an evening stroll.

He walked right into the Thing. Suddenly, as it enveloped him, Lisa saw that a faint light was issuing from his body, a pale phosphorescence which kindled warmly as he went. She saw the edges of the Thing contract, as if they were sucked inwards. This proceeded, and the light became intense. About a burning ovoid core dawned and vibrated the flashing colours of the rainbow. The Thing disappeared completely; at the same moment the light went out. Simon Iff was once again merely an old gentleman taking an evening stroll. But she heard a soft voice, almost as faint as an echo; it murmured: "Love is the law, love under will."

"Let us go in," said he as he rejoined them. "You must not catch a chill."

Lisa went to the divan. She said nothing; she was stupefied by what she had seen. Perhaps she even lost full consciousness for a moment; for her next impression was of the two men arguing.

"I agree," Cyril was saying, "it is very neat, and shows the restraint of the great artist; but I am thinking of the Man behind the gun. I should have struck terror into him."

"But fear is failure!" protested Iff mildly, as if surprised.

"But we want them to fail!"

"Oh no! I want them to succeed."

Cyril turned rather angrily to Lisa. "He's impossible! I fancy myself at paradox, you know; but he goes beyond my understanding every time. I'm an amateur, and a rotten amateur at that."

"Let me explain!" said Simple Simon. "If everybody did his Will, there would be no collision. Every man and every woman is a star. It is when we get off our orbits that the clashes come. Now if a Thing gets off its orbit, and comes into my sphere of attraction, I absorb it as quietly as possible, and the stars sing together again."

"Whew!" said Cyril, and pretended to wipe the sweat from his brow.

"But weren't you in danger from that devilish Thing?" asked Lisa, with the memory of a great anxiety. She had trembled like an aspen during the scene in the garden.

"The rhinoceros," quoted Simon Iff, "finds no place in him into which to thrust its horn, nor the tiger a place in which to fix its claws, nor the weapon a place to admit its point. And for what reason? Because there is in him no place of death."

"But you did nothing. You were just acting like an ordinary man. But I think it would have been death for any one but you."

"An ordinary man would not have touched the Thing. It was on a different plane, and would no more have interfered with him than sound interferes with light. A young magician, one who had opened a gate on to that plane, but had not yet become master of that plane, might have been overcome. The Thing might even have dispossessed his ego, and used his body as its own. That is the beginner's danger in magick."

"And what is your secret?"

"To have assimilated all things so perfectly that there is no longer any possibility of struggle. To have destroyed the idea of duality. To have achieved Love and Will so that there is no longer any object to Love, or any aim for Will. To have killed desire at the root; to be one with every thing and with Nothing.

"Look!" he went on, with a change of tone, "why does a man die when he is struck by lightning? Because he has a gate open to lightning; he insists on being an electrical substance by possessing the quality of resistance to the passage of the electric current. If we could diminish that resistance to zero, lightning would no longer take notice of him.

"There are two ways of preventing a rise of temperature from the sun's heat. One is to oppose a shield of non-conducting and opaque material: that is Cyril's way, and at the best it is imperfect; some heat always gets through. The other is to remove every particle of matter from the space which you wish to be cold; then there is nothing there to become hot; and that is the Way of the Tao."

Lisa put an arm round Cyril's neck, and rested her head on his shoulder. "I shouldn't know how to begin!" she said: "and – I know it would mean giving up Cyril."

"It would mean giving up yourself," retorted the mystic, "and you'll have to do it one day: But be reassured! Everybody has to go through your stage – and unless I'm mistaken, you are about to go through it in a particularly acute form."

"I've tried the Tao," said Cyril, half regretful, "but I can't manage it."

The old man laughed. "You're like the old man in the storm who realised that he would be warmer elsewhere. So he decided to diminish the amount of himself by removing his clothes, and only found it colder. It gets worse and worse till the moment when you vanish utterly and for ever. But you have only tried half-measures. Naturally, you have found your will divided against itself – the will to live against the will to Nirvana, if I may call it so – and that is not even good magick."

The boy groaned inwardly. He could understand just enough to realise how far the heights reached above him. His heart almost failed him at the thought – which was instinctive knowledge – that he must scale them, whether he would or no.

"Take care!" suddenly cried Simon Iff.

At almost the same instant a terrible scream shrilled out from a neighbouring studio. "It is my fault," murmured the old man, humbly. "I divided his will. I have been talking like an old fool. I must have been identified with Simon Iff for a moment. Oh, pride! Oh, pride!"

But Cyril Grey had understood the warning. He rose to his full height, and made a curious gesture. Then, with a grim face, he ran out of the studio. In a moment he was battering at the door of his neighbour. It burst open under the momentum of his shoulder.

A woman lay upon the floor. Over her stood the sculptor, a blood-stained hammer in his hand. He seemed absolutely dazed. Grey shook him. He looked round stupidly. "What have I done?" he said. "Nothing!" snarled Cyril. "I did it, I. Quick! can't we save her?" But the sculptor burst into lamentation: he was incapable of anything but tears. He flung himself upon the body of his model, and wept passionately. Cyril gritted his teeth; the girl was on the borderland. "Master!" he cried, in a terrible voice.

"In a case of this kind," said Simple Simon, who was standing unperceived within a foot of him, "where Nature has been outraged, an attempt made to interfere violently with her laws, it is permissible to act – or rather, to counteract just so much as is necessary to restore equilibrium. There was a seed of quarrel in the hearts of these young people; the blow aimed at you, when your own will became divided, struck aslant; their own division attracted the murder-force to them.

"I will administer The Medicine." He took a flask from his pocket, put a drop of the contents on the lips of the girl, and one in each nostril. He then sprinkled a little upon a handkerchief, and put it to the wound on her head.

Suddenly the sculptor rose to his feet with a great cry. His hands were covered in blood, which streamed from his own scalp.

"Quick! back to the studio!" said Simon. "We don't want to make explanations. They'll both be all right in five minutes, and they'll think it all a dream. As, indeed, like the rest of things, it is!"

But Cyril had to carry la Giuffria. The rapid successions of these mysterious events had ended by throwing her consciousness completely out of gear. She lay in a deep trance.

"A very fortunate circumstance!" remarked Simon, when he observed it. "This is the time to take her over to the Profess-House." Cyril wrapped her in her furs; between them they carried her to the boulevard, where Simon Iff's automobile was in waiting.

The old mystic held up his left hand, with two of the fingers crossed. It was a signal to the chauffeur. In another moment they were running on easy speed up the Boulevard Arago.

Lisa came to herself as the car, crossing the Seine, pointed at the heights of Montmartre; and she was perfectly recovered as it stopped before a modest house of quite modern type, which was set against the steepest part of the hill.

The door opened, without alarm being given. Lisa learnt later that in this house no orders needed to be issued, that simplicity had reached so serene a level that all things operated together without question. Only when unusual accidents took place was there need for speech; and little, even then.

The door stood open, and a quite ordinary butler presented himself, bowing. Simon Iff returned the salute, and walked on, when a second door opened, also spontaneously. Lisa found herself in a small lobby. The man who had opened the inner door was clad from neck to knee in a single black robe, without sleeves. From his belt hung a heavy sword with a cross-hilt. This man held up three fingers. Simon Iff again nodded, and led his guests to the room on the left.

Here were the three guests indicated by the gesture of the guard. Lord Antony Bowling was a familiar friend of the old mystic. He was a stout and strong man of nearly fifty years of age, with a gaze both intrepid and acute. His nose was of the extreme aristocratic type, his mouth sensual and strong.

Cyril Grey had nicknamed him "The Merman of Mayfair" and claimed that Rodin got the idea for his "Centaur" the day that he met him.

He was the younger brother of the Duke of Flint, his race probably Norman in the main: but he gave the impression of a Roman Emperor. Haughtiness was here, and great good-nature; the intellect was evidently developed to the highest possible pitch of which man as man is capable; and one could read the judicial habit on his deep wide brows. Against this one could see the huge force of the man's soul, the passionate desire for knowledge which burnt in that great brain. One could conceive him capable of monstrous deeds, for he would let no man, no prejudice of men, stand in his way. He would certainly have fiddled while Rome was burning if it had been his hobby to play the violin.

This man was the mainstay of the Society for Psychical Research. He was the only absolutely competent man in it, perhaps; at least, he stood well above all others. He had the capacity for measuring the limits of error in any investigation with great accuracy. Just as the skilful climber can make his way on rotten chalk by trusting each crumbling fragment with just that fraction of his weight which will not quite dislodge it, so Lord Antony could prepare a sound case from worthless testimony. He knew the limits of fraud. He might catch a medium in the act of cheating a dozen times in a seance, and yet record some of the phenomena of that seance as evidential. He used to say that the fact of a medium having his hands free did not explain the earthquake at Messina.

If this man had ever caused people to distrust his judgment – nobody but an imbecile could have doubted his sincerity – the cause lay in his power to fool the mediums he was investigating to the top of their bent. He would enter into every phase of their strange moods as if he had been absolutely one with them in spirit; then, when they were gone, he would withdraw and look at the whole course of events from without, as if he had had no share in them.

But people who saw him only in the first phase thought him easily hoodwinked.

The second of the guests of Simon Iff, or, rather, of the Order to which he belonged, was a tall man bowed with ill-health. A shock of heavy black hair crowned a face pallid as death itself; but his eyes blazed formidably beneath their bushy brows. He had just returned from Burma, where he had lived for many years as a Buddhist monk. The indomitable moral valour of the man shone from him; one could see in every gesture the marks of his fierce fight against a dozen deadly sicknesses. With hardly a week of even tolerable health in any year, he had done work that might have frightened the staff of a great University. Almost single-handed, he had explored the inmost doctrine of the Buddha, and thrown light on many a tangled grove of thought. He had reorganised Buddhism as a missionary religion, and founded societies everywhere to study and practise it. He had even found time and strength, amid these labours, to pursue his own hobby of electrical research. Misunderstood, thwarted, hampered in every way, he had won through; and

he had never violated the precepts of his Teacher by raising his voice to denounce error. Even his enemies had been compelled to recognise him as a saint. Simon Iff had never met him, but he went to greet Cyril with the affection of a brother. The boy had been the greatest of his pupils, but the Mahathera Phang, as he was now called in his monastery, had long ago abandoned magick for a path not very different from that of Simon Iff.

The third man was of very inferior calibre to either of the others. He was of medium height and good build, though somewhat frail. But in him was no great development. One divined a restless intelligence fettered to mere cleverness, a failure to grasp the distinction between genius and talent. He was an expert conjurer, had all the facts of psychic research at his finger's end, was up in all the modern theories of psychology, but was little more than a machine. He was incapable of refuting his own logic by an appeal to his common sense. Some one having once remarked that we all dig our graves with our teeth, Wake Morningside had started to prove scientifically that eating was the direct cause of death; and that, consequently, absolute fasting would confer immortality. This was of course easy to prove – in America.

He had continued with experiments in weighing souls, photographing thoughts, and would probably have gone fishing for the Absolute if he had only thought of it! He was a prop to the editors of the New York Sunday Newspapers, and was at present engaged on writing a scenario for moving pictures in which he was to incorporate the facts of psychical research. Nobody in the world was better aware than he that everything reliable could be packed into a single reel, and rattle, but he had undauntedly contracted for a series of fifty five-part pictures. He chewed his chocolate – his latest specific for averting the perils of more complex nutrition – with no idea that these activities might damage his reputation as a research student. And he was really a very clever man, with a quick eye and brain. If he had possessed moral force, he might have been saved from many of his follies. But his belief in his own fads had impaired his health and made him somewhat hysterical; as a result of this, and of his tendency to exploit his knowledge in second-rate ways, people had begun to doubt the value of his testimony even in serious matters. For instance, some years before, he had been one of the signatories to a favourable report on a medium named Jansen; the following year he had brought the man over to America, and made a great deal of money out of the tour. The action destroyed both Jansen and the earlier report. In New York the Scandinavian medium had been exposed, and when Morningside had objected that this did not invalidate the earlier report, his opponent retorted: "No! *Your* presence there does that!"

But Bowling, with whom he had just crossed from England, knew him better than to think venality of him, and still valued his co-operation in the investigations of alleged spiritualistic phenomena for his extraordinary skill in conjuring, and his practically complete knowledge of every trick that ever had been played, or could be played. In fact, he was Bowling's expert witness on the question of the limits of possible fraud.

Until Simon Iff and his party entered, these three men had been entertained by a woman. She was dressed in a plain purple robe, made in a single piece. It fell to her feet. The sleeves were long and widening towards the wrist. A red rose, upon a cross of gold, was embroidered on the breast. Her rich brown hair was coiled over her ears.

The face of this woman was of extreme beauty, in a certain esoteric fancy. Like her whole body, it was sturdy and vigorous, but there was infinite delicacy, surprising in so strong a model. Her eyes were clear and fearless and true; but one could see that they must have served her ill indeed often enough, for they were evidently incapable of understanding falsity, and evil. The nose was straight and broad, full of energy; and the mouth passionate and firm. The lips were somewhat thick, but they were mobile and the whole expression of the face redeemed any defect of any feature. For while its general physical aspect was severe, even savage – she might have been a Tartar beauty, the bride of a Gengis Khan, or a South Sea Island Queen, tossing her lovers into the crater of Mauna Loa after killing them in the excess and fantasy of her passion – yet the soul within shone out and turned the swords to ploughshares. There was pride, indeed, but only of that kind which is (as it were) the buckler on the arm of nobility; the woman was incapable of meanness, of treachery, or even of unkindness.

There were terrible fires in the depths of that volcano; but they had been turned to human service; they had been used to heat the forge of art. For this woman was a great singer; and no one outside the Order knew of her secret aspirations, or that she retired from time to time to one or the other of the Profess-Houses of the Order, there to pursue a mightier transmutation of her being.

She greeted Cyril with peculiar warmth – indeed, it had been she to whom he had once thrown a pair of socks. In a way, it was he that had made her a great artist; for his personality had broken down her dykes; not till she met him had she ever let herself go. And it was by a magical trick that he had shown her how to use her art as a vehicle for her soul.

Later, he had brought her into the Order, realising the inestimable value of her virtue; and if she was not its most advanced member she was its most beloved.

They called her Sister Cybele.

CHAPTER VI

OF A DINNER

WITH THE TALK OF DIVERS GUESTS

SIMON IFF and Cyril Grey had slipped out of the reception-room to clothe themselves according to their dignity in the Order.

They returned in a few moments. The old man was in a robe of the same pattern as Sister Cybele's – all the robes of the Order were thus fashioned – but it was of black silk, and on the breast was embroidered a golden eye within a radiant triangle.

Cyril Grey was in a similar robe, but the eye was enclosed in a six-pointed star, and swords with undulating blades issued from each re-entrant angle.

Their return broke up the conversation, and Sister Cybele led the way, with Lisa on her arm, to the lobby.

There the wonder of the house began. The wall facing the front door was masked by a group of statuary of heroic size.

It was a bronze, and represented Mercury leading Hercules into Hades. In the background stood Charon in his boat, one hand upon his oar, the other stretched to receive his obolus.

Sister Cybele waited until all the guests were in the boat. Then she made pretence to place the coin in Charon's hand.

In reality she touched a spring. The wall parted; the boat moved slowly through; it took its place beside another wharf.

They were in a vast hall; and Lisa realised that the hill behind the house must have been profoundly hollowed out. This hall was lofty, narrow and long. In the midst, a circular table awaited the guests. Behind each chair stood one of the Probationers of the Order in a white robe, on whose breast was a scarlet Pentagram. Neck, sleeves, and hem were trimmed with gold. Beyond this table, at which a number of other members, in variously coloured robes, were already seated, though they rose to salute the newcomers briefly and in silence, was a triangular

slab of black marble, the points truncated for convenience. Around this there were six seats, made of ebony inlaid with silver discs.

Sister Cybele left the others to take her seat as president of the circular table. Simon Iff himself sat at the head of the triangle, placing Cyril Grey and the Mahathera Phang at the other corners. Lord Antony Bowling was at his left, Lisa at his right; Morningside faced him from the base.

When all were seated, Sister Cybele rose, struck a bell that stood at her hand, and said: "Do what thou wilt shall be the whole of the Law. O Master of the Temple, what is thy will?"

Simon Iff rose in his place. "It is my will to eat and drink," said he.

"Why shouldst thou eat and drink?"

"To sustain my body in strength."

"Why is it thy will that thy body may be sustained in strength?"

"That it may aid me in the accomplishment of the Great Work."

At this word all rose, and chanted solemnly in chorus, "So mote it be."

"Love is the law, love under will," said Sister Cybele softly, and sat down.

"Of course it's a most absurd superstition," remarked Morningside to Simon Iff, "to think that Food sustains the body. It is sleep that does that. Food merely renews the tissues."

"I agree entirely," said Cyril, before Iff could answer, "and I am about to renew my tissues to the extent of a dozen of these excellent Cherbourg prawns – to begin with!"

"My dear man," said Lord Antony, "prawns are much better at the end of a dinner – as you'd know if you had been to Armenia lately."

When Morningside said something absurd, it merely meant that he was airing his fads; when Lord Antony did so, it meant a story. And all his stories were good ones. Simon Iff jumped at the opening. He turned immediately, and asked for the yarn.

"It's rather long," said Bowling, a little dubiously. "But it's very, very beautiful."

Unacknowledged quotations gave a curious fascination to his narrative style. People became interested through the psychological trick involved. They recognised, yet could not place, the remark, and they were stirred by the magick of association, just as one becomes interested in a stranger who reminds one of one can't quite think who.

"At the close of a dark afternoon," pursued Lord Antony, "a huntsman of sinister appearance might have been seen approaching the hamlet of Sitkab in Armenia. This was myself – or I should hardly think it worth while to tell the story. Why detain you with a lesser potentate? I was in pursuit of the most savage, elusive, and dangerous wild beast, with the exception of woman," (he smiled at Lisa so delightfully that she could only take it as a compliment) "that infests this globe. Need I say that I refer to the Poltergeist?"

"You must do more," laughed Lisa. "You must tell me what my rival is!"

"A Poltergeist is a variety of spook distinguished by its playful habit of throwing furniture about, and otherwise playing practical jokes of the clown-in-the-pantomime order. The particular specimen, whose hide – if they have hides – I was anxious to add to my collection of theosophical tea-cups, spirit cigarettes, and other articles of vertu, was an artist of singular refinement, for he performed upon only one instrument, as a rule; but of that instrument he

had acquired the most admirable mastery. It was a common broomstick. This genial spectre – or rather non-spectre, for they are but rarely seen, only heard, conditions precisely opposed, I beg you to note, to those that we require in little boys – this Poltergeist, then, was alleged to be the guest of the local lawyer in the aforesaid hamlet. It had annoyed him considerably for some two years; for while claiming, through an excellent medium in the locality, to be the spirit of a deceased Adept, it had merely thrown broomsticks at him as he went about his daily task of making mischief between the citizens of that deplorably peaceful corner of the earth, or misappropriating funds intrusted to him for investment. He was an honest lawyer, as lawyers go – I was called to the Bar myself in my unregenerate days – and he resented the interference, the more so as no writ of habeas broomstick seemed to abate the nuisance.

"The amiable creature, however, had recently taken pity upon his host, and sought to establish a claim upon his gratitude by saving him from death. For one day, as the lawyer was about to drive across the village bridge he saw the broomstick fall from the sky and stand erect, precisely in his path. His horse reared; a moment later the bridge was swept away by the torrent. (This is really excellent Bortsch, Mr. Iff.) Well, I had been called in to investigate this matter, and there I was, installed in the house of my brother brigand. The results of my stay of six weeks or so were inconclusive. I was convinced of the man's entire belief in his story, and the broomstick certainly moved in various ways for which I could not account; but I was not fortunate enough to observe anything of the kind when he was not somewhere in the offing. And one is bound to strain one's theories of the limits of fraud as far as it is humanly possible – especially when one is dealing with a lawyer or a broomstick. So I returned from the parts of the tribes even unto the modern Babylon, where I abode for a season. A little while later I received a card announcing my friend's marriage to the heiress of Sitkab, and, a year later again, in response to kind enquiries, he had the honour to announce that the manifestations of the Poltergeist had totally ceased since the day of the wedding. Some of these Adepts are of course fearfully particular on the sex-question, as we all know. Fall for an hour from the austerities of a Galahad, and devil a cigar will precipitate itself into your soup, nor will you be interrupted at billiards by the arrival of an urgent message from Tibet, written on notepaper of the kind you purchase in Walham Green if you are a real lady, to the effect that the secret Wisdom is beyond the Veil, or some other remark evidential of Supreme Enlightenment in too much of a hurry to use the regular post.

"No, the story does not end here; in fact, the above has been but the prelude to a mightier theme. Once more a year passed by. By a singular, and, in view of what happened later, I think an ominous, train of circumstance, it occupied exactly twelve calendar months in the process.

"I now received another letter from the lawyer. Whether love's moon had waned or no he did not say; but he announced the resumption of the phenomena, with additions and improvements. One encouraging point was that in the previous series nothing had ever happened outside his house, except in the case of the bridge incident; now the broomstick was ubiquitous indeed, and followed him about like Mary's lamb. His wife, too, had developed the most surprising powers of mediumship and was obtaining messages from Herr P. Geist, which seemed of unusual importance. A new world was open to our view. I have always fancied myself as a Columbus;

and, as I had recently made a considerable sum of money by a fortunate speculation in oil, I did not hesitate to go to the expense of a telegram. I have always fancied myself as a Caesar, and I endeavoured to emulate his conciseness. 'Come stay winter' was the expression employed. A week later those simple and pious souls, escaping the perils of the journey to Constantinople, were safely cloistered, if I may use the term, in the Orient Express. They were extricated from Paris by a friend whom I had thoughtfully sent to meet them; and the following day my heart was gladdened by the realisation of my dreams – the actual physical presence of my loved ones in my ancestral halls in Curzon Street – those which I rented two years ago from Barney Isaacs; or rather from his heirs, for the poor fellow was hanged, as you remember.

"Well, the conclusions of science appear to indicate that a Poltergeist of the better classes takes a fortnight or more to accustom himself to a new domicile; from which circumstance learned men have written many treatises to suggest that it may be of the cat tribe; though others equally learned have contended with great plausibility that its touching attachment to this lawyer shows its nature to conform rather with that of the dog.

"To me it has seemed possible that the light is not altogether withheld from either party to the discussion; I have in fact diffidently put forward the theory that the Poltergeist, for all its German name, is of an ambiguous nature, like the animals of Australia; and I have ventured to rely upon the analogy between the broomstick employed in this case and the throwing-stick of the aborigines of that continent. However this may be, friend Poltergeist began to rehearse exactly fourteen days after the arrival of the lawyer and his wife, and was so kind as to oblige with a full recital – Scherzo in A flat, or more accurately A house – three days later. I never really valued the Sèvres vase which was offered on this occasion to the infernal gods.

"The mediumistic powers of the lady began to develop at the same time. The spirit had devised an ingenious method of communication, known to science as Planchette. This instrument is probably familiar to you all; it is an inconvenient way of writing, but otherwise exhibits no marked peculiarity. Now that we have accepted 'automatic wrriting' as automatic, there is really no reason why mediums should pretend that a planchette is not under control.

"This planchette gave us much invaluable information as to the habits, mode of life, social and other pleasures, of various parties deceased; and added, free of all charge, advice which, followed out, would undoubtedly tend to make me an even better man than I am. It is, however, with regret that I find myself obliged to confess that scientific truth is an even dearer object of my heart than moral beauty, and at the moment I was wholly absorbed in the desire to verify the latest facts about the Poltergeist, for these lent great weight to the theory that it was some kind of dog. Under the inspiring intuition of its charming mistress, it had developed those qualities which we associate with the spaniel or the retriever.

"Even in Armenia it had been wont, when weary of its solos upon the broomstick, to gladden and instruct humanity by putting small articles in places where they should not be. I would occasionally find my socks stuffed tightly into my trousers' pockets, or my razor poised upon a mirror, when I realised that morning in the bowl of night had flung the stone that puts the stars to flight, and that the Hunter of the East had caught the Sultan's Turret in a noose of light. But in

the second series of phenomena the faithful and intelligent animal had done far more than this, bringing into the house various objects from afar. It was evidently appreciated in the Beyond that a Poltergeist's reach should exceed his grasp.

"One day, in the wonderful month of May with all its flowers a-blossom, the planchette produced an exceedingly mysterious message. So far as we could understand him, he would bring more evidence of his presence. 'Proof' was one of the words used, I remember; yes, I remember that very distinctly. And the message ended, with a sudden transition, 'Look out for game!' There could hardly have been a more superfluous injunction so far as I was concerned!

"I must now describe my dining-room. It is very like any other room of the sort, I dare say; the point is that there is a big table, over which is suspended a cluster of electric lamps, a flat shade covering these from above. The top of this shade is just about on the level of the eyes of a fairly tall man, standing. I can see clear over it from the edge of the table without straining.

"Well, we went down to dinner, and the Poltergeist was exceptionally active all through the meal. The medium was exceedingly distressed by his insistence on the mysterious injunction to look out for game. It was only at dessert that the problem was solved. The medium screamed out suddenly, 'Oh! he's pinching my neck!' – and a second later – lightning in a clear sky – a large quail fell from the empyrean upon my humble mahogany.

"I only wished I could have had Rear Admiral Moore, Sir Oliver Lodge, Colonel Olcott, Sir Alfred Turner, Mr. A. P. Sinnett, and Sir Arthur Conan Doyle present on that sublime occasion. There could have been no dissentient voice to say that this was not 'evidential' – save, possibly, what is negligible, my own. A poor thing, but mine own!

"I wonder if you have ever reflected upon the halo of excitement and romance which must gild the lives of the members of the worshipful Company of Poulterers. They are the true sportsmen of our times; theirs to beard the turkey in his den, theirs to grapple the lordly pheasant, to close in deadly combat with the grouse, to wrest the plover's egg from its lonely nest upon the moors, to dare a thousand deaths in their grim heroism, the fulfilment of their oaths to supply us with sparrow, cat or rabbit. Think, too, of their relations with the mysterious bazaars of Baghdad; their traffickings with wily orientals, the counting-out of secret gold by moonlight in the shadow of the mosques; think of Mason, as he painfully deciphers the code cablegram from Fortnum, burns the message, and armed with a dagger and a bag of uncut rubies, plunges from the Ghezireh Palace Hotel to his rendezvous with Achmet Abdullah in the Fishmarket, where, with no eye to see, the hideous bargain is concluded, and, handing over his rubies, Mason sallies from that dreadful alley, clutching beneath his gaberdine – a quail.

"You have not thought such thoughts? Nor, until now, had I. But I knew that quails were cold storage products of the burning East, and I knew that the number of poulterers in my vicinity was limited. Early the next morning I visited in turn these respectable tradesmen, the third of whom remembered the sale of a quail to a lady on the previous day. Both quail and lady answered to the descriptions I had in mind.

"It had been the custom of my guests to walk abroad in the afternoons, now singly, now together, now with one or another of the members of my household.

"On this particular day, I begged the medium to permit me the honour of escorting her. She agreed with characteristic amiability; and, once in the street, I pleaded with her, like a child, to tell me a story. I said that I was sure she had a nice story to tell me. But no; it appeared not.

"In the course of our ambulation, we came – surely led by some mysterious Providence – to the very poulterer whom I had seen in the morning. I led her to that worthy man. 'Yes, my lord,' he replied to my urbane question with affable obsequience, 'this is the lady to whom I sold the quail.' She contradicted the statement brusquely; she had never been in the shop in her life. We proceeded on our walk. 'Tell me,' I said, 'exactly what you did do when you were out yesterday.' 'Nothing at all,' she answered. 'I went and sat in the park for a little. Presently my sister came and sat down with me, and we talked for a little. Then she went away, and came back in about half-an-hour. We talked some more, and them I came away back to Curzon Street.'

"On our return I questioned her husband. 'Sister!' he exclaimed, 'she never had a sister!'

"The mystery was cleared up. It was a case of Double Personality! There was, however, still one small point. How did that Spirit Quail get on to the table? It had fallen very straight, or so it seemed to us; and the butler said that he could hardly believe that a quail could have been concealed on the lamp-shade; he would have noticed it, he thought, while laying the table.

"The experiments continued. Some time later Brother Poltergeist permitted himself some allusions to fish – in the best possible taste – and I took my precautions accordingly. Before dinner I slipped downstairs and made a thorough search of the dining room. Alas! to what treacheries are the most virtuous of us liable to be subjected? That medium's saucy Sister Second Personality had again betrayed her to a most unjustifiable suspicion! For one dozen prawns, of the best quality, were distributed in most excellent symmetry about the lamp-shade.

"A hasty reference to the dictionary not yet published by the Society for Psychical Research assured me that this sort of thing was a 'prepared phenomenon'.

"Now, if you are going to prepare a phenomenon, you may as well prepare it properly; and I attended – you shall soon learn how – alike to decency and to asthetics.

"Dinner was served; the Poltergeist supplied the conversation. Never before had he been so light, so genial, so anxious to assure us of our future in Summerland; but ever and anon he touched the minor chord, spoke darkly of 'proof,' and of fish! (I beg you all to bear witness that I have not degraded myself by the evident pun). The dessert arrived. And now the Poltergeist was imminent. The lawyer thought to touch him and to hold him; he saw signs of him all over the room; he ran about after him, like a boy with a butterfly-net. But of all this I took no heed; I was watching the lady's face.

"Professor Freud would perhaps explain my motive as 'infantile psycho-sexual pre-sexuality'; but no matter: I watched her face.

"The lawyer, like what's his name pursuing Priam, was close on the heels of the Poltergeist – 'jam, jam' as used by Vergil in the sense of prolonging the suspense – at last he made one grab in empty air. He overbalanced; must have touched the lamp-shade, I suppose – for a shower of prawns fell upon us like the gentle rain from heaven, blessing both him that gives and him that takes.

"And oh! those spirit prawns were beautiful upon the table-cloth; for each had a bunch of blue ribbon, blue ribbon, to tie up its bonny red hair. I had not moved my eyes from that fair lady's face; and I am sorry to conclude this abstract and brief chronicle of the prawn by saying that I cannot swear that she betrayed any guilty knowledge!"

Lord Antony stopped with a jerk; and lifting his liqueur glass, drained it suddenly.

Sister Cybele rose and bowed to Simon Iff.

But Cyril Grey's voice rose in a high-pitched drawl: "Better a dinner of herbs where love is, than a stalled prawn, and discontentment therewith!"

The Master frowned him down. "Gentlemen!" he said, "It is the custom of this House that its guests pay for their entertainment. Lord Antony Bowling has done so by his delightful story; Mr. Morningside by his brilliant theory upon the function of food; and the Mahathera Phang by his silence. I may say that I expected no less, and no different, from any one of you; we are overpaid; and the debt of gratitude is ours."

Morningside was pleased; he thought the compliment sincere; Bowling understood something of the soul which had escaped him until that moment; the Mahathera Phang remained in his superb indifference.

Lisa addressed the Master: "I'm afraid I haven't paid; and I've had a perfectly wonderful dinner!"

Simon Iff replied with weight: "My dear young lady, you are not a guest – you are a candidate."

Suddenly conscious of herself, she blanched, and became rigid in her chair.

Simon Iff bade farewell to the three guests; Cyril and Sister Cybele conducted them to the boat, and bade them God-speed. The other brethren of the Order dispersed, one to one task, one to another.

Presently Simon and Cyril, Cybele and Lisa were together alone. The old man led the way to a cell cunningly hidden in the wall. There they took seats.

Lisa la Giuffria recognised that the critical moment of her life was come upon her.

CHAPTER VII

OF THE OATH OF LISA LA GIUFFRIA

AND OF HER VIGIL IN THE CHAPEL OF ABOMINATIONS

"**B**EFORE we go further," began Cyril Grey, "I think it right to express a doubt as to the advisability of our procedure. We have already seen the most determined opposition to our plans; and for my part, I would say frankly that it might be wiser, certainly safer, to abandon them."

Lisa turned on him like a tigress. "I don't know what your plans are, and don't care. But I didn't think you'd go back on them."

"Impulsive ladies," returned Cyril, "rush in where angels fear to tread."

"I'll go," said she. "I'm sorry for all that has happened – all!" and she fixed her lover with a look of infinite contempt.

Cyril shrugged his shoulders. "If you feel like that, of course, we can continue. But when the pinch comes, don't squeal! I have warned you."

"Brother Cyril could not draw back if he wished," put in Sister Cybele. "He is bound by his oath – as, in a little while, you will be."

Lisa read upon the woman's face a smile, as of triumphant malice. It disturbed her far more than Cyril's protest. Was she indeed in a trap? It might be so; then, Cyril, who had tried to save her, was in the trap too. She must go on, if only to be able to save him when opportunity occurred. At present she was wholly in the dark. She could feel the atmosphere of constraint, of subtle and terrible forces in the abyss which she was treading blindfold upon some razor-edge whose supports she could not even imagine; the adventure was to her a supreme excitement, and she lived first and last for that. Had she known herself better, she would have understood that

her love for Cyril was little more than a passion for the bizarre. But at the moment she was Joan of Arc and Juliet in one.

Moreover, she had the instinctive feeling that wherever these people might be going it was certainly somewhere. They were engineers building a bridge to an unknown land, just as methodically and purposefully as the builders of an earthly bridge. There was no doubt as to the validity of their knowledge or their powers. She perceived that Lord Antony Bowling had spent his life in the investigation of disjointed, purposeless items of mostly plain fraud; while under his very nose the Brethren of this Order were proceeding calmly with some stupendous task, not troubling even to acquaint the world with their results. And she could dimly guess why this was so, and must be so. They did not wish to be dragged into foolish controversies with the ignorant.

And just then Simon Iff took up the conversation with a remark in tune with that thought.

"We shall not ask you for any pledge of secrecy," he said, "for you have only to say what you see and hear to be laughed at for a liar. If this be our last meeting, we are quits. You will be taken to a little chapel leading from this room. There you will find a circle, which you must enter, being careful not to touch it, even with your dress; for that would be dangerous. Within that circle you must remain until we send for you, unless you wish to leave, in which case you have only to pass through the white curtains in the north. You will find yourself in a lighted passage; open the door at the end, you will be in the street, where my automobile awaits your orders. Your use of this exit will, however, close your career in magick; in any future relations we should merely be good friends – or I hope so – but we should not consider any proposal to reconstruct the present situation."

"I will wait until you send for me," cried Lisa. "I swear it."

Simon Iff placed his hand upon her brow; in another instant he was gone from the room.

Sister Cybele rose and took her by the hand. "Come!" said she; "but you had better bid farewell to your lover." The girl once again thrilled to the undertone of malice in the voice. But Cyril took her fondly in his arms, and crushed her to him.

"Tomorrow," he said, "brave heart, true heart! Tomorrow we shall be alone together!"

Trembling, la Giuffria returned to Sister Cybele, and followed her to the door of the chapel. She threw a last look over her shoulder: to her amazement Cyril was regarding her with a cynical smile of amusement. Her heart went deadly cold; she felt the pull of Sister Cybele's hand, suddenly grown iron and inexorable. The door shut behind her with a monstrous clang; and she found herself in a room at once obscure and menacing.

She wondered why they called it a chapel. It was a bell-shaped cave. She dimly saw the white curtains of which Iff had spoken; there was nothing else in the room but a square thin altar whose surface was of polished silver, around whose base ran a broad copper band, evidently the circle referred to, and ten lamps, set in little stars of iron, which gave a faint blue light. The entire chamber was cut out of the solid rock. Only that part of it which lay within the circle had been dressed; the rest of the floor, and the walls, which bent over to meet in a point, were rough.

She stepped carefully into the circle, raising her dress. Sister Cybele faced her squarely. In the woman's face Lisa read a thousand evil purposes, a cruelty devilishly hot as Cyril's was devilishly cold, and the assurance in those grey eyes that she had fallen into the power of creatures utterly abominable. Sister Cybele suddenly broke into a short harsh laugh, then stepped aside, and Lisa, turning quickly, only saw the door close behind her. Heedless of caution, she leapt after her in the impulse of self-preservation – but the door was entirely smooth on the inside. She beat against it, uttering a horrible, fierce cry: but only silence answered her.

The impulse passed as quickly as it had come. Mechanically she stepped back into the circle. And as she did so the thought of Simon Iff came to calm her. The other two might puzzle her, but she felt that Iff would neither do nor suffer wrong.

During dinner, too, she had fixed her gaze, fascinated, upon the Mahathera Phang. She knew that he was more than friendly to the Order, though not a member of it; and his face, coupled with the fact that he had not spoken even once in her presence, redoubled that confidence.

In front of the little altar, she discovered, as her eyes accommodated themselves to the dimness, a curiously shapen stool covered with leather. She squatted on it, and found it a very Paradise of ease. And then it dawned upon her that she had to wait. To wait!

There was no sound or movement to fix her attention; presently she began to amuse herself by making faces at herself in the polished silver of the altar. It was not long before she tired of that; and once again she found herself waiting.

Her imagination soon began to people the little room with phantoms; the memory of the Thing in the Garden began to obsess her. Once again Simon Iff came to the rescue. She knew that her imagination was at work, and that, even had the shapes about her been real, they could not harm her. She heard herself repeating the old mystic's words: "Because there is in him no place of death."

She became perfectly calm; for a little while her thoughts occupied her. Suddenly they fled, and she found herself (so to speak) in a small open boat, without provisions, in the midst of a limitless ocean of unutterable boredom.

She had a period of fidgets; that over, she became listless, and merely prayed for sleep.

Then she noticed that a square pencil of light had entered from the apex of the chapel, and was casting glory upon the top of the altar. She rose instantly – and gasped in amazement, for figures were moving on the silver.

Three men, with strange musical instruments, species respectively of flute, viol, and drum, were walking across a room. This room was hung with rose-coloured curtains, and lit with silver candelabra. At one end was a dais, and on this the men took their seats. They began to tune their instruments, and so strong was her fancy, that she thought she heard them. It was a fantastic Oriental dance-music. Presently a small boy, a negro, dressed in a yellow tunic and baggy breeches of pale blue, entered the room. He carried a salver, on which were a great flask of wine and two goblets of gold.

Then, to her utter amazement, Cyril Grey stepped into the room with Sister Cybele. They took the wine from the boy, and, each placing the left hand on the left shoulder of the other, they

touched their goblets, and, throwing their heads back, drained them. The boy took the empty cups and disappeared.

She saw Cyril and Cybele draw together; they gave a laugh which (once again) she fancied she could hear. It rang demoniac in her very inmost soul. An instant more, and their mouths met in a kiss.

Lisa felt her knees give way. She caught the altar, and saved herself from falling; but she must have lost consciousness for a second or two, for when her eyes opened she saw that they had discarded their robes, and were dancing together. It was wild and horrible beyond all imagination; the dancers were locked so closely that they appeared like a single monster of fable, a thing with two heads and four legs which writhed or leapt in hideous ecstasy.

She was so shaken that she did not even ask herself the nature of the vision, whether it was a dream, an hallucination, a picture of the past, or an actual happening. The bacchanal obscenity of it was overwhelming. Again and again she turned her eyes away; but they always returned to the gaze, and every gesture shot a pang of agony to her soul. She understood the ambiguities of her lover; his strange behaviour seemed like an open book to her; and the malice of Sister Cybele, her elfin laughter, her satanic sneer, sank into her bleeding heart like acid, burning, fuming.

The revel did not diminish; instead, it took novel and more atrocious forms. All that she had ever conceived of sensuality, of bestiality, was a thousandfold surpassed. It was an infinite refinement of abomination joined with an exaggeration of grossness that might have turned Georges Sand to stone. The light went out.

The thought of flight from that abominable chapel never came to her. It was Cyril – the man to whom she had given herself utterly at the first touch – who was plunging this poisoned dagger into her soul. And she could not even die; it was ferocity and madness that awoke in her. She would wait until the morning – and she would find a way to be avenged. Yet she felt that she was slowly bleeding to death; it did not seem that any morning could ever come to her. She would not be able to face Cyril; it seemed somehow as if the shame were hers.

And then she screamed aloud – a soft hand was on her shoulder. "Hush! Hush!" came a gentle voice in her ear. It was the girl who had waited on her at dinner. Even at the time Lisa had noticed that she was very different to the others; for they were of most cheerful countenance, and this girl's eyes were red with weeping. "Come away!" said the girl, "come away while it is time. This is the first chance I have ever had to escape; I was set to watch the chapel door tonight; and I found the spring. Oh, come away quickly! They're criminals; they corrupt you and they torture you. Oh do come, sister! I can't escape without you; the man in the automobile would stop me. But if you come, I can slip away. It's only a step through the passage. Oh God! Oh God! if I had only gone when I was as you are!" Lisa's whole soul went out in sympathy to the gentle creature. "Look what they've done to me!" "Feel all down my back!" The girl winced with pain even at Lisa's gentle fingertips. Her back was a mass of knotted weals; she must have been beaten savagely with a sjambok or a knout.

"And see my arms!" The girl lifted her hands, and the loose sleeves of her robe fell back. From wrist to elbow she was a mass of parallel cuts. "I wouldn't do what they wanted," she moaned, "it

was too horrible. You'd think no woman would; but they do. Sister Cybele's the worst. O come! Do come from this abominable house!"

Lisa had touched the summit of the mountain of hysteria. Her feelings were far beyond all expression; she was living in a world deeper than feeling. She gained the consciousness of her own nature, something far deeper than anything she had ever known, and she expressed its will in words of absolute despair. "I can't leave Cyril Grey."

"I'm afraid of him more than all the others," whispered the girl. "I loved him too. And when I came to him two days ago, thinking that he still loved me – he laughed and he had me whipped. Oh come away!"

"I can't," said Lisa, brokenly. "But you shall go. Here, take my dress; give me your robe. The chauffeur won't know the difference. Tell him to drive to the Grand Hotel; ask for Lavinia King; I'll get word to you tomorrow, and money if you need it. But – I – can't – go."

The last words dripped out icily from the frozen waters of her soul. Quickly the girl dressed herself in Lisa's clothes: then she threw the white robe over her – La Giuffria never thought of the symbolism of the action; she would have rather stood naked before a thousand men than appear in that garment of infamy –

The girl pressed one soft kiss upon her forehead: then was gone headlong through the curtains. Lisa heard the clang of the outer door, and a breath of cold air swept round the room.

It dizzied her, as if she had been drunk; she remembered no more; probably she slept.

At last, she came to consciousness again in a most strange state of being. A peculiar smell was in the air, something as of the sea; she felt a physical exhilaration incomparable. Her mind was still quite blank as to the past; she was not even surprised at her surroundings. She rose and began to stretch her arms in a dozen physical exercises. Just as she touched her toes for the tenth time the door behind her opened. Sister Cybele was standing there. "Come, Sister!" she cried, "it will be dawn in three minutes; first we must make the Adoration of the Sun, and then comes breakfast!"

The horror of the night returned to Lisa in a flash. But somehow it had receded into a deeper stratum of her being; when it came to a question of any possible action, she seemed remote. She had the horrible fancy that she had died in the night. She followed Sister Cybele as she would have followed her executioner to the block.

Together they went up a spiral staircase. They came to a large room, circular in shape; it was full of the members of the Order, in their robes. At the East, where an oriel opened toward the dawn, she could see the figure of Simon Iff, his eyes fixed, awaiting the rising of the Sun.

A beam touched his face; and he began:

"Hail unto thee that art Ra in thy rising; even unto thee that art Ra in thy strength, that travellest over the Heavens in thy Bark in the uprising of the Sun! Tahuti standeth in his splendour at the prow, and Ra-Hoor abideth at the helm; hail unto thee from the abodes of night!"

It seemed to her that the whole assembly, uniting in the singular gesture with which Simon Iff accompanied his words, was uplifted in some subtle way beyond her understanding. The crowd-psychology assailed her; and she gritted her teeth to curse this hypocrisy of devilry.

But at that moment the crowd broke like a wave upon the beach; and she saw a girl running upon her.

"Oh, you were splendid, sister!" cried a voice, and two scarred arms were thrown about her neck. It was the girl of the night before!

"Didn't you escape?" babbled Lisa, incoherent.

But the child's ringing laughter silenced her. "I forgive you for spoiling my record," she bubbled over. "You know, I'm supposed to get them five times in six."

Lisa stood bewildered. But Sister Cybele was wringing her hands and kissing her, and Cyril Grey was telling the child that he had first claim on the strangle-hold –

And then they all suddenly melted from her. Simon Iff was walking toward her, and his hand was open.

"I congratulate you, sister," he said solemnly, "upon your initiation to our Holy Order. You have well earned the robe in which you stand, for you have paid its price – service to others without thought of the consequence to yourself. Let us break our fast!"

And he took Lisa's arm; presently they came to the refectory. As in a well-rehearsed play, every one fell into his place; and before Lisa realised the utter subversion that had taken place in her being, Sister Cybele was on her feet, proclaiming:

"Do what thou wilt shall be the whole of the Law."

Lisa thought that breakfast the most delicious she had ever tasted in her life.

A great reaction from the strain of the previous twenty-four hours was upon her. She had lived a lifetime in that period; and in a sense she had most surely died and been reborn. She felt like a little child. She wanted to climb on to everybody's knee, and be hugged! She had regained at a single stroke the infant's faith in human nature; she looked at the universe as simply as a great artist does. (For in him too lives and rejoices the Eternal Babe.)

But her greatest surprise was in her physical health and energy. She had passed through a fierce and furious day, a night of infernal torture; yet she was unaccountably buoyant, eager, assiduous in every act, from her smiled word of pleasure to the drinking of her coffee.

Everything at that meal seemed matter of intoxication. She had not previously realised that toast, properly understood, was a superior stimulant to brandy.

When breakfast ended, she could not have walked across the room. It was dancing or nothing, so she said to herself.

Somehow she found herself once more in the Chapel of Abominations. On the altar was laid a sprig of gorse, and the sunlight, streaming through the apex of the vault, made its thorny bloom of the very fire and colour of day.

Simon Iff stood behind the altar; Cyril Grey was on her right hand, Sister Cybele on her left. They joined their hands about her.

"I will now complete the formality of your reception," said the old man. "Say after me: 'I (your name).'"

"I, Lisa la Giuffria –

"Solemnly promise to devote myself –"

She repeated the phrase.

"To the discovery of my true purpose in this life."

She echoed in a lower tone.

All three concluded "So mote it be."

"I receive you into this Order," Simon Iff added, "I confirm you in the robe which you have won; I greet you with the right hand of fellowship; and I induct you to the Gate of the Great Work." Still holding the hand which he had grasped, he led her from the chapel.

They passed through the refectory, and entered a room on its other side. This room was furnished as a library; there was nothing in it to suggest magick.

"This is the Hall of Learning," said Simon Iff. "Here must your work begin. And, innocent as it seems, it is a thousandfold more dangerous than the chapel from which you have come forth with so much credit."

Lisa seated herself, and prepared to listen to the exposition of her task in life which she expected to follow.

But she could not know why the old mystic was at such great pains (as he afterwards proved) to make every syllable of his discourse intelligible; for she had not heard his conference with Cyril Grey at the moment when Sister Cybele had called her.

"Brother Cyril!" the old mystic had said, "I shall go on – I shall even put more than the necessary care into the work – as if this were victory and not defeat.

"I tell you that you will never do anything yourself, still less anything for others, so long as you rely on women. This victory of the woman's is only the chance resultant of a chaos of emotional states. She's in it for the fun of the thing; she's not even an artist; she's merely the female of the species; and I do not alleviate the situation by one further precision – your species!"

"Are women no use? Why were they made?" asked Cyril, angry. He did not know that his question was prompted by a desire yet unconquered in himself. But Simon Iff answered him with mock humility.

"I am unskilled to unravel the mysteries of the Universe. Like Sir Isaac Newton, I am." But seeing the muffled rage in the boy's eyes, he spared him the conclusion.

CHAPTER VIII

OF THE HOMUNCULUS

CONCLUSION OF THE FORMER ARGUMENT

CONCERNING THE NATURE OF THE SOUL

"I AM going to be perfectly horrid," said Simon Iff, leaning over to Lisa, and measuring his words with the minutest care. "I am going to do everything possible to damp your enthusiasm. I would rather have you start from cold and spark up well as you go, than have you go off with a spurt, and find yourself without petrol in the middle of the big rise.

"I want you to take up this research because of your real love of knowledge, not because of your passion for Brother Cyril. And I tell you honestly that I am mortally afraid for you, because you live in extremes. It is good for a swift push to have that sudden energy of yours; but no research in science is to be taken by storm. You need infinite patience, nay, even infinite indifference to the very thing on which your heart is set:

"Well, I have prated. The old man must utter his distrust of fiery youth. So we'll go on.

"I'm going to talk to you about the soul again. Remember our conception of it, the idea that seemed to do away with all the difficulties at a blow. We had the idea of a soul, of a real physical substance, one of whose surfaces, or rather boundary-solids, was what we call body and mind. Body and mind are real, too, and truly belong to the soul, but are only minute aspects of it, just as any ellipse or hyperbola is an aspect of the section of a cone.

"We'll take just one more analogy in the lower dimensions as we pass.

"How do solids know one another? Almost entirely by their surfaces! Except in chemistry, which we have reason to believe to be a fourth-dimensional science, witness the phenomena of polarisation and geometrical isomerism, solids only make contact superficially.

"Then, shifting the analogy as we did before, how do fourth-dimensional beings know one another? By their bounding solids. In other words, my soul speaks to yours through the medium of our minds and bodies.

"That is the common phrase? Quite so; but I am using it in an absolute physical sense. A line can only be aware of another line at a point of contact; a plane of another plane at the line where they cut; a cube of another cube at the surface common to both; and a soul of another soul where their ideas are in conjunction.

"I do want you to grasp this with every fibre in your being; I believe it to be the most important thesis ever enunciated, and you will be proud to learn that it is wholly Brother Cyril's, with no help from me. Hinton, Rouse Ball, and others, laid the foundations; but it was he that put it in such a clear light, and correlated it with occult science."

"You must give the honour to the Mahathera Phang!" interjected Cyril. "I was proving to him the metaphysical nature of the soul – and he regarded me with so amused a smile that I perceived my asininity. Of course there can be but one order of Nature!"

"In any case," continued Iff, "this theory of Cyril's wipes the slate clean of every metaphysical speculation. Good and evil vanish instantly, with Realism and Nominalism, and Free will and Determinism – and all the 'isms' and all the 'ologies'! Life is reduced to mathematical formulae, indeed, as the Victorian scientists rightly wished to do; but at the same time mathematics is restored to her royal pre-eminence as not only the most exact, but the most exalted of the sciences. The intelligible order of things, moreover, becomes natural and inevitable; and such moral problems as the cruelty of organic life return to their real insignificance. The almost comic antinomy between man's size and his intelligence is reduced; and although the mystery of the Universe remains unsolved, at least it is a rational mystery, and neither senseless nor intolerable.

"Let us now come down to a simple practical point. Here is a soul anxious to communicate with other souls. He can only do it by obtaining a mind and body. Now you'll notice, taking that cone image of ours again, that any section of it is always one of three regular curves. It would not fit into a square, for example, however you turned it. And so our soul has to look about for some mind which will fit one of his sections. There is a great deal of latitude, no doubt; for the mind grows, and is at first very plastic. But there must be some sort of relation. If I am a wandering soul, and wish to communicate with the soul now manifesting a section of itself as Professor of Electricity at Oxford, it is useless for me to take the mind of a Hottentot. (Cyril sighed a doubt.)

"I'm going to digress for a moment. Look at the finished product, the soul 'incarnated,' as we may call it. There are three forces at work upon it; the soul itself, the heredity and the environment. A clever soul will therefore be careful to choose the embryo which seems most likely to be fairly free in the two latter respects. It will look for a healthy stock, for parents who will, and can, give the child every chance in life. You must remember that every soul is, from our point of view, a 'genius', for its world is so incalculably greater than ours that one spark of its knowledge is enough to kindle a new epoch in mankind.

"But heredity and environment usually manage to prevent any of this coming to light. No matter how full of whisky a flask may be, you will never make it drunk!

"So we may perhaps conceive of some competition between souls for possession of different minds and bodies; or, let us say, to combine the ideas, different embryos. I hope you notice how this theory removes the objection to reincarnation, that one's mind does not remember 'the last

time'. Why should our cone make connexion between its different curves? Each is so unimportant to it that it would hardly think of doing so. Yet there might be some similarity between successive curves (in our case, lives) that might make an historian suspect that they were connected; just as a poet's style would be constant in some respects, whether he wrote a war story or a love lyric.

"You see, of course, by the way, how this theory does away with all the nonsense about 'Are the planets inhabited?' with its implication of idiotic waste if they be not. To us every grain of dust, every jet of hydrogen on the sun's envelope, is the manifestation of a section of some soul:

"And here we find ourselves quite suddenly and unexpectedly in line with some of the old Rosicrucian doctrines.

"This brings us to the consideration of certain experiments made by our predecessors. They had quite another theory of souls; at least, their language was very different to ours; but they wanted very much to produce a man who should not be bound up in his heredity, and should have the environment which they desired for him.

"They started in paraphysical ways; that is, they repudiated natural generation altogether. They made figures of brass, and tried to induce souls to indwell them. In some accounts we read that they succeeded; Friar Bacon was credited with one such Homunculus; so was Albertus Magnus, and, I think, Paracelsus.

"He had, at least, a devil in his long sword 'which taught him all the cunning pranks of past and future mountebanks', or Samuel Butler, first of that dynasty, has lied.

"But other magicians sought to make this Homunculus in a way closer to nature. In all these cases they had held that environment could be modified at will by the application of telesmata or sympathetic figures. For example, a nine-pointed star would attract the influence which they called Luna – not meaning the actual moon, but an idea similar to the poets' ideas of her. By surrounding an object with such stars, with similarly disposed herbs, perfumes, metals, talismans, and so on, and by carefully keeping off all other influences by parallel methods, they hoped to invest the original object so treated with the Lunar qualities, and no others. (I am giving the briefest outline of an immense subject.) Now then they proceeded to try to make the Homunculus on very curious lines.

"Man, said they, is merely a fertilised ovum properly incubated. Heredity is there even at first, of course, but in a feeble degree. Anyhow, they could arrange any desired environment from the beginning, if they could only manage to nourish the embryo in some artificial way – incubate it, in fact, as is done with chickens today. Furthermore, and this is the crucial point, they thought that by performing this experiment in a specially prepared place, a place protected magically against all incompatible forces, and by invoking into that place some one force which they desired, some tremendously powerful being, angel or archangel – and they had conjurations which they thought capable of doing this – that they would be able to cause the incarnation of beings of infinite knowledge and power, who would be able to bring the whole world into Light and Truth.

"I may conclude this little sketch by saying that the idea has been almost universal in one form or another; the wish has always been for a Messiah or Superman, and the method some

attempt to produce man by artificial or at least abnormal means. Greek and Roman legend is full of stories in which this mystery is thinly veiled; they seem mostly to derive from Asia Minor and Syria. Here exogamic principles have been pushed to an amusing extreme. I need not remind you of the Persian formula for producing a magician, or of the Egyptian routine in the matter of Pharaoh, or of the Mohammedan device for inaugurating the Millenium. I did remind Brother Cyril, by the way, of this last point, and he did need it; but it did him no good, for here we are at the threshold of a Great Experiment on yet another false track!"

"He is only taunting me to put me on my mettle," laughed Cyril.

"Now I'm going to bring all this to a point," went on the old mystic. "The Greeks, as you know, practised a kind of eugenics. (Of course, all tribal marriage laws are primarily eugenic in intention.) But like the mediaeval magicians we were speaking of, with their Homunculus, the Greeks attached the greatest possible importance to the condition of the mother during gestation. She was encouraged to look only on beautiful statues, to read only beautiful books. The Mohammedans, again, whose marriage system makes Christian marriage by comparison a thing for cattle, shut up a woman during that period, keep her perfectly quiet and free from the interference of her husband.

"This is all very good, but it falls short of Brother Cyril's latest lunacy. As I understand him, he wishes indeed to proceed normally in a physical sense, but to prepare the way by making the heredity, and environment as attractive as possible to one special type of soul, and then – to go soul-fishing in the Fourth Dimension!

"Thus he will have a perfectly normal child, which yet is also a Homunculus in the mediaeval sense of the word!

"And he has asked me to lend you the villa of the Order at Naples for the purpose."

Lisa had lent forward; her face, between her hands was burning.

Slowly she spoke: "You know that you are asking me to sacrifice my humanity?" She was not silly enough to pretend to misunderstand the proposal and Simon liked her better for the way she took it.

He thought a moment. "I see now; I never thought of it before, and I am foolish, The conservatism of woman calls this sort of thing a 'heartless experiment.' Yet nothing is farther from our thoughts. There will be no action to annoy or offend you on the contrary. But I understand the feeling – it is the swift natural repugnance to discuss what is sacred."

"Tut – tut – my memory is always failing me these days," muttered Cyril; "I've quite forgotten the percentage of children that were born blind in 1861."

Lisa started to her feet. She did not know what he meant, but in some way it stung her like a serpent.

Simon Iff intervened. "Brother Cyril, you always use strong medicine!" he said, shaking his head; "I sometimes think you're too keen to see your results."

"I hate to beat about the bush. I say the thing that can never be forgotten."

"Or forgiven, sometimes," said the old man in gentle reproof.

"But come, my dear, sit down; he meant truth, after all, and truth cuts only to cure. It's a brutal fact that children used to be born blind, literally by the thousand, because it wasn't quite nice to publish the facts about certain diseases; and precautions against them were called 'heartless experiments'. What Cyril is asking you to do is no more than what your whole heart craves for; only he wants to crown that with a gift to humanity such as has never yet been given. Suppose that you succeed, that you can attract a soul to you who will find a way to abolish poverty, or to cure cancer, or to – oh! surely you glow with vision, a thousand heights of human progress thrusting their sunlit snows through the clouds of doubt!"

Lisa rose again to her feet, but her mood was no longer the same. She put her hands in Simon Iff's. "I think you're a very noble man," she said, "and it's an honour to work in such a cause." Cyril took her in his arms. "Then you will come with me to Naples? To the Master's own villa?"

She looked at Iff with a queer smile. "May I make a joke?" she said. "I should like to rechristen the villa – The Butterfly-Net!"

Simple Simon laughed with her like a child. It was just the delicate humour that appealed to him; and the classical allusion to the Butterfly as allegorical of the Soul showed him a side of the girl that he had hardly suspected.

But Cyril Grey swerved instantly to the serious aspect of the problem. "We have merely been discussing an A. B. case," he said; "we have forgotten where we stand. Somewhere or other I have made a blunder already, mark you! – and we have the Black Lodge on our trail. You may possibly recall some of the events of yesterday?" he concluded, with a touch of his old airy manner.

"Yes," said Simon, "I think you had better get to business."

"We discussed the thing on general lines during your vigil last night," said Cyril. "Our first need is defence. The strongest form of defence is counter-attack; but you should arrange for that to take shape as far as possible from the place you are defending, In this game you are keeping goal, Lisa; I am full back; Simple Simon is the captain playing at half-back; and I think we have a fairly fit eleven! So that's all right. There is reason to believe that the enemy's goal is in Paris itself. And if we can keep the ball in their half all through the game, you and I can spend a very quiet year in Italy."

"I can't follow all that football slang; but do explain why anyone should want to interfere with us. It's too silly."

"It's only silly when you get to the very distant end of a most abstruse philosophy. On the surface it's obvious. It's the objection of the burglar to electric lights and bells. You can imagine him having enough foresight to vote against a town councillor who proposed an appropriation for the study of science in general. Something might turn up which would put him out of business."

"But what is their business?"

"Ultimately, you may call it selfishness – only that's a dreadful word, and will mislead you. We're just as selfish; only we realise that other things beyond our own consciousnesses are equally ourselves. For instance, I try to unite myself as intimately as I can with every other mind, or body, or idea, that comes in my way. To take that cone simile, I want to be all the different curves I can,

so as to have a better chance of realising the cone. The Black Lodge magician clings to his one curve, tries to make it permanent, to exalt it above all other curves. And of course the moment the cone shifts, out he goes: pop!"

"Observe the poet!" remarked Simon Iff. "He values himself enormously; but his idea of perpetuating himself is to make the beauty that is inherent in his own soul radiate beyond him so as to illumine every other mind in the world. But your Black Magician is secret, and difficult of access; he isn't going to tell anyone anything, not he! So even his knowledge tends to extinction, in the long run."

"But you are yourselves a secret society!" exclaimed Lisa.

"Only to secure freedom from interruption. It is merely the same idea as that which makes every householder close his doors at night; or, better, as public libraries are guarded by certain regulations. We can't allow lunatics to scrawl over our unique manuscripts, and tear the pages out of all our books. Shallow people are always chattering about science being free to all; the truth is that it is guarded as no other secret ever was in all history, by the simple fact that, with all the help in the world, it takes half a lifetime to begin to master even one small section of it. We guard our magick just as much and as little as our other branches of physics; but people are so stupid that, though they know it requires years of training to use so simple an instrument as a microscope, they are indignant that we cannot teach them to use the Verendum in an hour."

"Ah, but they complain that you have never proved the use of the Verendum at all."

"Only those who have not learnt its use. I can read Homer, but I can only prove the fact to another man by teaching him Greek; and he is then obliged to do the same to a third party, and so on. People generally acquiesce that some men can read Homer because – well, it's their intellectual laziness. A really stout intelligence would doubt it.

"Spiritualism and Christian Science, which are either fraud or bluff or misinterpretation of facts, have spread all over the Anglo-Saxon world because there is no true critical spirit among the half-educated. But we are not willing to have our laboratories invaded by reporters and curiosity-mongers; we are dealing with delicate forces; we have to train our minds with an intensity which no other study in the world demands. Public indifference and incredulity suit us perfectly. The only object of advertisement would be to get suitable members; but we have methods of finding them without publicity. We make no secret of our methods and results, on the other hand; but only the right man knows how to discover them.

"It is not as if we were working in an old field where all the terms were defined, and the main laws ascertained. In Magick, even more than in any other science, the student must keep his practice level with his theory."

"Don't you ever do magick under test conditions?"

"Unfortunately, my child, creative magick, which is the thaumaturgic side of the business, depends on a peculiar excitation which objects to 'test conditions' very strongly. You might as well ask Cyril to prove his poetic gift, or even his manhood, before a set of fools. He will produce you poems, and infants, and events, as the case may be; but you have more or less to take his word for it that he did the acts responsible primarily for them. Another difficulty about true magick is

that it is so perfectly a natural process that its phenomena never excite surprise except by their timeliness – so that one has to record hundreds of experiments to set up a case which will even begin to exclude coincidence. For instance, I want a certain book. I use my book-producing talisman. The following day, a bookseller offers me the volume. One experiment proves nothing. My ability to do it every time is the proof. And I can't even do that under 'test conditions'; for it is necessary that I should really want the book, in my subconsciousness, whose will works the miracle. It is useless for me to think, or pretend, that I want it. Any man may fluke a ten-shot at billiards, but you call him a player only when he can average a break of thirty or so every time he goes to the table.

"But in some branches of magick we can give proof on the spot; in any branch, that is, where the female, and not the male, part of us is concerned. The analogy is quite perfect. Thus, in my guess at your birth-hour – was not that a test? I will do it all day, and be right five times in six. Further, in the event of error, I will show exactly why I was wrong. It's a case where one is sometimes right to be wrong, as I'll explain one day. Then again, your own clairvoyance; I did not tell you that sort of a Thing to look for; yet you saw it under the same form as I did. You shall practise these things daily with Cyril if you like, always checking your results in a way which he will show you; and in a month you will be an expert. Then, if you feel you want to advertise, do. But you won't.

"Besides, the real trouble is that not one person in a thousand cares for any form of science whatever; even such base applications of science as the steam-engine and all its family, from the telegraph to the automobile, were only thrust upon the unwilling people by bullies who knew that there was money in them. Who are your 'men of science' in the popular notion of today? Edison and Marconi, neither of whom ever invented anything, but were smart businessmen, with the capacity to exploit the brains of others, and turn science to commercially useful and profitable ends. Heigho!"

"We're a long way from our subject," said Cyril. "I have had a delightful morning – I have felt like Plato with the Good, the True, and the Beautiful in contemplating you three – but we have work before us. I propose in this emergency to copy the tactics of Washington at Valley Forge. We will make a direct and vehement attack on the Black Lodge: they will expect me to be in my usual position in the van – I will slip away with Lisa while the fires blaze brightest."

"A sound plan," said Simon. "Let us break up this conference, and put it immediately into execution. You had better not attract attention by collecting luggage, and you must certainly take no person outside the Order into your circle. So after dinner you will put on your other clothes, walk down to the Métro, cross to the Gare de Lyon, and jump into the Rome *rapide*. Wire me when you arrive at The Butterfly-Net!"

CHAPTER IX

HOW THEY BROUGHT THE BAD NEWS FROM ARAGO TO QUINCAMPOIX

AND WHAT ACTION WAS TAKEN THEREUPON

JUST as Lord Antony Bowling turned into the Grands Boulevards from the Faubourg Montmartre, Akbar Pasha was leaving them. The Turk did not see the genially flourished cane; he was preoccupied – and perhaps he did not wish to be recognised. For he dodged among the obscure and dangerous streets of "The Belly of Paris" with many a look behind him. To be sure, this is but a reasonable precaution in a district so favourable to Apache activities. At last he came out into the great open square of the markets; and, crossing obliquely, came to a drinking den of the type which seeks to attract foreigners, preferably Americans. It bore the quite incongruous name *Au Père Tranquille*. Akbar mounted the stairs. It was too early for revellers; even the musicians had not arrived; but an old man sat in one corner of the room, sipping a concoction of gin, whisky and rum which goes in certain circles by the name of a Nantucket Cocktail.

This individual was of some sixty years of age; his hair and beard were white; his dress was that of a professional man, and he endeavoured to give dignity to his appearance by the assumption of a certain paternal or even patriarchal manner. But his eye was pale and cold as a murderer's, shifty and furtive as a thief's. His hands trembled continually with a kind of palsy; and the white knuckles told a tale of gout. Self-indulgence had bloated his body; unhealthy fat was everywhere upon him.

The trembling of his hands seemed in sympathy with that of his mind; one would have said that he was in deadly fear, or the prey to a consuming anxiety.

At the Turk's entrance he rose clumsily, then fell back into his chair. He was more than half intoxicated.

Akbar took the chair opposite to him. "We couldn't get it," he said; in a whisper, though there was nobody within earshot. "Oh, Dr. Balloch, Dr. Balloch! do try to understand! It was impossible. We tried all sorts of ways."

The doctor's voice had a soft suavity. Though a licensed physician, he had long since abandoned legitimate practice, and under the guise of homeopathy pursued various courses which would have been but ill regarded by more regular practitioners.

His reply was horrible, uttered as it was in feline falseness, like a caress. "You foul ass!" he said. "I have to take this up with S.R.M.D., you know! What will he say and do?"

"I tell you I couldn't. There was an old man there who spoilt everything, in my idea."

"An old man?" Dr. Balloch almost dropped his hypocritical bedside voice in his rage. "Oh curse, oh curse it all!" He leant over to the Turk, caught his beard, and deliberately pulled it. There is no grosser insult that you can offer to a Mussulman, but Akbar accepted it without resentment. Yet so savage was the assault that a sharp cry of pain escaped him.

"You dog! you Turkish swine!" hissed Balloch. "Do you know what has happened? S.R.M.D. sent a Watcher – a bit of himself, do you understand what that means, you piece of dirt? – and it hasn't returned. It must have been killed, but we can't find out how, and S.R.M.D. is lying half dead in his house. You pig! Why didn't you come with your story at once? I know now what is wrong."

"You know I don't know your address," said the Turk humbly. "Please, oh please, leave go of my beard!"

Balloch contemptuously released his victim – who was a brave enough man in an ordinary way, and would have had the blood of his own Sultan, though he knew that the guards would cut him to pieces within the next ten seconds, for the least of such words as had been addressed to him. But Balloch was his Superior in the Black Lodge, which rules by terror and by torture; its first principle was to enslave its members. The bully Balloch became a whimpering cur at the slightest glance of the dreaded S.R.M.D.

"Tell me what the old man was like," he said. "Did you get his name?"

"Yes," said Akbar, "I got that. It was Simon Iff."

Balloch dashed his glass upon the ground. "Oh hell! Oh hell! Oh hell!" he said, not so much as a curse but as an invocation. "Hear, oh hear this creature! The ignorant, blind swine! You had him – Him! – under your hand; oh hell, you fool, you fool!"

"I felt sure he was somebody," said Akbar, "but I had no orders."

"And no brains, no brains," snarled the other. "Look here; I'll tell you how to get your step in the Lodge if you'll give me a hundred pounds."

"Do you mean it?" cried Akbar, entirely his own man in a moment, for abject fear and

obsessing ambition combined to make his advancement the tyrant of his whole tormented mind. "Will you swear it?"

Balloch made an ugly face. "By the black sow's udder, I will."

His whole frame trembling with excitement, Akbar Pasha drew a cheque-book from his pocket, and filled in a blank for the required sum.

Balloch snatched it greedily. "This is worth your money," he said. "That man Iff is in the second grade, perhaps even the first, of their dirty Order; and we sometimes think he's the most powerful of the whole damned crew. That fool Grey's a child to him. I know now how the Watcher was destroyed. Oh! S.R.M.D. will pay somebody for this! But listen, man – you bring that old beast's head on a charger – or Grey's, either! – and you can have any grade you dare ask for! And that's no lie, curse it! Why," he went on with increasing vehemence, "the whole thing's a plant of ours. Monet-Knott's one of us; we use him to blackmail Lavinia King – about all he's fit for, the prig! And we got him to drag that dago woman in front of Master Grey's dog nose! And now they bring in Simon Iff. Oh, it's too much! We've even lost their trail. Ten to one they're safe in their Abbey tonight. Be off! No, wait for me here; I'll bring back orders. And while I'm gone, get that son of yours here – he's got more sense than you. We'll have to trace Grey somehow – and astral watchers won't do the trick when Simon Iff's about."

Balloch rose to his feet, buttoned his coat around him, put on a tall silk hat, and was gone without wasting another word upon his subordinate.

The Turk would have given his ears to have dared to follow him. The mystery of S.R.M.D.'s personality and abode were shrouded in the blackest secrecy. Akbar had but the vaguest ideas of the man; he was a formless ideal of terrific power and knowledge, a sort of incarnated Satan, the epitome of successful iniquity. The episode of the "Watcher" had not diminished the chief's prestige in his eyes; it was evidently an "accident"; S.R.M.D. had sent out a patrol and it had been ambushed by a whole division, as it were. So trivial a "regrettable incident" was negligibly normal.

Akbar had no thought but of S.R.M.D. as a Being infinitely great in himself; he had no conception of the price paid by the members of the Black Lodge. The truth is, that as its intimates advance, their power and knowledge becomes enormously greater; but such progress is not a mark of general growth, as it is in the case of the White Brotherhood; it is like a cancer, which indeed grows apace, but at the expense of the man on whom it feeds, and will destroy both him and itself in the long run. The process may be slow; it may extend over a series of incarnations; but it is sure enough. The analogy of the cancer is a close one; for the man knows his doom, suffers continual torture; but to this is added the horrible delusion that if only the disease can be induced to advance far enough, all is saved. Thus he hugs the fearful growth, cherishes it as his one dearest possession, stimulates it by every means in his power. Yet all the time he nurses in his heart an agonising certainty that this is the way of death.

Balloch knew S.R.M.D. well; had known him for years. He hoped to supplant him, and while he feared him with hideous and unmanly fear, hated him with most hellish hatred. He was under no delusion as to the nature of the Path of the Black Lodge. Akbar Pasha, a mere outsider, without a crime on his hands as yet, was a rich and honoured officer in the service of the

Sultan; he, Balloch, was an ill-reputed doctor, living on the fears of old maids, on doubtful and even criminal services to foolish people, from the supply of morphia to the suppression of the evidence of scandal, and on the harvest of half-disguised blackmail that goes with such pursuits. But he was respectability itself compared to S.R.M.D.

This man, who called himself the Count Macgregor of Glenlyon, was in reality a Hampshire man, of lowland Scottish extraction, of the name of Douglas. He had been well educated, became a good scholar, and developed an astounding taste and capacity for magic. For some time he had kept straight; then he had fallen, chosen the wrong road. His powers had increased at a bound; but they were solely used for base ends. He had established the Black Lodge far more firmly than ever before, jockeyed his seniors out of office by superior villainy, and proceeded to forge the whole weapon to his own liking. He had had one terrible setback.

Cyril Grey, when only twenty years of age, a freelance magician, had entered the Lodge; for it worked to attract innocent people under a false pretence of wisdom and of virtue. Cyril, discovering the trick, had not withdrawn; he had played the game of the Lodge, and made himself Douglas's right-hand man. This being achieved, he had suddenly put a match to the arsenal.

The Lodge was always seething with hate; Theosophists themselves might have taken lessons from this exponent; and the result of Cyril's intervention had been to disintegrate the entire structure. Douglas found his prestige gone, and his income with it. Addiction to drink, which had accompanied his magical fall, now became an all-absorbing vice. He was never able to rebuild his Lodge on its former lines; but those who thirsted for knowledge and power – and these he still possessed in ever increasing abundance as he himself decayed – clung to him, hating and envying him, as a young ruffian of the streets will envy the fame of some robber or murderer who happens to fill the public eye.

It was with this clot of perverse feelings that Balloch approached the Rue Quincampoix, one of the lowest streets in Paris, and turned in at the den where Douglas lodged.

S.R.M.D. was lying on a torn soiled sofa, his face white as death; a mottled and empurpled nose, still showing trace of its original aggressive and haughty model, alone made for colour. For his eyes were even paler than the doctor's. In his hand was a bottle half full of raw whisky, with which he was seeking to restore his vitality.

"I brought you some whisky," said Balloch, who knew the way to favour.

"Put it down, over there. You've got some money."

Balloch did not dare to lie. S.R.M.D. had spotted the fact without a word.

"Only a cheque. You shall have half tomorrow when I've cashed it."

"Come here at noon."

Despite the obvious degradation of his whole being, S.R.M.D. was still somebody. He was a wreck, but he was the wreck of something indubitably big. He had not only the habit of command, but the tone of fine manners. In his palmy days he had associated with some very highly placed people. It was said that the Third Section of the Russian Police Bureau had once found a use for him.

MOONCHILD

"Is the Countess at home?" asked Balloch, apparently in courtesy.

"She's on the Boulevard. Where else should she be, at this time of night?"

It was the vilest thing charged against that vile parody of a man, his treatment of his wife, a young, beautiful, talented, and charming girl, the sister of a famous Professor at the Sorbonne. He had delighted to reduce her to the bedraggled street-walker that she now was. Nobody knew what Douglas did with his money. The contributions of his Lodge were large; blackmail and his wife's earnings aided the exchequer; he had probably a dozen other sources of income. Yet he never extricated himself from his sordidness; and he was always in need of money. It was no feigned need, either; for he was sometimes short of whisky.

The man's knowledge of the minds of others was uncanny; he read Balloch at a gesture.

"Grey never struck the Watcher," he said; "it was not his style; who was it?"

"Simon Iff."

"I shall see to that."

Balloch understood that, though S.R.M.D. feared Iff and loathed him, his great preoccupation was with Cyril Grey. He hated the young magician with a perfect hatred; he would never forget his ruin at those boyish hands. Also, he forgave nothing, from a kindness to an insult; he was malignant for the sake of malice.

"They will have gone over to their house on Montmartre," continued Douglas, in a voice of absolute certitude. "We must have the exits watched by Abdul Bey and his men. But I know what Grey will do as well as if he had told me; he will bolt somewhere warm for his damned honeymoon. You and Akbar watch the Gare de Lyon. Now, look here! with a bit of luck, we'll finish off this game; I'm weary of it. Mark me well!"

Douglas rose. The whisky he had drunk was impotent to affect him, head or legs. He went over to a small table on which were painted certain curious figures. He took a saucer, poured some whisky into it, and dropped a five-franc piece into the middle. Then he began to make weird gestures, and to utter a long conjuration, harsh-sounding, and apparently in gibberish. Lastly, he set fire to the whisky in the saucer. When it was nearly burnt through, he blew it out. He took the coin, wrapped it in a piece of dark-red silk, and gave it to his pupil.

"When Grey boards a train," he ordered, "go up to the engine-driver, give him this, and tell him to drive carefully. Let me know what the fellow looks like; get his name, if you can; say you want to drink his health. Then come straight here in a cab."

Balloch nodded. The type of magic proposed was familiar enough to him. He took the coin and made off.

At the Sign of the Tranquil Father, Akbar was awaiting him with his son Abdul Bey. The latter was in charge of the Turkish Secret Service in Paris, and he did not hesitate to use the facilities thus at his disposal to his own magical advancement. All his resources were constantly at the service of Balloch. Now that S.R.M.D. himself was employing him, he was beside himself with pride and pleasure.

Balloch gave his instructions. An hour later the house where Lisa was even then undergoing her ordeal would be surrounded by spies; additional men would be placed at all the big terminals

of Paris; for Abdul Bey meant to do the thing thoroughly. He would not take a chance; for all his fanatical faith in Douglas, he thought it prudent to provide against the possibility of an error in the chief's occult calculations. Also, his action would prove his zeal. Besides, Cyril might deliberately lay a false trail – was almost sure to play some trick of the sort.

Balloch and Akbar Pasha were stationed in a restaurant facing the Gare de Lyon, ready to answer the telephone at any moment. "Now," said Abdul, "have you photographs of these people to show my men?"

Balloch produced them.

"I've seen this man Grey somewhere," remarked the young Turk casually. And then he gave a sudden and terrible cry. In Lisa he recognised an unknown woman whom he had admired the year before at a dance – and whom he had craved ever since. "Tell S.R.M.D.," he roared, "that I'm in this thing for life or death; but I ask the girl for a trophy."

"You'll get that, or anything else," said Balloch, "if you can put an end to the activities of Mr. Cyril Grey."

Abdul Bey rushed off without another word spoken; and Balloch and the Pasha went to the rendezvous appointed. They passed that night and the next day in alternate bouts of drink and sleep. About half-past eight on the following evening the telephone rang. Douglas had judged rightly; the lovers had arrived at the Gare de Lyon.

Balloch and his pupil sprang to life – fresh and vigorous at the prick of the summons to action.

It was easy to mark the tall figure of the magician, with the lovely girl upon his arm; at the barrier their distinction touched the humanity of the collector. Tickets through to Rome – and no luggage! Most evidently an elopement!

With romantic sympathy, the kind man determined to oppose the passage of Balloch, whom he supposed to be an angry father or an outraged husband. But the manner of the Englishman disarmed him; besides, he had a ticket to Dijon.

Concealing himself as best he could, the doctor walked rapidly to the head of the train. There, assuming the character of a timid old man, he implored the driver, with the gift of the bewitched "cart-wheel", to be sure to drive carefully. He would drink the good fellow's health, to be sure – what name? Oh! Marcel Dufour. "Of the furnace – that is appropriate!" laughed the genial passenger, apparently reassured as to his security.

But he did not enter the train. He dashed out of the station, and into a motor-cab, overjoyed to return to Douglas with so clean a record of work accomplished.

He never gave the Turk another thought.

But Akbar Pasha had had an idea. Balloch had taken a ticket for Dijon – he would take one, too. And he would go – he would retrieve his error of yesterday. He was not in the least afraid of that cub Grey, when Simon Iff was not there to back him. It would go hard, but he should get a drop of Lisa's blood – if he had to bribe the wagon-lit man. Then – who knows? – there might even be a chance to kill Grey. He waited till the last moment before he boarded the train.

The train would stop at Moret-les-Sablons; by that time the beds would be made up; he would have plenty of time to act; he could go on to Rome if necessary.

Cyril Grey, away from the influence of Simon Iff, had become the sarcastic sphinx once more. He was wearing a travelling suit with knickerbockers, but he still affected the ultra-pontifical diplomatist.

"The upholstery of these cars is revolting," he said to Lisa, with a glance of disgust. And he suddenly opened the door away from the platform and lifted her on to the permanent way; thence into a stuffy compartment in the train that was standing at the next *Voie*.

"A frosty moonlight night like this," he said, pulling a large black pipe from his pocket and filling it, "indicates (to romantic lovers like ourselves) the propriety of a descent at Moret, a walk to Barbizon through the forest, a return to Moret by a similar route in a day or so, and the pursuance of our journey to Naples. See Naples and die!" he added musingly, "Decidedly a superior programme." Lisa would have listened to a proposition to begin their travels by swimming the Seine, on the ground that the day after tomorrow would be Friday; so she raised no objection. But she could not help saying that they would have reached Moret more quickly by the *rapide*.

"My infant child!" he returned; "the celebrated Latin poet Quintus Horatius Flaccus has observed, for our edification and behoof, '*Festina lente*'. This epigram has been translated by a famous Spanish author, '*mañana*'. Dante adds his testimony to truth in his grandiose outburst, '*Domani*'. Also, an Arab philosopher, whom I personally revere, remarks, if we may trust the assertion of Sir Richard Francis Burton, K.C.M.G. – and why should we not? – 'Conceal thy tenets, thy treasure, and thy travelling!' This I do. More so," he concluded cryptically, "than you imagine!"

They were still waiting for their local funeral (which the French grandiloquently describe as a train) to start when Dr. Balloch returned radiant to the Rue Quincampoix.

Douglas was on the alert to receive him. The news took only a second to communicate.

"Marcel Dufour!" cried S.R.M.D. "We shall drink for him, as he may not drink on duty."

He carefully opened two bottles of whisky, mixed the stale spirit in the magic saucer with their contents, and bade Balloch join him at the table.

"Your very good health, Marcel Dufour!" cried Douglas. "And mind you drive carefully!" Balloch and he now set to work steadily to drain the two bottles – a stiff nip every minute – but the stuff had no effect on them. It was far otherwise with the man on the engine.

Almost before he had well left Paris behind him, he began to fret about the furnace, and told his fireman to keep up the fullest head of steam. At Melun the train should have slackened speed; instead, it increased it. The signalman at Fontainebleau was amazed to see the *rapide* rush through the station, eight minutes ahead of time, against the signals. He saw the driver grappling with the fireman, who was thrown from the footplate a moment after, but escaped with a broken leg.

"My mate went suddenly mad," the injured man explained later. "He held up a five-franc piece which some old gentleman had given him, and swore that the devil had promised him another if he made Dijon in two hours. (And, as you know, it is five, what horror!)"

He grew afraid, saw the signals set at danger, and sprang to the lever. Then that poor crazed Dufour had thrown him off the train.

The guard was new to that section of the line, and so, no doubt, too timid to take the initiative; he certainly should have applied the brakes, even at Melun.

An hour later Cyril Grey and Lisa and all their fellow passengers were turned out at Fontainebleau. There had been a terrible disaster to the Paris-Rome *rapide* at Moret. The line would be blocked all night.

"This contretemps," said Cyril, as if he had heard of a change of programme at a theatre, "will add appreciably to the length and, may I add, to the romance – of our proposed walk."

When they reached Moret more than three hours later, they found the *rapide* inextricably tangled with a heavy freight train. It had left the line at the curve and crashed into the slower train. Cyril Grey had still a surprise in store. He produced a paper of some sort from his pocket, which the officer of the police cordon received in the manner of the infant Samuel when overwhelmed by the gift of prophecy. He made way for them with proud deference.

They had not to walk far before the magician found what he was seeking. Beneath the ruins of the rear compartment were the remains of the late Akbar Pasha.

"I wonder how that happened," he said. "However, here is a guess at your epitaph: 'a little learning is a dangerous thing.' I think, Lisa, that we should sup at the Cheval Blanc before we start our walk to Barbizon. It is a long way, especially at night, and we want to cut away to the west so as to avoid Fontainebleau, for the sake of the romance of the thing."

Lisa did not mind whether she supped at the White Horse, or on one. She realised that she had hold of a man of strength, wisdom, and foresight, far more than a match for their enemies.

He stopped to speak to the officer in charge of the cordon as they passed him. "Among the dead: Mr. and Mrs. Cyril Grey. English people. No flowers. Service of the minister."

The officer promised to record the lie officially. His deference was amazing.

Lisa perceived that her lover had been at the pains to arm himself with more than one kind of weapon. Lisa pressed his arm, and murmured her appreciation of his cleverness.

"It won't deceive Douglas for two minutes, if he be, as I suspect, the immediate Hound of the Baskervilles, but he may waste some time rejoicing over my being such an ass as to try it; and that's always a gain."

Lisa began to wonder whether her best chance of ever saying the right thing would not be to choose the wrong. His point of view was always round the corner of her street!

CHAPTER X

HOW THEY GATHERED THE SILK

FOR THE WEAVING OF THE BUTTERFLY-NET

CYRIL GREY made the midnight invocation to the Sun-God, Khephra, the Winged Beetle, upon the crest of the Long Rocher; and he made the morning invocation to the Sun-God, Ra, the Hawk, upon the heights that overlooked the hamlet of Barbizon.

Thence, like Chanticleer himself, he woke the people of the Inn, who, in memory of the days Stevenson had spent with them, honour his ashes by emulating the morality of Long John Silver.

They were prepared for the breakfast order; but Cyril's requirement, a long-distance call to Paris, struck them as unseasonable and calculated to disturb the balance of the Republic. They asked themselves if the Dreyfus case were come again. However, Cyril got his call, and Simon Iff his information, before seven o'clock. Long before Douglas, who had waited until midnight for the news of his triumph, had recovered from the sleep following its celebration, Iff in his fastest automobile had picked up the lovers at an agreed spot in the forest, the Croix du Grand Maître, whirled them to Dijon, and put them into the train for Marseilles. There they took ship, and came to Naples by sea, without adventure.

The enemy, in one way or another, had been thrown utterly off the track. It was early in the morning when they landed; at three o'clock they had visited such local deities as commanded their more urgent piety; the Museum, Vergil's Tomb, also Michaelsen the bookseller and vendor of images of the Ineffable. At four they started, hand in hand, along the shore, towards their new home.

An hour's walk brought them to the foot of a long stairway, damp stonework, narrow, between high walls, that led vertical and steep to the very crest of Posilippo. One could see the

old church amid its cluster of houses. Cyril pointed to a house a couple of hundred yards north of the church. It was the most attractive building on the hillside.

The house itself was not large, but it was built like a toy imitation of one of those old castles that one sees everywhere on difficult heights, throughout most of Southern and even Central Europe; in a word, like a castle in a fairy-story. It looked from below, owing to foreshortening, as if it were built over a sheer rampart, like the Potala at Lhassa; but this was only the effect of merging a series of walls which divided the garden by terraces.

"Is that the Butterfly-net?" cried Lisa, slapping her hands with delight.

"That," he dissented, "is The Net."

Once again Lisa felt a pang of something like distrust. His trick of saying the simplest things as if they bore a second meaning, hidden from her, annoyed her. He had been strangely silent on the voyage, and wholly aloof from her on those planes where she most needed him; that was a necessary condition of the experiment, of course; but none the less it tended to disturb her happiness. Such talks as they had had were either purely educative, Magick in Six Easy Lessons, he called it, or Magick without Tears, or else they were conventional lover's chats, which she felt sure he despised. He would tell her that her eyes were like the stars; and she would think that he meant: "What am I to say to this piece of wood?" Even nature seemed to stir his contempt in some way. One night she had noticed him rapt in a poetic trance leaning over the bows watching the foam. For a long while he remained motionless, his breast rising quickly and falling, his lips trembling with passion – and then he turned to her and said in cold blood: "Ought that to be used to advertise a dentifrice or a shaving soap?" She was sure that he had rehearsed the whole scene merely to work her up in order to have the fun of dropping her again. Only the next morning she woke early, to find a pencilled sonnet on his table, a poem so spiritual, so profound, and of such jewelcraft, that she knew why the few people whom he had allowed to read his work thought him the match of Milton. So apt were the similes that there could be no doubt that he had thought it out line by line, in that trance which he had marred, for her, by his brutal anti-climax.

She had asked him about it.

"Some people," he had said quite seriously, "have one brain; some have two. I have two." A minute later: "Oh, I forgot. Some have none."

She had refused to be snubbed. "What do you mean by your having two brains?"

"I really have. It seems as if, in order to grasp anything, I were obliged to take its extremes. I see both the sublime and the ridiculous at once, and I can't imagine one existing apart from the other, any more than you can have a stick with only one end. So I use one point of view to overbalance the other, like a child starting to swing itself. I am never happy until I have identified an idea with its opposite. I take the idea of murder – just a plain, horrid idea. But I don't stop there. I multiply that murder, and intensify it a millionfold, and then a millionfold again. Suddenly one comes out into the sublime idea of the Opening of the Eye of Shiva, when the Universe is annihilated in an instant. Then I swing back, and make the whole thing comic by having the hero chloroform Shiva in the nick of time, so that he can marry the beautiful American heiress."

"Until I have been all round the clock like that, I don't feel that I have the idea at all. If you had only let me go on about the shaving soap, I should have made it into something lovely again – and all the time I should have perceived the absolute identity of even the two contradictory phases."

But it was beyond her still, in each case as it came up "That is the Net!" A riddle? It might mean a thousand things; and to a woman of her positive and prosaic temperament (which she had, for all her hysteria and romanticism) doubt was torture. Love itself always torments women of this type; they want their lovers under lock and key. They would like love itself to be a more substantial commodity, a thing that one could buy by the pound, and store in a safe or an ice-chest.

Doubt and jealousy, those other hand-maidens of love, are also the children of imagination. But people wrongly use the word "imagination" to mean abstraction of ideas from concrete facts. And this is the reverse of the truth. Imagination makes ideas visible, clothes Being in form. It is, in short, very much like the "faith" of which Paul speaks. When true imagination makes true images of the Unseen, we have true love, and all true gods; when false imagination makes false images – then come the idols, Moloch, Jahveh, Jaganath, and their kindred, attended by all shapes of vice, of crime, of misery.

Lisa was thinking, as she climbed the apparently unending staircase, that she had taken pretty long odds. She had not hesitated to buck the Tiger, Life. Simon Iff had warned her that she was acting on impulse. But – on the top of that – he had merely urged her to be true to it. She swore once more that she would stick to her guns. The black mood fell from her. She turned and looked upon the sea, now far below. The sun, a hollow orb of molten glory, hung quivering in the mist of the Mediterranean; and Lisa entered for a moment into a perfect peace of spirit. She became one with Nature, instead of a being eternally at war with it.

But Cyril turned his face again to the mountain; she knew that he wanted to perform the evening adoration from the terrace of the house itself.

At last they came out from their narrow gangway to the by-street behind the church. It was an old and neglected thoroughfare, far from the main automobile road that runs along the crest. It was a place that the centuries had forgotten. Lisa realised that it was a haven of calm – and in a sense she resented the fact. Her highly coloured nature demanded constant stimulus. She was an emotion-fiend, if one may construct the term by analogy with another branch of pathology.

The lovers turned to the left through the village; in a few minutes the road opened, and they saw the villa before them. It stood on a spur of rock, separated from the main hill by a sharply cut chasm. This was spanned by an old stone bridge, a flying arch set steeply from the road to the house. It almost gave the effect of a frozen cascade issuing from the great doorway.

Cyril led Lisa across the bridge. This house was not served like that they had left behind them in Paris. Visitors were not expected or desired at any time, and the inmates rarely left the grounds, except on duty.

It was therefore some time before an answer to the summons reached them. Cyril's hand, dragging down an iron rope, had set swinging a great bell, deep and solemn, like a tocsin, in the turret which overlooked the chasm. Not until its last echo was dumb did a small Judas in

the door slide back. Cyril held up his left hand, and showed his seal-ring. Immediately the door swung open; a man of fifty odd years of age, dressed in black, with a great sword, like his brother guard at the Profess-House in Paris, stood bowing before them.

"Do what thou wilt shall be the whole of the Law. I enter the house."

With these words Cyril Grey assumed possession. "Lead me to Sister Clara." The man turned and went before them down a long corridor which opened upon a stone terrace, flagged with porphyry. A circular fountain in the middle had for its centre a copy of the Venus Callipyge in black marble. The parapet was decorated with statues of satyrs, fauns, and nymphs.

The woman who came to meet them was assuredly kin to that ancient company. She was about forty years of age, robust and hardy, burnt dark with years of outdoor life, her face slightly pitted with smallpox, her eyes black, stern, and true. Her whole aspect and demeanour expressed devoting capacity and determination. It was she who ruled the house in the absence of Simon Iff.

A brief colloquy between this woman and Cyril Grey followed their first greetings, whose austere formality inexplicably conveyed the most cordial kindness. He explained that he wished her to continue in full control of the house, only modifying its rules so far as might be necessary for the success of a certain experiment in magick which he had come to carry out. Sister Clara acquiesced with the slightest of nods; then she raised her voice, and summoned the others to the evening adoration of the Sun.

Cyril performed this as leader; the duty done, he was free to meet his new brothers and sisters.

Sister Clara was assisted by two young women, both of the slender willowy type – rather babyish even, one might say, with their light brown fluffiness and their full, red soft lips. They remained standing apart from the men, who numbered five. First in rank came the burly Brother Onofrio, a man of some thirty-five years, strong as a bull, with every muscle like iron from constant physical toil. Two men of thirty stood beside him, and behind them two lads of about sixteen.

They were all devoted – so far as the outer world was aware – to the healing of humanity in respect of its physical ills. The men were doctors, or students, the women nurses; though in fact Sister Clara was herself the most brilliant of them all, a surgeon who could have held her own against any man in Europe.

But it was contrary to the rule of the house for any sick person to lodge there; the private hospital which was attached to it was situated some three hundred yards further back from the hillside.

At a glance Lisa perceived that she had come into a circle where discipline was the first consideration.

Every one moved as if a Prussian sergeant had been in charge of him from infancy. Every one looked as if his responsibility were ever present to his mind. These manners sat naturally enough upon Clara and Onofrio; on the others the idea was hardly yet assimilated. But there was no evidence of any outward constraint; even the youngest of the boys was proud to take himself so seriously as he did.

A touch of frost was in the air; Cyril led Lisa within. A special set of rooms had been prepared for their reception; but Lisa was displeased to find that they had been arranged entirely with reference to feminine tastes and requirements. A single scheme of colour embraced the whole suite; white, blue and silver. The tapestries, the carpets, the very ceilings, were wholly in these and no other lights.

The pictures and statues were of Artemis, no other goddess; the very objects in the apartment were crescent shaped, and the only metal in evidence was silver. Where the crescent could not serve the purpose, the surfaces had been engraved with stars of nine points.

Only three books lay upon the table; they were the *Endymion* of Keats, the *Atalanta in Calydon* of Swinburne, and one other. But in a small bookshelf were several other volumes; and Lisa found later that each one described, suggested, or had been more or less directly inspired by the moon. In a silver censer, too, burnt an incense whose predominating ingredient was camphor. Everything present was designed or chosen so that it might turn the girl's mind to the earth's satellite. Subsequently she discovered that this plan extended even to her diet – she was to live exclusively on those foods which wise men of old classified as lunar in nature, on account either of their inherent qualities, or because they are traditionally sacred to Diana.

After the beginning of the experiment, no male was to enter that apartment.

She was a little frightened on grasping the fact that Cyril must have forseen her perfect compliance from the beginning. He noticed it with a slow smile, and began to explain to her why he had chosen the moon as the type of "butterfly" they were going to snare.

"The moon is the most powerful influence in your horoscope," he said. "She stands, in her own sign Cancer, in the mid-heaven. The Sun and Mercury are rising in square to her, which is not specially good; it may bring trouble of a certain kind. But Neptune is sextile to her, Jupiter and Venus trine. It is about as good a horoscope as one could hope for in such a case. The worst danger is the conjunction of Luna and Uranus – they are much too close to be comfortable. My own nativity goes well with yours, for I am primarily solar by nature, though (Heaven knows!) Herschel in the ascendant modifies it; and so I make the complement to you. But I am not to influence you or associate with you too much. I shall sleep with the men in the square tower yonder, which is kept magically separate from the rest of the house. We shall all be working constantly to invoke the moon's influence and to keep off intruders. Sister Clara is egregiously powerful in work of this special kind; she has made a particular study of it for twenty years; and during the past ten she has never spoken to a man, except in strict necessity. Her pupils have taken a similar resolution. There is no question of vows, which imply self-distrust – fear of weakness and of vacillation; the women of our order execute their own wills, with no need of external pressure. Go thou and do likewise!" Suddenly he had become stern and gloomy; and she felt how terrible would be his anger or contempt.

The morning broke brilliant; and Lisa found, not for the first time, that the most bracing influence resulted from the routine peculiar to the Profess-houses. To rise before dawn; to make a ceremonial ablution with the intention of so purifying both body and mind that they should be as it were new-born; then the joyous outburst of adoration as the sun rose to sight: this was

a true Opening of the Day. Insensibly the years slipped from her; she became like a maiden in thought and in activity.

About a week was to elapse before the new moon, at the moment of which the operation was timed to commence; but it was a busy week for Cyril Grey. With Brother Onofrio, for whom he had taken an immense liking, he inspected every inch of the defences of the house. It was already a kind of fortress; the terraces were bounded by ramparts angled or rounded so as to suggest that old-fashioned pattern of military work of which Fort William in Calcutta is said to be the most perfect example.

But the defence of which the magicians were thinking was of a different order; the problem was to convert the whole place as it stood into an impregnable magical circle. For years, of course, the place had been defended, but not as against its present dangers. It had been hitherto sufficient to exclude evil and ignorant beings, things of the same class as Douglas' watcher; but now a far more formidable problem was in view, how to dissuade a Soul, a being armed with the imperial right to enter, from approaching. Demons and elementals and intelligences were only fractions of true Entities, according to the theory; they were illusions, things merely three-dimensional, with no core of substance in themselves. In yet another figure, they were adjectives, and not nouns. But a human soul is a complete reality. "Every man and every woman is a star."

To repel one such from its demand to issue into the world of matter was a serious difficulty – and, also, possibly involved no mean responsibility. However, Cyril's main hope was that any passing souls would be reasonable, and not try to force themselves into uncongenial company, or plant themselves in unsuitable soil. He had always held that incarnation was balked when the soul discovered that the heredity and environment of the embryo it had chosen were too hostile to allow the desired manifestation; the soul would then withdraw, with the physical result of miscarriage, still-birth, or, where the embryo, deserted by the human soul, becomes open to the obsession of some other thing, such as a Vampire or what the Bible calls a "dumb spirit", the production of monsters or idiots.

Cyril Grey, by insisting upon constant devotion to the human ideal, hoped to ward off all other types of soul, just as the presence of a pack of wolves would frighten away a lamb; and he further trusted to attract potent forces, who would serve as a kind of lighthouse to his harbour. He imagined his desired Moon-soul, afloat in space, vehemently spurred towards the choir of sympathetic intelligences whom it could hardly fail to perceive, by reason of the intensity of the concentration of the magical forces of the operators upon the human idea.

Two days before the beginning of the operation, a telegram from Paris reached him. It stated that, as he suspected, Balloch and Douglas were the forces behind the attack; further, that Grey's presence in Naples was known, and that three members of the Black Lodge had left Paris for Italy.

He thought it undesirable to communicate the news to Lisa.

But he renewed his general warnings to her.

"Child!" he said, "you are now ready for our great experiment. On Monday, the day of the New Moon, you take the oath of dedication; and we shall be able to resume those relations which we temporarily renounced. Now let me say to you that you are absolutely guarded in every way

but one. The weak spot is this: we cannot abolish unsuitable thoughts entirely from your mind. It is for you to do that, and we have done our best to make the conditions as favourable as possible; but I warn you that the struggle may be bitter. You will be amazed at the possibilities of your own mind, its fertility of cunning, its fatally false logic, its power of blinding you to facts that ought to be as clear as daylight – yes, even to the things before your very eyes. It will seek to bewilder you, to make you lose your mental balance – every trick is possible. And you will be so beaten and so blind that you have only one safeguard; which is, to adhere desperately to the literal terms of your oath.

"Do that, and in a little while the mind will clear; you will understand what empty phantoms they were that assailed you. But if you fail, your only standard is gone; the waters will swirl about you and carry you away to the abyss of madness. Above all, never distinguish between the spirit and the letter of your oath! The most exquisite deceit of the devil is to lure you from the plain meaning of words. So, though your instinct, and your reason, and your common sense, and your intelligence all urge you to interpret some duty otherwise than in the plain original sense; don't do it!"

"I don't see what you mean."

"Here's a case. Suppose you swore 'not to touch alcohol'. The devil would come with a sickness, and an alcholic medicine; he would tempt you to say that of course your oath didn't mean 'medicinally'. Or you would wish to rub your skin with *eau-de-cologne*; of course 'touch' really meant 'drink'."

"And I should really be right to be stupidly literal, like that?"

"Yes, in a case where the mind, being under a magical strain, becomes unfit to judge. It's the story of Bluebeard; only you must alter it so that the contents of the fatal chamber exist only in the woman's imagination, that she had so worked herself up by what she thought she might see that she also thought she saw it. So be on your guard!"

On the last day of the old moon he gave her an idea of the main programme.

First, the honeymoon; their normal relations were to endure until there was evidence of the need to emphasise the crucial point of the operation. From that moment she was to see nothing of Cyril save in the ceremonies of invocation; all other relations were to cease. The lover would become the hermit. The magician had calculated the probable moment of incarnation as about six months before the day of birth. Once it became certain that the soul had taken possession of the embryo, the hermit would become the elder brother.

It was clearly the middle period that was critical; not only because of the magical difficulties, but because Lisa herself would be under intense strain, and isolated from her lover's active sympathy. But Cyril thought it best to dare these dangers rather than to allow his own soul to influence her atmosphere, as his solar personality might possibly drive away the very "butterfly" which they wished to collect. In fact, his human individuality was one of the things that had to be banished from her neighbourhood. She must know nothing of him but the purely magical side, when, clothed in robes suitable to the invocations of Luna and with word and gesture concentrated wholly upon the work, he sank Cyril Grey utterly in the Priest of Artemis – "thy shrine, thine oracle, thine heat of pale-mouthed prophet dreaming".

CHAPTER XI

OF THE MOON OF HONEY, AND ITS EVENTS

WITH SUNDRY REMARKS ON MAGICK;

THE WHOLE ADORNED WITH MORAL

REFLECTIONS USEFUL TO THE YOUNG

THE many-terraced garden of the villa was planted with olive and tamarind, orange and cypress; but in the lowest of them all, a crescent over whose wall one could look down upon one of the paths that threaded the hillside, there was a pavement of white marble. A spring wept from the naked rock, and fell into a circular basin; from this small streamlets issued, and watered the terrace in narrow grooves, between the slabs. This garden was sacred to lilies; and because of its apt symbolism, Cyril Grey had chosen it for the scene of Lisa's dedication to Artemis. He had set up a small triangular altar of silver; and it was upon this that Sister Clara and her disciples came thrice nightly to make their incantations. The ritual of the moon might never be celebrated during daylight.

Upon the evening of Monday, after the adoration of the setting sun, Sister Clara called Lisa aside, and led her to this garden.

There she and the hand-maidens unclothed her, and washed her from head to foot in the waters of the sacred spring. Then she put upon her a solemn oath that she would follow out the rules of the ritual, not speaking to any man except her chosen, not leaving the protection of the

circle, not communicating with the outer and uninitiated world; but, on the other hand, devoting herself wholly to the invocation of the Moon.

Then she clothed her in a specially prepared and consecrated garment. It was not of the same pattern as those of the Order; it was a loose vestment of pale blue covered with silver tissue; and the secret sigils of the moon were woven cunningly upon its hem. It was frail, but of great volume; and the effect was that the wearer seemed to be wrapped in a mist of moonlight.

In a languid and mysterious chant Sister Clara raised her voice, and her acolytes kept accord on their mandolins; it was an incantation of fervour and of madness, the madness of things chaste, remote, and inscrutable. At the conclusion she took Lisa by the hand, and gave her a new name, a mystic name, engraved upon a moonstone, set in a silver ring which she put upon her finger. This name was Iliel. It had been chosen on account of its sympathy of number to the moon; for the name is Hebrew, in which language its characters have the value of 81, the square of 9, the sacred number of the moon. But other considerations helped to determine the choice of this name. The letter L in Hebrew refers to Libra, the sign under which she had been born; and it was surrounded with two letters, I, to indicate her envelopment by the force of creation and chastity which the wise men of old hid in that hieroglyph.

The final "EL" signified the divinity of her new being; for this is the Hebrew word for God, and is commonly attached by the sages to divers roots, to imply that these ideas have been manifested in individuals of angelic nature.

This instruction had been given to Lisa in advance; now that it was ceremonially conferred upon her, she was struck to the heart by its great meaning. Her passion for Cyril Grey had been gross and vehement, almost vulgar; he had translated it into terms of hunger after holiness, of awful aspiration, of utter purity. Nor Rhea Silvia, nor Semele, nor any other mortal virgin had ever glowed to inherit more glorious a destiny, to feel such infinite exaltation of chastity. Even the thought of Cyril himself fell from her like a stain. He had become no more than a necessary evil. At that moment she could have shaken off the trammels of humanity itself, and joined Sister Clara in her ecstatic mood, passed on, imperial votaress, in maiden meditation fancy-free. Only the knowledge of her sublime task inured her to its bitter taste. From these meditations she was awakened by the voice of Sister Clara.

"Oh, Iliel! Oh, Iliel! Oh, Iliel! there is a cloud upon the sea."

The, two girls chimed in with the music of their mandolins.

"It is growing dark. I am afraid," cried Sister Clara.

The girls quavered in their melody.

"We are alone in the sacred grove. Oh, Artemis, be near us, protect us from all evil!"

"Protect us from all evil!" echoed the two children. "There is a shape in the cloud; there is a stirring in the darkness; there is a stranger in the sacred grove!"

"Artemis! Artemis! Artemis!" shrilled the girls, their instruments fierce and agitated.

At that moment a great cry arose from the men, who were in waiting on the upper Terrace. It was a scream of abject fear, inarticulate, save for the one word "Pan"! They fled shrieking in every direction as Cyril Grey, clad in a rough dress of goatskins, bounded from the topmost

terrace into their midst. In another moment, leaping down the garden, he reached the parapet that overlooked the little terrace where the girls crouched, moaning.

He sprang down among them; Sister Clara and her disciples fled with cries like startled sea-birds; but he crushed Iliel to his breast, then flung her over his shoulder, and strode triumphant to the house.

Such was the magical ceremony devised by the adept, a commemoration or dramatic representation of the legend of the capture of Diana by Pan. It is, of course, from such rites that all dramatic performance developed. The idea is to identify oneself, in thought by means of action, with the deities whom one desires to invoke.

The idea of presenting a story ceremonially may have preceded the ritual, and the Gods may have been mere sublimations of eponymous heroes or personifications of abstract ideas; but ultimately it is much the same. Admit that the genius of man is divine, and the question "Which is the cart, and which the horse?" becomes as pointless as if one asked it about an automobile.

The ensuing month, from the middle of November until the week before Christmas, was a honeymoon. But animal appetite was scarce more than an accidental adjunct; the human love of Cyril and Lisa had been raised to inconceivable heights by the backbone of spirituality and love of mankind that lay behind its manifestations. Moreover, everything was attuned to it; nothing detracted from it. The lovers never lost sight of each other for an hour; they had their fill and will of love; but in a way, and with an intensity, of which worldly lovers never dream. Even sleep was to them but as a veil of many colours cast upon their rapture; in their dreams they still pursued each other, and attained each other, beneath bluer skies, upon seas that laughed more melodiously than that which lay between them and Capri, through gardens of more gladness than their own, and upon slopes that stretched eternally to the palaces of the Empyrean.

For four weeks no word came from outside; with one exception, when Sister Clara brought a telegram to Cyril. It was unsigned, and the message curt. "About August First" was all its purport. "The better the day, the better the deed!" cried Cyril gaily. Iliel questioned him. "Just magick!" he answered. She did not pursue the subject: she divined that the matter did not concern her, and she regretted even that microscopical interruption.

But although Iliel was kept from all knowledge of external events, it was by dint of steel. The Black Lodge had not been idle; Brother Onofrio, in charge of the garrison, had found his hands full. But his manoeuvres had been successful; the enemy had not even secured their first point of vantage, a material link with the Brotherhood.

It is a law of magick that causes and effects lie on the same plane. You may be able to send a ghost to frighten someone you dislike, but you must not expect the ghost to use a club, or steal a pocket handkerchief. Also, most practical magick starts on the material plane, and proceeds to create images on other planes. Thus, to evoke a spirit, you first obtain the objects necessary for its manifestation, and create subtler forms of the same nature from them.

The Butterfly-net was worked on exactly the same lines. Morality enters into magick no more than into art or science. It is only when the effects react upon the moral nature of man that this question arises. The Venus de Medici is neither good nor bad; it is merely beautiful; but its

reaction on the mind of an Antony Comstock or a Harry Thaw may be disastrous, owing to the nature of such minds. One can settle the details of a murder over the telephone; but one should not blame the telephone.

The laws of magick are closely related to those of other physical sciences. A century or so ago men were ignorant of a dozen important properties of matter; thermal conductivity, electrical resistance, opacity to the X-ray, spectroscopic reaction, and others even more occult. Magick deals principally with certain physical forces still unrecognised by the vulgar; but those forces are just as real, just as material – if indeed you can call them so, for all things are ultimately spiritual – as properties like radio-activity, weight and hardness. The difficulty in defining and measuring them lies principally in the subtlety of their relation to life. Living protoplasm is identical with dead protoplasm in all but the fact of life. The Mass is a magical ceremony performed with the object of endowing a material substance with divine virtue; but there is no material difference between the consecrated and the unconsecrated wafer. Yet there is an enormous difference in the moral reaction upon the communicant. Recognising that its principal sacrament is only one of an infinite number of possible experiments in talismanic magic, the Church has never denied the reality of that Art, but treated its exponents as rivals. She dare not lop the branch on which she sits.

On the other hand, the sceptic, finding it impossible to deny the effects of ceremonial consecration, is compelled to refer the cause to "faith"; and sneers that Faith is the real miracle. Whereupon the Church smilingly agrees; but the magician, holding the balance between the disputants, and insisting upon the unity of Nature, asserts that all force is one in origin. He believes in the "miracle," but maintains that it is exactly the same kind of miracle as charging a Leyden Jar with electricity. You must use a moral indicator to test one, an electrical indicator to test the other; the balance and the test-tube will not reveal the change in either.

The Black Lodge knew well enough that the weak strand in the Butterfly-net was Lisa's untrained mind. Its white-hot flame of enthusiasm, radiating passionate love, was too active to assail directly, even could they have succeeded in communicating with it.

But they were content to watch and wait for the reaction, should it come, as they knew it must ultimately do. Eros finds Anteros always on his heels; soon or late, he will be supplanted, unless he have the wit to feed his fire with the fuel of Friendship. In the meanwhile, it was the best chance to work upon the mind through the body. Had they been able to procure a drop of Iliel's blood, she might have been as easy a prey as that unlucky engine-driver of the Paris-Rome *rapide*.

But Sister Clara saw to it that not so much as a nail-paring of Iliel escaped careful magical destruction; and Brother Onofrio organised a nightly patrol of the garden, so that no physical breach of the circle should be made.

The man in charge of the mission of the Black Lodge was one Arthwait, a dull and inaccurate pedant without imagination or real magical perception. Like most Black Magicians, he tippled habitually; and his capacity for inflicting damage upon others was limited by his inordinate conceit. He hated Cyril Grey as much as he hated any one, because his books had been reviewed

by that bright spirit, in his most bitterly ironical strain, in the *Emerald Tablet*, the famous literary review edited by Jack Flynn; and Grey had been at particular pains to point out elementary blunders in translation which showed that Arthwait was comically ignorant of the languages in which he boasted scholarship. But he was not the man for the task set him by Douglas; his pomposity always stood in his way; a man fighting for life is exceptionally a fool if he insists on stopping every moment to admire himself. Douglas had chosen him for one of the curious back-handed reasons which so often appeal to people of perverse intelligence: it was because he was harmless that he was selected to work harm. A democracy often chooses its generals on the same principle; a capable man might overthrow the republic. It apparently prefers to be overthrown by a capable enemy.

But Douglas had backed him with a strong executive.

Abdul Bey knew no magic, and never would; but he had a desperate passion for Lisa, and a fanatical hatred of Grey, whom he credited, at the suggestion of Balloch, with the death of his father. He had almost unlimited resources, social and financial; there could hardly have been a better man for the external part of the work.

The third commissioner was the brains of the business. He was a man highly skilled in black magic in his own way. He was a lean, cadaverous Protestant-Irishman named Gates, tall, with the scholar's stoop. He possessed real original talent, with now and then a flash of insight which came close to genius. But though his intellect was keen and fine, it was in some way confused; and there was a lack of virility in his make-up. His hair was long, lank and unkempt; his teeth were neglected; and he had a habit of physical dirt which was so obvious as to be repulsive even to a stranger.

But there was no harm in him; he had no business in the Black Lodge at all; it was but one of his romantic phantasies to pose as a terribly wicked fellow. Yet he took it seriously enough, and was ready to serve Douglas in any scheme, however atrocious, which would secure his advancement in the Lodge. He was only there through muddle-headedness; so far as he had an object beyond the satisfaction of his vanity, it was innocent in itself – the acquisition of knowledge and power. He was entirely the dupe of Douglas, who found him a useful stalking-horse, for Gates had a considerable reputation in some of the best circles in England.

Douglas had chosen him for this business on excellent points of cunning; for he neither hated nor loved his intended victims, and so was likely to interpret their actions without passion or prejudice. It was this interpretation that Douglas most desired. Douglas had seen him personally – rare privilege – before he left for Naples and explained his wishes somewhat as follows.

The fool Arthwait was to blunder pedantically along with the classical methods of magical assault, partly on the chance of a hit, partly to keep Grey busy, and possibly to lead him to believe that the main attack lay there. Meanwhile he, Gates, was to devote himself, on the quiet, to divining the true nature of Grey's purpose. This information was essential; Douglas knew that it must be something tremendous; that the forces which Cyril was working to evoke were cosmic in scope. He knew it not only from his own divinations, but deduced it from the fact of the intervention of Simon Iff. He knew well that the old Master would not have lifted a finger for

anything less than a world-war. Douglas therefore judged that if he could defeat Grey's purpose, it would involve the triumph of his own. Such forces, recoiling upon his head who had evoked them, would shatter him into a thousand fragments. Douglas, still weak from the destruction of his "watcher", was particularly clear on this point!

Arthwait was to be the nominal head of the party in all things, and Abdul Bey was to be urged to support him vigorously in all ways that lay in his power; but if necessary Gates was to thwart Arthwait, and secure the allegiance of the Turk, bound to secrecy on the matter, by showing him a card which Douglas then and there duly inscribed and handed over.

Louis XV tried a double-cross game of this sort on his ambassadors; but Douglas was not strong on history, and knew nothing of how those experiments resulted.

Nor, apparently, had he taken to heart the words of the gospel: "If Satan be divided against Satan, how shall his kingdom stand?"

Still less did he realise that this ingenious plan had been suggested to him by Simon Iff! Yet it was so: this was the head of the counter-attack which the old mystic had agreed to deliver on behalf of Cyril Grey. It was only a quarter of an hour's work; the Way of the Tao is the easiest as it is the surest.

This is what "Simple Simon" had done. Since all simple motion is one-pointed, and its enemy is inertia, the swordsmith brings his sword to a single sharp edge; the fletcher grinds his arrow-barb to a fine point. Your Dum-Dum bullet will not penetrate as does your nickel tip; and you cannot afford to use the former unless the power of penetration is so great as to reach the soft spots before the bullet expands and stops. This mechanical principle is perfectly applicable in magick. Therefore, when there is need to resist a magical attack, your best method will be to divide your antagonist's forces.

Douglas had already lost a pawn in the game, Akbar Pasha having gone to his destruction through setting up an idea of his own, apart from, and inconsistent with, the plan of his superior. The defect is inherent in all Black Magic, because that art is itself a thing set up against the Universal Will. If it were not negligibly small, it would destroy the Universe, just as the bomb-throwing Anarchist would succeed in destroying society if he amounted to, say, a third of the population.

Now Simple Simon, at this time, did not know Douglas for the enemy General; but he was in the closest possible magical touch with him. For he had absorbed the Thing in the garden into himself and that Thing had been a part of Douglas.

So he set himself to the complete assimilation of that Thing; he made certain that it should be part of himself for ever. His method of doing this was as simple as usual. He went over the Universe in his mind, and set himself to reconcile all contradictions in a higher Unity. Beginning with such gross things as the colours of the spectrum, which are only partialities of white light, he resolved everything that came into his mind until he reached such abstractions as matter and motion, being and form; and by this process worked himself up into a state of mind which was capable of grasping those sublime ideas which unite even these ultimate antinomies. That was all.

Douglas, still in magical touch with that "watcher", could feel it being slowly digested, so to say, by some other magician. This (incidentally) is the final fate of all black magicians, to be torn

piecemeal, for lack of the love which grows by giving itself to the beloved, again and again, until its "I" is continuous with existence itself. "Whoso loveth his life shall lose it" is the corresponding scriptural phrase.

So Douglas, who might at that moment have saved himself by resignation, was too blind to see the way – an acquired blindness resulting from repeated acts whose essence was the denial of the unity of himself with the rest of the universe. And so he fought desperately against the assimilation of his "watcher". "It's mine, not yours!" he raged. To the steady and continuous affirmation of true unity in all diversity which Simon Iff was making, he opposed the affirmation of duality. The result was that his whole mind was aflame with the passion of contrasting things, of playing forces off against each other. When it came to practical decisions, he divided his forces, and deliberately created jealousy and hatred where co-operation and loyalty should have been the first and last consideration.

Yet Simon Iff had used no spell but Love.

CHAPTER XII

OF BROTHER ONOFRIO

HIS STOUTNESS AND VALIANCE;

AND OF THE MISADVENTURES THAT

CAME THEREBY TO THE BLACK LODGE

THE ecclesiastic is a definite type of man. The Italian priest has changed his character in three thousand years as little as he has his costume.

Brother Onofrio's father happened to be a free-thinking Anti-clerical, a pillar of Masonry; otherwise, his son would assuredly have been a bishop. The type is perfectly pagan, whatever the creed; it is robust and subtle, spiritual and sensual, adroit in manipulation of inferiors and superiors alike. It has the courage which vigorous health and the consciousness of its own validity combine to give; and where courage will not serve the turn, astuteness deftly takes its place.

A stupid pedant like Edwin Arthwait is the very feeblest opponent for such a man.

Brother Onofrio, while successfully practising magick, was quite ready at a moment's notice to throw the whole theory overboard with a horse laugh – and at the same time to reckon his action in so doing a branch of magick also. It was the beginning of the duplicate brain-development which Cyril Grey had cultivated to so high a point of perfection.

But Arthwait was in the fetters of his own egoism; while he pronounced himself father and grandfather of all spiritual science, in language that would have seemed stilted and archaic to Henry James, or Osric, and presumptuous in the mouth of an archangel, he was the bondslave of utterly insignificant writers, fakers of magical "grimoires" of the fourteenth century, hawkers of spells and conjurations to a benighted peasantry who wished to bewitch cows or to prevent their neighbours from catching fish. Arthwait had published a book to show the folly of such works, but in practice they were his only guide. In particular, he swore by the "Black Pullet", which

seemed to him less dangerous than the "Grand Grimoire", or the forgery attributed to Pope Honorius. He wanted to evoke the devil, but was terrified lest he should be successful. However, nobody could be more pedantically pious than he in following out the practical prescriptions of these absurd charm-books.

This individual might usually have been discovered during that honeymoon in the Naples villa, seated in the armchair of the apartment which he had rented in the Galeria Vittoria. He would be clad in a frockcoat of City cut, for he affected the "professional man", and his air would be preoccupied. The arrival of his colleagues for consultation would apparently startle him from a profound speculation upon the weightier matters of the law.

It would be only by an effort that he spoke in English; the least distraction would send him back into Latin, Greek, or Hebrew, none of which languages he understood. He was a peddler of words; his mind was a rag-and-bone shop of worthless and disjointed mediaevalism.

After a severe struggle, he would "proceed to an allocution". He never "spoke"; he "monologised".

The first formal conference took place when they had been about a week in Naples.

"My fathers learned in Art Magic," he began, addressing Gates and Abdul, "venerable and archetypal doctors of the Hermetic Arcanum, it hath been sacramentally imposed upon our sophistic Tebunah by the monumentally aggregated psycho-mentality of Those whose names in respect of known dedications must here – *juxta nos* – be *heled ob Danaos* (as I should adumbrate advisedly, for is it not script, concerning cowans, in the archives of the Clermont Harodim?) that a term, *in fine*, should mete the orbit and currency of the heretic and apostate, *quem in Tartarum conjuro*, high Grey, in his areopagus of the averse hierarchy. I exiterate, *clam populo*, that all warrants of precursors fait no ratification, peradventure, in the actual concatenation, *sed, me judice*, it is meliorated that by virtue and cosmodominicy of Satanas – *cognomen ineffabile, quod reverentissime proloquor!* – the opus confronts the Sir Knights of the Black Chapter – *in via sua propria* – in the authentic valley and this *lucus tenebrosa Neapolitanensis*, as the near – nay, the next! – conflagration of barbaric pilum against retiarial ludibry. Worthy Fathers and reverend in the doctrine, *salutatio in summo imperio – per totam orbem* – in the supranominal Donner of Orcus and of Phlegethon – *sufficit!*"

The Turkish diplomat spoke nine languages, but not this one. Gates, who had known Arthwait for many years, explained that these remarks, formidable in appearance, meant only that Grey ought to be killed at any time, on general principles, but that as they were specially charged with that task by their leaders, so much the better.

The conference, thus prosperously inaugurated, proved a lengthy one. How, indeed, could it be otherwise? For Arthwait was naturally slow of thought and speech; it took him some time to warm up to real eloquence; and then he became so long-winded, and lost himself so completely in his words and phrases, that he would speak for many hours without conveying a single idea of any kind to his hearers, or even having one to convey.

But the upshot of his conversation upon this occasion was that an attempt should be made to poison the household magically by bewitching the food supplied to them from the market.

Certain succulent shell-fish, called *vongole*, very popular in Naples, were selected as a material basis, "because their appurtenance and charter was be-Yekl Klippoth", as Arthwait explained.

Into these molluscs, therefore, might be conjured a spirit of Mars "of them that bear witness unto Bartzabel", in the hope that those who partook of them might be stricken with some type of fever, fevers and all acute diseases being classified as Martial.

It was unfortunate for these plans that Brother Onofrio habitually took the precaution to purify and consecrate all food that came into the house before it reached the kitchen; and further, anticipating some such attempt, he had everything tested psychometrically by one of his acolytes, whom he had trained especially in sensitiveness to all such subtle impressions.

The shell-fish were consequently discovered to be charged with the Martial current; Brother Onofrio smiled hugely and proceeded to call upon the divine forces of Mars, before which even Bartzabel "trembles every day", and, thus having converted himself into a high-power engine of war, sat down to a Gargantuan banquet, eating the entire consignment himself. The result was that the unfortunate Arthwait was seized with violent and intractable colic, which kept him twisted in agony on his bed for forty-eight hours.

Gates had taken no part in this performance; he knew how dangerous it was, and how likely to recoil upon the rash practitioner. But he did some genuinely useful work. He had been to the church in the village, near Posilippo, whose tower overlooked the Butterfly-net; and he had persuaded the priest to allow him continual access to that tower, on the pretext of being an artist. And indeed he had a pretty amateur talent for painting in water-colours: some people thought it stronger than his verses. For ten days he watched the Butterfly-net with extreme care, and he wrote down the routine of the inhabitants hour by hour. Nothing escaped him of their doings in the garden; and (as it happened) the preponderating portion of their work lay out-of-doors. He could make nor head nor tail of the fact that the most important people were apparently doing no magick of any kind, but, careless lovers, enjoying the first fruits of their flight to the South.

But Douglas put two and two together very cleverly, even from the first report; he noted, also, the intelligence and ability of Gates, and made a memorandum to use him up quickly and destroy him.

Without divining the exact intention of Cyril Grey, he rightly concluded that this "honeymoon" was not so simple as it seemed; in fact, he recognised it as the core of the apple. He telegraphed Gates to redouble his watch upon the lovers, and to report instantly if any marked change occurred in their habits.

Meanwhile, Edwin Arthwait was busy with the "Black Pullet". There is a method of describing a pentagram upon a doorstep which is infallible. The first person who crosses it receives a shock which may drive him insane, or even kill him. A magician would naturally be suspicious if he found anything of this kind on his front doorstep, so Arthwait cleverly determined to paint the pentagram in Gum Arabic, which would hardly be visible. Accordingly he went to the Butterfly-net at dead of night, armed with this means of grace, and set to work by the light of a candle-lamp. He was careful to make the pentagram so large that it was impossible to cross the bridge without stepping over it. Absorbed in his inspiring task, he did not notice, until the last stroke

was in place, that he was himself hemmed in between his pentagram and the door of the villa. He crouched in terror for the best part of an hour; then a hint of daylight made him fearful of discovery. He was forced to make a move of some sort; and he found that by careful sidling he could escape to the parapet of the bridge. But he was no climber; he overbalanced and fell into the chasm, being lucky to escape with a severe shaking. On his limping way back to Naples he was overtaken by an icy shower of rain; and as he got into bed, too late to avoid a nasty chill, which kept him in bed for a week, he had the irritating reflexion that his pentagram must have been washed away.

But he had not become known as the most voluminous of modern pedants without perseverance. His literary method was that of the "tank". It was not agile, it was not versatile, it was exposed to artillery attack; but it proceeded. He was as comprehensive as the Catalogue of the British Museum – and almost as extensive. But he was not arranged. Such a man was not to be deterred by two failures, or forty-two. Indeed, but for the frank criticism of Gates, he would have counted them successes.

For his third experiment he chose "The Wonder-working Serpent", whose possession confers the power of attracting love. The appeal lay in the failure of Abdul to make any impression upon Lisa, whom he had courted in characteristically local manner by appearing, guitar in hand, below the terrace where she had been dedicated to the moon. He caught her there alone, and called her by her name. She recognised him instantly; she had been violently attracted to him at the ball where they had originally met; and, until she had seen Cyril, regretted constantly that she had missed the opportunity.

The memory of that thwarted desire sprang vehement upon her; but she was at the white heat of her passion for Cyril. Even so, she half hesitated; she wanted to keep Abdul on ice, so to speak, for a future occasion; such action was as instinctive with her as breathing. But her obligation was still fresh in her mind; she was pledged not to communicate with the outer world. She ignored him; she turned and left the garden without so much as a gesture; and he went back to Naples in a black fury against her. "The Wonder-working Serpent" was, therefore, an operation entirely to his taste. Gates thought the line of attack hopeful; he was totally sceptical of Lisa's virtue, or any woman's; and he had lived on women long enough to make his view arguable, within the limits of his experience. He bade Abdul try again. Good – then let magic aid!

In order to possess "The Wonder-working Serpent", it is necessary, in the words of the Grimoire, "to buy an egg without haggling", which (by the way) indicates the class of person for and by whom the book was written. This egg is to be buried in a cemetery at midnight, and every morning at sunrise it must be watered with brandy. On the ninth day a spirit appears, and demands your purpose. You reply, "I am watering my plant." This occurs on three successive days; at the midnight following the egg is dug up, and found to contain a serpent, with a cock's head. This amiable animal answers to the name of Ambrosiel. Carry it in your bosom, and your suit inevitably prospers.

Arthwait put this scheme into careful rehearsal, and having got the conjurations and ceremonies perfect – for the egg must be buried with full military honours, as it were – he

reached the third day without mishap. But at this point a spirit appeared – a guardian of the cemetery – and, dissatisfied with his answers, took him to the police-station as a wandering lunatic. A less other-worldly master of the dark sciences might have bribed the official; but Arthwait's self-importance once again stood in his way. He got in deeper, and in the end it was Gates who offered to be responsible for him, and persuaded the British Consul to use influence for his release.

As so many workers of magic have done, from the Yukon and Basutoland to Tonga and Mongolia, Arthwait attributed his defeats to the superior cunning and wickedness of his opponents.

Gates himself had varied his pleasures by a much more serious attempt to create a magical link with the garrison. From his tower he had observed many pigeons upon the hillside, and he began to tame these, spreading corn upon the tower. In three days they were eating out of his hand. He then trained them to recognise him and follow him from place to place. A week later he found a moment when the garden was deserted save for a single patrol, and threw his grain over the wall. The pigeons flocked to it and fed. Now it so happened that the patrolling magician was unsuspicious. He was aware that the benign influence of the house made its gardens attractive. There flowers bloomed brighter than elsewhere; and all Nature's wanderers seemed to look to it as their refuge. They felt instinctively the innocence and goodwill of the inhabitants, and thronged those hospitable terraces.

When Gates moved on, the pigeons followed his next throw; round the first corner, he placed the remains of his supply of corn in a small heap on the ground; the pigeons unsuspectingly approached, and he threw a net over half a dozen of them.

This was a great point gained; for the Black Lodge was in possession of living things that had come from within the guarded precinct; it would be easy to attack the inmates by means of sympathetic magic. As it chanced, two of the birds were male; but pigeons being of the general nature of Venus, it was decided to try to identify them with the least male persons of the garrison, namely the four women and the two boys. Accordingly, ribbons were tied to the necks of the birds, and the names of the intended victims inscribed upon them. Magical ceremonies were now made, Gates, who took a real interest in the experiment, being the leader.

When he considered the identification adequate, he placed red pepper on the tongues of the birds; and was rewarded the following morning by seeing Sister Clara turn upon one of her girls with a gesture of rage; he could even hear faintly the tones of anger in her voice. But Brother Onofrio had not failed to observe the same thing; and he divined instantly that a breach had been made in his circle. He went immediately to Sister Clara, and compelled her attention by a sign of such authority that no initiate dare overlook it.

"Sister," he said very gently, "you do not speak with man; what cause, then, can there be for bitterness?"

She answered him, still angrily. "The house is upside down," she said. "Iliel is as irritable as an eczema; the boys have both made insulting faces at every one they have seen this morning; and the girls are absolutely impudent."

"This is a matter for me, as in charge of the defence of the circle."

Sister Clara uttered a sharp exclamation. It had not occurred to her to think of it in that way. "I should be obliged," continued Brother Onofrio, "if you could see your way to impose a rule of silence for seven days from sunset tonight. Excepting, of course, in the invocations. I will warn the boys; do you take up the matter with Iliel and the girls."

"It shall be done."

Brother Onofrio went off to the private room where he did his own particular magick. He saw that a serious inroad had been made; but his divination, on this occasion, failed to enlighten him. His favourite device was the Tarot, those mysterious cards with their twenty-two hieroglyphic trumps; and as a rule he was able to discover all kinds of unknown matters by their use. But on this attempt he was baffled by the monotony of his answer.

However he used the cards, they always reverted to a single symbol, the trump numbered XVI, which is called "The Blasted Tower", and has some reference to the legend of Babel.

"I know," he muttered, himself irritated by the persistence of the card, "I know it's Mars" – which is the planet signified by that particular hieroglyph. "But I wanted a lot more than that. I asked 'What is the trouble?' 'From whom is the trouble?' 'Where is the trouble?' 'What shall I do?' And the same card answers all the questions!"

The next day Gates found that the tongues of the birds were shrivelled up, and he divined that his mode of attack had been detected, and precaution taken. He proceeded by drugging the pigeons with the vapour of ether.

In the house the result was immediate. The six people affected showed signs of intoxication and dizziness, coupled with a strong feeling of suffocation. Sister Clara was less troubled than the others, and she recognised the magical cause of the symptoms. She ran quickly to Brother Onofrio; he saw instantly that a new attack was in progress, and gave the sign agreed upon for retirement to a specially consecrated room in the square tower, a sort of inner circle, or citadel. The victims gathered in this room within a few minutes, and their symptoms abated on the instant.

But Brother Onofrio had a glimpse of light, as he assisted one of the two boys, who was almost choking, to reach the refuge. The tower caught his eye, and it flashed upon him that perhaps the Tarot was referring to an actual tower. It was only one step to think of the tower of the church; and, running into the garden, he saw that a man was standing there, evidently engaged in watching the house of the magicians. Brother Onofrio's quick insight decided him instantly upon the course to follow.

The Tarot Trump in question represents a tower struck by lightning, from which figures of men are seen falling.

He laughed joyously; his favourite method of divination had vindicated itself supremely. His four questions had indeed a single answer.

W. S. Gilbert informs us that "a deed of blood, and fire, and flames, was meat and drink to Simple James"; and to find himself approached upon the plane of Mars was like mother's milk to Brother Onofrio.

For he was himself of the strongest Martial type, having been born with Scorpio, the night house of Mars, rising, and the planet himself conjoined with Herschel in the mid-heaven in the sign of the Lion, with the Sun rising in trine and Jupiter conjoined with Saturn making an additional trine from the sixth house, which governs secret things such as magick. It was as formidable a combination as Mars could make in a thousand years.

He happened also to belong to that grade of the Order – Adeptus Major – which specialises in Mars; Arthwait and Company had unwittingly come to meet him where he was strongest.

To invoke Mars is to establish a connection with that order of nature which we class as martial. It may be remembered how a man once came to a doctor, suffering internal pangs of no mean order from having swallowed by mistake some pills intended for a horse. Asked how it came to happen, he explained that he had been administering them to the horse by blowing them down its throat through a tube; but the horse had blown first. This is of course the danger in every magical experiment; and this constitutes the evergreen glory of every man who adventures upon it; for at each new portal he enters, naked and new-born, to confront he knows not what malignant enemies. The sole excuse for the existence of our miserable species lies not in intelligence, but in this masterful courage, this aspiration to extend the empire of the spirit. Even the blackest of magicians, like Douglas, or the stupidest, like Arthwait, is a higher type of being than the bourgeois who goes along with his nose on the ground picking up gold bricks in the mire.

Now when Brother Onofrio found Gates perched upon the campanile, he saw the Martial symbol complete – only awaiting the lightning-flash. There was no need for him to produce a thunderstorm, as it would have been if Gates had been an ordinary man, accessible only to coarse influences; no, Brother Onofrio knew how to assimilate the church tower to The Blasted Tower of the Tarot without appealing to the material forces of nature, so-called, as if "matter" were not comprehensive as "nature" herself; but the English language is full of these booby-traps.

He went to his laboratory, took out the Tarot card XVI and set it up on the altar. He lighted the fire upon the tripod, and he kindled the incense of dragon's blood that stood ready in the iron censer. He then put upon his head the steel crown of Mars, thorny with its four flashing pentagrams, and he took in his hands the heavy sword, as long as himself, with a two-edged blade tapering from a width, at the junction of the hilt, of no less than five inches.

Chanting the terrible conjurations of Mars, fierce war-songs of the olden peoples of the world, invocations of mighty deities throned upon the thunder – "He sent out his arrows and scattered them; he sent forth his lightnings, and consumed them" – Brother Onofrio began the war-dance of the Serpent, the invoking dance of Mars. Close coiled about the altar at first, he took gradually a wider sweep, constantly revolving on himself but his feet tracing a complex spiral curve. On reaching the door of the room, he allowed the "Serpent" to stretch out its length, and, ever twisting on himself, came out upon the terrace.

Gates was still at his post upon the campanile; he had been about to go, but this new feature of the routine of the house riveted him to his place. This was just what Douglas needed to know! He leant upon the parapet of the tower, watching with infinite eagerness and minuteness the convolutions of the adept.

Once upon the terrace, Brother Onofrio proceeded to coil up his "Serpent" after him, diminishing the sweep of his spirals until he was at zero, merely rotating on himself.

Then he began the second part of his work, the Dance of the Sword.

Slowly he began to cause his feet to trace a pentagram, and he allowed the Sword to leave his body as he quickened his pace, just as one sees the weights of the ball-governor of a steam-engine fly outwards as pressure and speed leap higher.

Gates was altogether fascinated by the sight. In the sunlight, this scarlet figure with lights darting from every brilliance of its steel was a magnificent spectacle, almost bewildering in its intensity.

Faster and faster whirled the adept, his sword swaying about him like a garment of light; and his voice, louder and fiercer with every turn, assumed the very majesty of thunder.

Gates watched with open mouth; he was learning much from this man. He began to perceive the primaeval energy of the universe, under a veil, the magical clang and rush of blazing stars in the blind emptiness of space. And suddenly Brother Onofrio stopped dead; his voice snapped short into a silence far more terrible than any word; and his long sword was still, fearfully still, stretched out like a shaft of murderous light – the point towards the tower.

Gates was suddenly aware that he had all along been the object of the dance; and then his brain began to reel. Had the whirling flashes hypnotised him? He could not think; the world went black for him. Automatically he clutched at the parapet; but he pitched headlong over it, and crashed upon the ground a hundred feet below.

On the terrace Brother Onofrio was beginning the banishing spirals of Mars, with songs of triumph into which stole, as if surreptitiously, some hint of that joy of love which, from the beginning of time, has welcomed the victorious soldier.

MOONCHILD

CHAPTER XIII
OF THE PROGRESS OF THE GREAT EXPERIMENT

NOT FORGETTING OUR FRIENDS LAST SEEN

IN PARIS, ABOUT WHOSE WELFARE MUCH

ANXIETY MUST HAVE BEEN FELT

EARLY in January Cyril Grey received a letter from Lord Antony Bowling. "My good Grey," it began, "may the New Year bring you courage to break your resolutions early! My own plan is to swear off every kind of virtue, so that I triumph even when I fail!

"Morningside is off to America with his New Discovery in Science. It is that all crime is due to breathing. Statistics show (a) that all convicts are guilty of this disgusting habit; (b) it is characteristic of all the inmates of our insane asylums.

"On the other hand, neither crime nor insanity has ever been proved against any person who was not an habitual breather. The case, as you see, is complete. Morningside has gone even further, and shown that breathing is akin to drug-habits; he has made numerous experiments upon addicts, and finds that suppression leads to mental and physical distress of an even more acute type than that which follows the removal of morphia or cocaine from their slaves. There is little doubt that Congress will take immediate action to penalise this filthy vice as it deserves, and Fresh Air will be included among the drugs to which the Harrison Law applies. Hot Air, as the natural food of the People, will of course be permitted.

"I saw Sister Cybele the other day. She was passing through London to visit friends in Scotland. I tried to alleviate that dreadful destiny by asking her to dinner, and we had an amusing

180

seance with my new toy, a youth named Roger Blunt, who is controlled by a spirit called Wooloo, has eight secondary personalities, and causes pencils to adhere to walls. It cannot be that this is varnish, or surface tension, or a little of both; it would be too, too cruel!

"The Mahathera Phang has vanished from our gaze; he has probably gone to the Equator to correct the obliquity of the Ecliptic in the interest of the Law of Righteousness. I'm sorry; I believe in that man; I know he's got something that I haven't, and I want it. However, Simple Simon has been nice to me; only he won't talk Phenomena – says that, like a certain Pope, he has seen too many miracles to believe in them. Which is my own case, only he is referring to genuine ones. Hence difficulty in comprehension of his attitude.

"I hope you're having a great time with the devil; I envy your blue skies; London is wrapped in fog, and even on fine days I have to go to the War Office. But isn't it a pity those wicked bad naughty men know where you are? I have my doubts about magick; but I know Balloch, and he's the rottenest egg in London. I gather he's at the back of it. Some blackmailing articles on you, again; but as Morningside would say, you should worry. Come along and see me before, in a moment of madness and despair, you plunge into Vesuvius in the hope of exciting a future Matthew Arnold to immortalise you.

"Well, here's the best to you! – ANTONY BOWLING."

There was a brief note, too, from Simon Iff. "It's to be supposed all's well; rumours of disaster to enemy offensive current in Paris. You had better worry along on your own now; there's other fish frying in this kitchen. An old man may possibly drop in on you early in August; you may recognise him – with a strong pair of glasses – as your old friend – SIMON IFF."

Simple Simon never spoke of himself as "I" in a letter; he only used the pronoun in conversation as a concession to custom.

The Black Commissioners had also heard from headquarters; Gates was replaced, as quick as rail could carry, by a man of superior advancement in the Black Lodge.

This was the celebrated Dr. Victor Vesquit, the most famous necromancer of his age. There was really little harm in the man beyond his extraordinary perversion in the matter of corpses. His house in Hampden Road was not only a rendezvous of spiritualists, but a Home for Lost Mummies. He based all his magical operations upon dead bodies, or detached portions of the same, believing that to endow dead matter with life – the essential of nearly all magick, as he quite rightly saw – it was best to choose matter in which life had recently been manifest. An obvious corollary is that the best bodies are those that have met a violent death, rather than those which have been subjected to illness and decay. Also, it followed that the best corpses of all were those of executed murderers, whose vitality may be assumed as very great – though on this last point Cyril Grey, for one, would have disagreed with him, saying that the most vital people would have too much respect for the principle of life to commit murder in cold blood.

However, Dr Vesquit had obtained an appointment as coroner in the most murderous district of London; and uncanny were the rumours that circulated among occult sympathisers.

His career had nearly been ruined on two occasions by scandal. The notorious Diana Vaughan, it had been said, was his mistress; and he had become her accomplice in the introduction of the frightful sect of the Palladists.

The rumour was not widespread, and Vesquit need not have suffered; but he took alarm, and had the unlucky thought of employing Arthwait to write a book clearing him from all suspicion, by which it naturally was fixed on him for ever.

The second trouble was his little quarrel with Douglas. Vesquit was Senior in the Black Lodge, and Douglas overthrew him by "carelessly" leaving, in a hansom cab, some documents belonging to the Lodge, with Vesquit's name and address attached to them, which made some exceedingly grim revelations of the necromantic practices carried on in Hampden Road.

The honest cabby had turned over the papers to Scotland Yard, as his duty was; and the police had sent them on to those in authority over coroners; and Vesquit received, with his documents, an intimation that he must drop that sort of thing at once. To be chief in the Lodge seemed less than to be always in a Paradise of corpses; so he resigned office, and Douglas pushed his advantage by making him an abject tool, under the perpetual threat of exposure.

No sooner did Douglas learn of the death of Gates than he telegraphed to Arthwait to get the inquest adjourned "so that the relatives of the deceased in England might attend, and take possession of the body", and to Vesquit to attend the same. On this occasion the coroner needed no threat – the job was after his own heart.

Douglas met him in Paris in high glee, for he was not sorry to be rid of Gates; and, on the other hand, the man had died in full tide of battle, and should be the very corpse that Vesquit most needed; as Douglas himself said, with a certain grim humour in which he excelled, he was, morally speaking, an executed criminal; while, being in actual magical contact with Grey and his friends, so much so that he had evidently been killed by them, he was an ideal magical link.

Vesquit's task was, if possible, to learn from Gates exactly what had happened, and so expert a necromancer had no fear of the result. He was also to create a semi-material ghost of Gates from the remains, and send it to the person who had dealt out death to that unlucky wizard.

On his arrival at Naples, there was no difficulty in the way of the Black Lodge; the authorities were only too glad to return a formal verdict of death by misadventure, and to hand over the corpse to the rejoicing Vesquit.

Gates had fortunately left memoranda, a rough diary of the various procedures hitherto adopted; so that Vesquit was not committed to the task of acquiring information from Arthwait, which might easily have occupied a season; and from these notes the old necromancer came to the conclusion that the enemy was to be respected. Gates had done pretty well in the matter of the pigeons, at first; his procedure was not to be compared with his colleague's pedantic idiocies; but the first touch of riposte had been indeed deadly. Gates had been the clairvoyant of the party; he had gauged clearly enough the result of his operation; but naturally he had left no note of the last act, and neither Arthwait nor Abdul Bey had been able to do anything. Arthwait had been scared badly until his pompous vanity came to the rescue, and showed him that accidents of that kind must be expected when one is handicapped with an assistant of inferior ability.

Vesquit decided that the battle should be properly prepared, and no trouble spared to make it a success. His fondness for corpses had not gone to the length of desiring to become one.

In him there had been the makings of a fairly strong man; and, with Douglas to push him on, he was still capable of acting with spirit and determination. Also, he had the habit of authority. He set Arthwait to work on the Grimoire; for, in an operation of this importance, one must make all one's instruments.

Beginning with a magic knife, which one is allowed to buy, one cuts the magic wand from a hazel, the magic quill from a goose, and so on. The idea is to confirm the will to perform the operation by a long series of acts ad hoc. It is even desirable to procure parchment by killing a consecrated animal with the magic knife, and making ready the skin with similarly prepared utensils; one might for instance, cut and consecrate even the pegs which stretched the skin. However, in this case Arthwait had plenty of "Virgin parchment" in stock, with quills of a black vulture, and ink made by burning human bones, and mixing the carbonised products with the soot of the magic dark-lantern, whose candles were prepared with human fat.

But the Grimoire of any great operation must be thought out and composed; according to elaborate rules, indeed, but with the purpose of the work constantly in mind. Even when all this is done, the Grimoire is hardly begun; for it must be copied out in the way above indicated; and it should be illuminated with every kind of appropriate design. This was an ideal task for Arthwait; he was able to wallow in dog-Latin and corrupt Greek-Coptic; he made sentences so complicated that the complete works of George Meredith, Thomas Carlyle, and Henry James, tangled together, would have seemed in comparison like a word of three letters.

His Grimoire was in reality excellent for its purpose; for the infernal hierarchy delights in unintelligible images, in every kind of confusion and obscurity. This particular lucubration was calculated to drag the Archdemon of Bad Syntax himself from the most remote corner of his lair.

For Arthwait could not speak with becoming unintelligibility; to knot a sentence up properly it has to be thought out carefully, and revised. New phrases have to be put in; sudden changes of subject must be introduced; verbs must be shifted to unsuspected localities; short words must be excised with ruthless hand; archaisms must be sprinkled like sugar-plums upon the concoction; the fatal human tendency to say things straightforwardly must be detected and defeated by adroit reversals; and, if a glimmer of meaning yet remain under close scrutiny, it must be removed by replacing all the principal verbs by paraphrases in some dead language.

This is not to be achieved in a moment; it is not enough to write disconnected nonsense; it must be possible for anyone acquainted with the tortuosities of the author's mind to resolve the sentence into its elements, and reproduce – not the meaning, for there is none, but the same mental fog from which he was originally suffering. An illustration is appended.

Pneumaticals	Omnient
(spirits)	(all)
Tabernacular	Subinfractically
(dwelling)	(Below)

Homotopic	hermeneutical
(this)	(magic)
Ru-volvolimperipunct,	suprorientalise,
(circle)	(arise)
factote	kinematodrastically,
(move)	(soon)
overplus	phenomenise!
(and)	(appear)

Upon this skeleton, a fair example of his earlier manner, for no man attains the summit of an art in a day, he would build a superstructure by the deft introduction of parentheses, amplifying each word until the original coherence of the paragraph was diluted to such an extent that the true trail was undiscoverable. The effect upon his public was to impress them with the universality of his learning.

Arthwait being thus well out of harm's way, Vesquit and Abdul set to work on the less arduous of the preparations. Four black cats were needed for the four points of the compass, and it was desirable to massacre a goat upon the altar, which would be no less than the corpse itself. Vesquit, declaring that the body was to be sent to England, had a dummy shipped off in a coffin, and kept Gates on ice, which may or may not have been a great comfort to him.

Abdul had no difficulty in procuring the cats which, much to their dissatisfaction, were caged in Arthwait's study, and fed on human flesh, which Vesquit easily procured from the dissecting-rooms of the local hospitals.

But the goat was a more serious matter. An ordinary goat will not do; it had to qualify in certain respects; Abdul succeeded in his quest only after a series of intrigues with the lowest ruffians in Naples, which brought him into more vulgar and unpleasant dangers than he had contemplated "when he first put that uniform on". It was, however, at least temporarily, a very amusing situation for the goat. The requisite bat, which must be fed on a woman's blood, was easily arranged for, a courageous country girl offering to accommodate with a toe, for a consideration. The nails from a suicide's coffin, and the skull of the parricide, were of course no trouble; for Vesquit never travelled without these household requisites.

There were many other details to arrange; the consideration of a proper place for the operation gave rise to much mental labour. It is, generally speaking, desirable to choose the locality of a recent battle; and the greater the number of slain the better. (There should be some very desirable spots in the vicinity of Verdun for black magicians who happen to flourish after the vulgar year 1917.) But the Grimoires were written in other times with other manners; now-a-days there is risk of disturbance if one sets up one's paraphernalia of goats and cats at a cross-roads, in the hope of helping oneself out with a recently interred suicide, or a ceremonially annihilated vampire; where the peasant of the fourteenth century would have fled shrieking, the motorist of the twentieth century stops to observe, or, more likely, runs you over; so that unless your property includes a private battlefield, it is a point of valour to choose a more retired site for one's

necromancy than the stricken field of the Marne. Cross-roads, again, are not so thickly planted with suicides and vampires as in happier days. Reflecting solidly and ably upon these points of modern degeneracy, Vesquit made up his mind to compromise, and accept the most agreeable substitute, a profaned chapel; it was easy to rent a villa with a chapel attached, and, to a man of Vesquit's ability, the work of a moment to profane it.

This he accordingly arranged through Abdul Bey.

The mind of this youth was very forcibly impressed by the preparations of the old coroner. He had been brought up in the modern school, and could laugh at superstition with the best of us; but there were traces of hereditary faith in Islam, and he was not sceptical enough to spoil the magic of Vesquit.

No man knew better than the necromancer that all this insane ceremonial was irrational. But it so happens that everything on this planet is, ultimately, irrational; there is not, and cannot be, any reason for the causal connexion of things, if only because our use of the word "reason" already implies the idea of causal connexion. But, even if we avoid this fundamental difficulty, Hume said that causal connexion was not merely unprovable, but unthinkable; and, in shallower waters still, one cannot assign a true reason why water should flow downhill, or sugar taste sweet in the mouth. Attempts to explain these simple matters always progress into a learned lucidity, and on further analysis retire to a remote stronghold where every thing is irrational and unthinkable.

If you cut off a man's head, he dies. Why? Because it kills him. That is really the whole answer. Learned excursions into anatomy and physiology only beg the question; it does not explain why the heart is necessary to life to say that it is a vital organ. Yet that is exactly what is done, the trick that is played on every inquiring mind. Why cannot I see in the dark? Because light is necessary to sight. No confusion of that issue by talk of rods and cones, and optical centres, and foci, and lenses, and vibrations is very different to Edwin Arthwait's treatment of the long-suffering English language.

Knowledge is really confined to experience. The laws of Nature are, as Kant said, the laws of our minds, and, as Huxley said, the generalisation of observed facts.

It is, therefore, no argument against ceremonial magic to say that it is "absurd" to try to raise a thunderstorm by beating a drum; it is not even fair to say that you have tried the experiment, found it would not work, and so perceived it to be "impossible". You might as well claim that, as you had taken paint and canvas, and not produced a Rembrandt, it was evident that the pictures attributed to his painting were really produced in quite a different way.

You do not see why the skull of a parricide should help you to raise a dead man, as you do not see why the mercury in a thermometer should rise and fall, though you elaborately pretend that you do; and you could not raise a dead man by the aid of the skull of a parricide, just as you could not play the violin like Kreisler; though in the latter case you might modestly add that you thought you could learn.

This is not the special pleading of a professed magician; it boils down to the advice not to judge subjects of which you are perfectly ignorant, and is to be found, stated in clearer and

lovelier language, in the Essays of Thomas Henry Huxley. Dr. Victor Vesquit, to whom the whole of these ideas was perfectly familiar, proceeded with his quaint preparations unperturbed by the least doubt of their efficacy.

He had found that they worked; and he cared no more for the opinion of those who, whatever their knowledge in other branches of science might be, were not experts in necromancy, than does Harry Vardon when it is proved to him, with the utmost scientific precision, that he cannot possibly hit a golf ball so long as he swings as he does, and uses that mechanically defective grip.

It is also to be remarked that the contrary holds good; no method of doing anything has yet been found which cannot be bungled by the inept.

So, as the Persian poet says: "Who hath the How is careless of the Why."

It was early in the course of Dr. Vesquit's preliminaries that (what Arthwait called the "antilan-thanetical douleskeiarchy") the secret service which had been established reported to him a complete change in the routine of the people of the Butterfly net. On the seventh of January Iliel reported that the first point of the work was in all probability attained; all that was now necessary was to concentrate upon the real crux of the case, the catching of the Butterfly.

The household was reorganised accordingly; Cyril Grey withdrew himself completely from the company of Iliel, and joined the Church Militant Here On Earth; while Iliel herself came under the direct care of Sister Clara, the point within the triangle of women. She took part in their invocations, as the focus to which they were directed; while the men were wholly busied in watching over the safety of the fortress, their faces turned inexorably outward, their sole business to assure the security of the three women and their treasure.

Upon these facts being brought to the notice of Edwin Arthwait, he smiled. He had redeemed his earlier failures – due to the incapacity of his assistants – by a sweeping success.

For to his magic, evidently, was due the observed change in nature! Shortly after the arrival of Vesquit, he had completed his latest operation, the bewitchment of three nails in such a manner that, if struck into the door of a room of a house, the occupants would be thereby debarred from the enjoyment of conjugal felicity. And here was the result, shining before him, beautiful with banners. Even the pretence of amity had been abandoned. As a matter of fact, Brother Onofrio had discovered the nails, and taken the proper measures to return the current to its sender; but on this occasion it was as "tae tak' the breeks aff a Hielan' mon"!

Arthwait was totally insensible to the malice of his adversary, and remained in the enjoyment of his supposed victory. He resolved to steal a march on Vesquit. Why should he share his glory with another? He had the enemy on the run; he had better pursue them forthwith. Vesquit's slow methods would only give them time to recover.

So he resolved upon the chivalrous if perilous course of Cat's Cradle. This magical operation, the relics of which are familiar even to the most unspiritually minded children, is exceedingly widespread, especially among nations which live principally by fishing, as, for example, the South Sea Islanders. Many most intricate and beautiful patterns have been devised, and of these the wayfaring man may partake by a perusal of Dr. W. W. R. Ball's monograph upon the subject. That able mathematician, however, neglects unpardonably the magical side of the matter.

The theory is apparently based upon the fact that the most elusive objects, birds, butterflies, and fishes, may be taken by means of a net. It is argued, therefore, that anything whatever, no matter how elusive, such as the ghost of one's father or the soul of one's enemy, may be caught similarly, though of course the net must be adapted to the special game that one is after.

With these things Arthwait was familiar, and it occurred to him that it should be easy to identify string, or, preferably, cat-gut, with the viscera of his victims. There could then be no difficulty in knotting up the cords in such a pattern, for example, as the Many Stars, or the Owl, or the Zigzag Lightning; and assuredly the magicians thus assailed would find similar re-arrangements of the contents of their peritonea.

After various preliminary exercises, annoying to the objects of this solicitude, Arthwait proposed to proceed to the grand operation of all, tying up his gut in the Elusive Yam pattern, which, from the greatest complexity, dissolves like a dream at a single last twist; the persons thus sympathetically treated would obviously perish no less miserably than did Eglon, King of Moab, or Judas Iscariot.

The advantage of this operation is evidently its extreme simplicity and economy; while, if it works at all, it surely leaves nothing to be desired in such Teutonic qualities as thoroughness and frightfulness.

Whether from any difficulty in identification or otherwise, it was some little while before Arthwait began to feel that his plan was working out. The trouble with all these operations was in the absence of a direct link with the principals; the currents invariably struck the outer defences, in the person of Brother Onofrio, before penetrating. When, therefore, Arthwait's efforts began to show results, they were first noticed by that sturdy warrior. And he, considering the situation, argued that the observed phenomena were due to Nature or to Magick, and that in either case the remedy lay in opposing no resistance to the forces, but allowing them to operate in a laudable manner. Accordingly, he took a large dose of a medicine known to the pharmacist as Hydrarg. Subchlor, adding the remark "If this be nature, may it do *me* good; and if this be magic, may it do *him* good!"

This occurred just as Arthwait reached his final operation, the evisceration of his enemy.

That night both parties were successful in causing things to happen; and the morning after Arthwait was securely incarcerated in the Quarantine Hospital of the city, and the newspapers were paragraphing a suspected case of Asiatic Cholera.

However, in five days the symptoms abated; the case was declared non-infectious; and the pallid shadow of the disconcerted sorcerer was restored to the more congenial atmosphere of his Grimoire.

CHAPTER XIV

AN INFORMATIVE DISCOURSE UPON THE OCCULT CHARACTER OF THE MOON

HER THREEFOLD NATURE, HER FOURFOLD PHASES,

AND HER EIGHT-AND-TWENTY MANSIONS; WITH

AN ACCOUNT OF THE EVENTS THAT PRECEDED

THE CLIMAX OF THE GREAT EXPERIMENT,

BUT ESPECIALLY OF THE VISION OF ILIEL

T HE Ancients, whose wisdom is so much despised by those who have never studied it, but content themselves with a pretence of understanding modern science which deceives nobody, would have smiled to observe how often the "latest discoveries" are equivalent to some fancy of Aristotle, or some speculation of Heracleitus. The remoter Picay-universities of America, which teach farming or mining, with a little "useless" knowledge as a side-course, for show, are full of bumptious little professors who would not be allowed to sweep out a laboratory in London or Berlin. The ambition of such persons is to obtain an illustrated interview in a Sunday supplement, with a full account of their wonderful discoveries, which have revolutionised the art of sucking eggs. They are peculiarly severe upon back numbers like Charles Darwin. Their ignorance leads them to believe the bombast of democracy-flatterers, who scream weekly of

Progress, and it really appears to them that anything more than six months old is out-of-date. They do not know that this is only true of loud-shouted mushroom rubbish such as they call truth.

The fundamental difference between ancient and modern science is not at all in the field of theory. Sir William Thomson was just as metaphysical as Pythagoras or Raymond Lully, and Lucretius quite as materialistic as Ernst Haeckel or Buchner.

But we have devised means of accurate measurement which they had not, and in consequence of this our methods of classification are more quantitative than qualitative. The result has been to make much of their science unintelligible; we no longer know exactly what they meant by the four elements, or by the three active principles, sulphur, mercury, and salt. Some tradition has been preserved by societies of wise men, who, because of the persecutions, when to possess any other book than a missal might be construed as heresy, concealed themselves and whispered the old teaching one to another.

The nineteenth century saw the overthrow of most of the old ecclesiastical tyranny, and in the beginning of the twentieth it was found once more possible to make public the knowledge. The wise men gathered together, discovered a student who was trustworthy and possessed of the requisite literary ability; and by him the old knowledge was revised and made secure; it was finally published in a sort of periodical encyclopedia (already almost impossible to find, such was the demand for it) entitled *The Equinox*.

Now in the science of antiquity, much classification depended upon the planets. Those things which were hot and fiery in their nature, lions, and pepper, and fevers, were classed under the Sun or Jupiter or Mars; things swift and subtle under Mercury; things cold and heavy under Saturn, and so forth.

Yet the principles of most of the planets appeared in varying proportions in almost everything; and the more equally these proportions were balanced and combined, the more complete was anything supposed to be, the nearer modelled on the divine perfection. Man himself was called a microcosm, a little universe, an image of the Creator. In him all the planets and elements had course, and even the Signs of the Zodiac were represented in his nature. The energy of the ram was in his head; the bull gave the laborious endurance to his shoulders; the lion represented the courage of his heart, and the fire of his temper; his knees, which help him to spring, are under the goat – all works in, and is divided and subdivided in, beauty and harmony.

In this curious language the moon signifies primarily all receptive things, because moonlight is only reflected sunlight. Hence "lunar" is almost a synonym of "feminine". Woman changes; all depends upon the influence of the man; and she is now fertile, now barren, according to her phase. But on each day of her course she passes through a certain section of the Zodiac; and according to the supposed nature of the stars beyond her was her influence in that phase, or, as they called it, mansion. It was in order to bring Iliel into harmony with every quality of the moon that her daily routine was ordered.

But beyond such minuteness of detail is the grand character of the Moon, which is threefold. For she is Artemis or Diana, sister of the Sun, a shining Virgin Goddess; then Isis-initiatrix, who brings to man all light and purity, and is the link of his animal soul with his eternal self; and she

is Persephone or Proserpine, a soul of double nature, living half upon earth and half in Hades, because, having eaten the pomegranate offered her by its lord, her mother could not bring her wholly back to earth; and thirdly, she is Hecate, a thing altogether of Hell, barren, hideous and malicious, the queen of death and evil witchcraft.

All these natures are combined in woman. Artemis is unassailable, a being fine and radiant; Hecate is the crone, the woman past all hope of motherhood, her soul black with envy and hatred of happier mortals; the woman in the fullness of life is the sublime Persephone, for whose sake Demeter cursed the fields that they brought forth no more corn, until Hades consented to restore her to earth for half the year. So this "moon" of the ancients has a true psychological meaning, as sound today as when the priest of Mithras slew the bull; she is the soul, not the eternal and undying sun of the true soul, but the animal soul which is a projection of it, and is subject to change and sorrow, to the play of all the forces of the universe, and whose "redemption" is the solution of the cosmic problem. For it is the seed of the woman that shall bruise the serpent's head; and this is done symbolically by every woman who wins to motherhood.

Others may indeed be chaste unto Artemis, priestesses of a holy and ineffable rite; but with this exception, failure to attain the appointed goal brings them into the dark side of the moon, the cold and barren house of Hecate the accursed.

It will be seen how wide is the range of these ideas, how sensitive is the formula of woman, that can touch such extremes, springing often from one to the other in a moment – according to the nature of the influence then at work upon her.

Cyril Grey had once said, speaking at a Woman's Suffrage Meeting:

"Woman has no soul, only sex; no morals, only moods; her mind is mob-rule; therefore she, and she only, ought to Vote."

He had sat down amid a storm of hisses; and received fourteen proposals of marriage within the next twenty-four hours.

Ever since the beginning of the second stage of the Great Experiment, Iliel had become definitely a Spirit of the Moon while Cyril was with her, she reflected him, she clung to him, she was one with him, Isis to his Osiris, sister as well as spouse; and every thought of her mind being but the harmonic of his, there was no possibility of any internal disturbance.

But now she was torn suddenly from her support; she could not even speak to her man; and she discovered her own position as the mere centre of an Experiment.

She knew now that she was not of scientific mind; that her aspirations to the Unknown had been fully satisfied by mere love; and that she would have been much happier in a commonplace cottage. It says much for the personality of Sister Clara, and the force of her invocations, that this first impulse never came to so much as a word. But the priestess of Artemis took hold of her almost with the violence of a lover, and whisked her away into a languid ecstasy of reverie. She communicated her own enthusiasm to the girl, and kept her mind occupied with dreams, faery-fervid, of uncharted seas of glory on which her galleon might sail, undiscovered countries of spice and sweetness, Eldorado and Utopia and the City of God.

The hour of the rising of the moon was always celebrated by an invocation upon the terrace consecrated to that planet. A few minutes earlier Iliel rose and bathed, then dressed herself in the robes, and placed upon her head the crescent-shaped tiara, with its nine great moonstones. In this the younger girls took turns to assist her. When she was ready, she joined the other girl, and together they went down to the terrace, where Sister Clara would be ready to begin the invocations.

Of course, owing to the nature of the ceremony, it took place an hour later every day; and at first Iliel found a difficulty in accommodating herself to the ritual. The setting of the moon witnessed a second ceremony, directly from which she retired to her bed. It was part of the general theory of the operation thus to keep her concealed and recumbent for the greater part of the day; which, as has been seen, really lasted nearer 25 hours than 24.

But with soft singing and music, or with the recital of slow voluptuous poetry, her natural disinclination to sleep was overcome, and she began to enjoy the delicious laziness of her existence, and to sleep the clock round without turning in her bed. She lived almost entirely upon milk, and cream, and cheese soft-curded and mild, with little crescent cakes made of rye with white of egg and cane sugar; as for meat, venison, as sacred to the huntress Artemis, was her only dish. But certain shell-fish were permitted, and all soft and succulent vegetables and fruits.

She put on flesh rapidly; the fierce, active, impetuous girl of October, with taut muscles and dark-flushed mobile face, had become pale, heavy, languid, and indifferent to events, all before the beginning of February.

And it was early in this month that she was encouraged by her first waking vision of the Moon. Naturally her sleep had already been haunted by this idea from the beginning; it could hardly have been otherwise with the inveterate persistence of the ceremonies. The three women always chanted a sacred sentence, *Epelthon Epelthon Artemis*, continuously for an hour after her couching; and then one of them went on while the others slept. They would each take a shift of three hours. The words were rather droned than sung, to an old magical chant, which Sister Clara, who was half-Greek, half-Italian, born of a noble family of Mitylene, had inherited from some of the women of the island at her initiation as a young girl into some of their mysteries. They claimed that it had come down unaltered from the great singers of history. It was a drowsy lilt, yet in it was a current of fierce heat like that of the sun, and an undertone of sobbing like the sea.

So Iliel's dreams were always of the moon. If the watcher beheld trouble upon her face, as if disturbing influences were upon her, she would breathe softly in her ear, and bring her thoughts back to the infinite calm which was desired for her.

For Cyril Grey in devising the operation had by no means been blind to the dangers involved in choosing a symbol so sensitive as Luna. There is all the universe between her good and evil sides; in the case of a comparatively simple and straightforward planet like Saturn, this is not the case. And the planets with a backbone are far easier to control. If you once get Mars going, so to speak, it is easy to make him comply with Queensberry rules; but the moon is so passive that the slightest new influence throws her entirely out.

And, of course, the calmer the pool, the bigger the splash! Hence, in order to draw down to Iliel only the holiest and serenest of the lunar souls, no precaution could be too great, no assiduity too intense.

The waking vision which came to her after about a month of the changed routine was of good cheer and great encouragement.

It was an hour after sunset; the night was curiously warm, and a soft breeze blew from the sea. It was part of the duty of Iliel to remain in the moonlight, with her gaze and her desire fixed upon the orb, whenever possible. From her room a stairway led to a tall turret, circular, with a glass dome, so as to favour all such observations. But on this night the garden tempted her. *Nox erat et caelo fulgebat Luna sereno inter minora sidera.* The moon hung above Capri, two hours from her setting. Iliel held her vigil upon the terrace, by the side of the basin of the fountain. When the moon was not visible, she would always replace her by looking upon the sea, or upon still water, for these have much in common with the lunar influence.

Something – she never knew what – drew her eyes from the moon to the water. She was so placed that the reflexion appeared in the basin, at the very edge of the marble, where the water flowed over into the little rivulets that coursed the terrace. There was a tremulous movement, almost like a timid kiss, as the water touched the edge.

And, to the eye of Iliel, it seemed as if the trembling of the moon's image were a stirring of vitality.

The thought that followed was a mystery. She said that she looked up, as if recalled to her vigil, and found that the moon was no longer in the sky. Nor indeed was there any sky; she was in a grotto whose walls, fantastically draped with stalactites, glimmered a faint purplish blue – very much the effect, she explained, of luminous paint. She looked down again; the basin was gone; at her feet was a young fawn, snow-white, with a collar of silver. She was impelled to read the engraving upon the collar, and was able to make out these words:

> *Siderum regina bicornis audi,*
> *Luna, puellas.*

Iliel had learnt no Latin. But these words were not only Latin, but the Latin of Horace; and they were exactly appropriate to the nature of the Great Experiment, "*Luna*" she had heard, and "*regina*"; and she might have guessed "*puellas*" and even "*siderum*"; but that is one thing, and an accurate quotation from the *Carmen Saeculare* is another. Yet they stood in her mind as if she had always known them, perhaps even as if they were innate in her. She repeated aloud:

> "*Siderum regina bicornis audi,*
> *Luna, puellas.*
>
> "List, o moon, o queen of the stars, two-horned,
> List to the maidens!"

At the time, she had, of course, no idea of the meaning of the words.

When she had read the inscription, she stroked the fawn gently; and, looking up, perceived that a child, clad in a kirtle, with a bow and quiver slung from her shoulders, was standing by her.

But the vision passed in a flash; she drew her hand across her brow, as if to auscultate her mental condition, for she had a slight feeling of bewilderment. No, she was awake; for she recognised the sacred oak under which she was standing. It was only a few paces from the door of the temple where she was priestess. She remembered perfectly now: she had come out to bid the herald blow his horn. And at that moment its mountainous music greeted her.

But what was this? From every tree in the wood, from every blade of grass, from under every stone, came running little creatures in answer to the summons. They were pale, semi-transparent, with oval (but rather flattened) heads quite disproportionately large, thin, match-like bodies and limbs, and snake-like tails attached to the base of their skulls. They were extraordinarily light and active on their feet, and the tails kept up a lashing movement. The whole effect was comic, at the first sight; one might have said tadpoles on stilts.

But a closer inspection stayed her laughter. Each of these creatures had a single eye, and in this eye was expressed such force and energy that it was terrifying. The effect was heightened by the sagacity, the occult and profound knowledge of all possible things, which dwelt behind those fiery wills. In the carriage of the head was something leonine as well as serpentine; there was extraordinary pride and courage to match the fierce persistency.

Yet there seemed no object in the movements of these strange beings; their immense activity was unintelligible. It seemed as if they were going through physical exercises – yet it was something more than that. At one moment she fancied that she could distinguish leaders, that this was a body of troops being rallied to some assault.

And then her attention was distracted. From her feet arose a swan, and took wing over the forest. It must have been there for a long time, for it had laid an egg directly between her sandalled feet. She suddenly realised that she was dreadfully hungry. She would go into the temple and have the egg for breakfast. But no sooner had she picked it up than she saw that it, like the collar of the fawn in her dream, was inscribed with a Latin sentence. She read it aloud: the words were absolutely familiar. They were those of the labarum of Constantine "*In hoc signo vinces*". "In this sign thou shalt conquer." But her, eyes gave the lie to her ears; for the word "*signo*" was spelt "*Cygno*"! The phrase was then a pun – "In this Swan thou shalt conquer." At the time she did not understand; but she was sure of the spelling, when she came afterwards to report her vision to Sister Clara.

It then came into her mind that this egg was a great treasure, and that it was her duty to guard it against all comers; and at the same moment she saw that the creatures of the wood – "sons of the oak" she called them instinctively – were advancing toward her.

She prepared to fight or fly. But, with a fearful crackling, the lightning – which was, in the strange way of dreams, identical with the oak – burst in every direction, enveloping her with its blaze; and the crash of the thunder was the fall of the oak. It struck her to the ground. The world went out before her eyes, dissolved into a rainbow rush of stars; and she heard the shouts

of triumph of the "sons of the oak" as they dashed forward upon her ravished treasure. "*Mitos ho Theos*!" they shouted – Sister Clara did not know, or would not tell, its meaning.

As the iridiscent galaxy in which she was floating gradually faded, she became aware that she was no longer in the wood, but in a strange city. It was crowded with men and women, of many a race and colour. In front of her was a small house, very poor and squalid, in whose doorway an old man was sitting. A long staff was by his side, leaning against the door; and at his feet was a lantern – was it a lantern? It was more like the opposite of one; for in the full daylight it burned, and shed forth rays of darkness. The ancient was dressed in grey rags; his long unkempt hair and beard had lacked a barber for many a day. But his right arm was wholly bare, and around it was coiled a serpent, gold and green, with a triple crown sparkling with ruby, sapphire, and with it he was engraving a great square tablet of emerald.

She watched him for some time; when he had finished, he went away with the staff, and the lamp, and the tablet, to the sea shore. Along the coast he proceeded for some time, and came at last to a cave. Iliel followed him to its darkest corner; and there she saw a corpse lying. Strangely, it was the body of the old scribe himself. It came to her very intensely that he had two bodies, and that he always kept one of them buried, for safety. The old scribe left the tablet upon the breast of the dead man, and went very quickly out of the cave.

But Iliel remained to read what was written. It was afterwards translated by Cyril Grey, and there is no need to give the original.

> Utter the Word of Majesty and Terror!
> True without lie, and certain without error,
> And of the essence of The Truth. I know
> The things above are as the things below,
> The things below are as the things above,
> To wield the One Thing's Thaumaturgy – Love.
> As all from one sprang, by one contemplation,
> So all from one were born, by permutation.
> Sun sired, Moon bore, this unique Universe;
> Air was its chariot, and Earth its nurse.
> Here is the root of every talisman
> Of the whole world, since the whole world began.
> Here is the fount and source of every soul.
> Let it be spilt on earth! its strength is whole.
> Now gently, subtly, with thine Art conspire
> To fine the gross, dividing earth and fire.
> Lo! it ascendeth and descendeth, even
> And swift, an endless band of earth and heaven;
> Thus it receiveth might of duplex Love,
> The powers below conjoined with those above,

So shall the glory of the world be thine
And darkness flee before thy SOVRAN shrine.
This is the strong strength of all strength; surpass
The subtle and subdue it; pierce the crass
And salve it; so bring all things to their fated
Perfection: for by this was all created.
O marvel of miracle! O magic mode!
All things adapted to one circling code!
Since three parts of all wisdom I may claim,
Hermes thrice great, and greatest, is my name.
What I have written of the one sole Sun,
His work, is here divined, and dared, and done.

In this obscure and antique oracle, so Simon Iff himself subsequently agreed, the secret of the Universe is revealed to those who are worthy to partake of it.

Iliel could not understand a word of what was written, but she realised that it must be valuable, and, taking the tablet, she hid it in her robe and came out of the cave. Then she saw that the coast was changed: it was the familiar Posilippo which hung above her, and she could see Vesuvius away to the right. She turned to breast the steep slope between her and the road, when she found herself confronted by something that she could not see. She had only a feeling that it was black, that it was icy cold, and that it wished to take the tablet from her. Her first sentiment was that of acute hatred and repulsion; but the thing, whatever it was, seemed so wretched, that she felt she would like to help it. Then she suddenly glowed hot – the arms of Abdul Bey were round her, and his face was looking into hers. She dropped the tablet hastily; she was back again in a ball-room somewhere, thousands of miles and thousands of years away. And then she saw the moon, near her setting, over Capri; she was on the terrace, seated on the ground, perfectly awake, but with the silver crescent from her hair lying upon the marble before her.

Sister Clara, on her knees beside her, was trying to decipher the scratches that she had made.

"That is the writing on the tablet," said Iliel, as if Sister Clara already knew all about it, "that the old man hid in the cave."

It was now the hour for her to cradle her limbs in slumber; but, while the monotonous chant of her hand-maidens wooed the soft air, Cyril Grey and Brother Onofrio were at work upon the inscription.

Almost until dawn they toiled; and, down in another villa, another labour reached its climax. Arthwait had finished his Grimoire. He was just in time. For the great operation of necromancy should properly begin on the second day of the waning of the moon, and there were nine previous days of most arduous preparation, no longer of the materials, but of the sorcerers themselves.

They must eat dog's flesh, and black bread baked without salt or leaven, and they must drink unfermented grape-juice – the vilest of all black magical concoctions, for it implies the denial of the divine beatitude, and affirms God to be a thing of wood. There were many other precautions

also to be taken. The atmosphere of the charnel must be created about them; they must abstain from so much as the sight of women; their clothing might not be changed even for an hour, and its texture was to be that of cerements, for, filching the grave-clothes from corpses of the unassoiled, they must wrap themselves closely round in them, with some hideous travesty of the words of the Burial Service.

A visit to the Jewish graveyard put them in possession of the necessary garments; and Arthwait's palinode upon the "resurrection unto damnation" left in each mind due impression of the ghastliness of their projected rite.

And, in Paris, Douglas, smashing the neck of a bottle of whisky on the edge of the table, was drinking the good health of his visitor, an American woman of the name of Cremers.

Her squat stubborn figure was clad in rusty-black clothes, a man's except for the skirt; it was surmounted by a head of unusual size, and still more unusual shape, for the back of the skull was entirely flat, and the left frontal lobe much more developed than the right; one could have thought that it had been deliberately knocked out of shape, since nature, fond, it may be, of freaks, rarely pushes asymmetry to such a point.

There would have been more than idle speculation in such a theory; for she was the child of hate, and her mother had in vain attempted every violence against her before her birth.

The face was wrinkled parchment, yellow and hard; it was framed in short, thick hair, dirty white in colour; and her expression denoted that the utmost cunning and capacity were at the command of her rapacious instincts. But her poverty was no indication that they had served her; and those primitive qualities had in fact been swallowed up in the results of their disappointment. For in her eye raved bitter a hate of all things, born of the selfish envy which regarded the happiness of any other person as an outrage and affront upon her. Every thought in her mind was a curse – against God, against man, against love, or beauty, against life itself. She was a combination of the witch-burner with the witch; an incarnation of the spirit of Puritanism, from its sourness to its sexual degeneracy and perversion.

Douglas put the broken glass to his mouth, and gulped down a bumper of whisky. Then he offered the bottle to his visitor. She refused by saying that it "played hell with the astral body", and asked her host to give her the price of the drink instead. Douglas laughed like a madman – a somewhat disgusted madman, for in him was some memory of his former state, and even his fall had been comparatively decent, the floor of his hell a ceiling to her heaven.But he had a use for the hag, and he contemptuously tossed her a franc. She crawled over the floor, like some foul insect, in search of it, for it had rolled to a corner; and, having retrieved it, she forgot her mannish assumptions in her excitement at the touch of silver, and thrust it into her stocking.

CHAPTER XV

OF DR. VESQUIT AND HIS COMPANIONS

HOW THEY FARED IN THEIR WORK OF NECROMANCY; AND OF A COUNCIL OF WAR OF CYRIL GREY AND BROTHER ONOFRIO; WITH CERTAIN OPINIONS OF THE FORMER UPON THE ART OF MAGICK

T HE Neapolitan winter had overpassed its common clemency; save for a touch of frost, kindly and wholesome, on a few nights, it had no frown or rigour. Day after day the sun had enkindled the still air, and life had danced with love upon the hills.

But on the night of her fullness, the moon was tawny and obscure, with a reddish vapour about her, as if she had wrapped herself in a mantle of anger; and the next dawn broke grey with storm, the wind tearing its way across the mountain spine of Italy, as if some horde of demon bandits were raiding the peasantry of the plains. The Butterfly-Net was sheltered from its rage by the crest of Posilippo; but it was bitter cold in the house, and Iliel bade her maidens pile the brazier with hazel and white sandalwood and birch.

Across the ridge, the villa which Dr. Vesquit had taken for the winter was exposed to the senseless madness of the blast; and he too heaped his braziers, but with cypress and bituminous coal.

As the day passed the violence of the storm increased; the doctor even began to fear for the safety of his operation when, about an hour after noon, a window of the villa was broken by a torn branch of olive that came hurtling against it.

But a little later the speed of the hurricane abated; the sky was visible, through the earth-vapours, as a wrack of wrathful clouds – one might say the flight of Michael before Satan.

Though the gale was yet fierce, its heart broke in a torrent of sleet mixed with hail; for two hours more it drove almost horizontally against the hillside, and then, steadying and steepening, fell as a flood, a cataract of icy rain.

The slopes of Posilippo roared with their foaming load; gardens were washed clear of soil; walls broke down before the impetuosity of the waves they strove to dam; and the streets of lower Naples stood in water to the height of a man's thigh.

The hour for the beginning of the work of the necromancers was that of sunset; and at that moment the rain, after a last burst of vehemence, ceased entirely; nightfall, though black and bitter, was silent as the corpse of Gates itself.

In the chapel a portion of the marble floor had been torn up; for it was desired to touch the naked earth with the bare feet, and draw her powers directly up from their volcanic stratum.

This raw earth had been smeared with mire brought from the swamps of the Maremma; and upon this sulphur had been sprinkled until it formed a thick layer. In this sulphur the magick circle had been drawn with a two-pointed stick, and the grooves thus made had been filled with charcoal powder.

It was not a true circle; no figure of sanctity and perfection might enter into that accursed rite; it had been made somewhat in the shape of an old-fashioned keyhole, a combination of circle and triangle.

In the centre the body of Gates, his head toward the north, was laid; Arthwait stood on one side with the Grimoire in one hand, and a lighted taper of black wax in the other. On the opposite side was Abdul Bey, holding the goat in leash, and bearing the sickle which Vesquit was to use as the principal magical weapon of the ceremony.

The doctor was himself the last to enter the circle. In a basket he had the four black cats; and, when he had lighted the nine small candles about the circle, he pinned the four cats, at the four quarters, with black arrows of iron. He was careful not to kill them; it was important that their agony should frighten away any undesirable spirits.

All being now ready, the necromancers fell upon their knees; for this servile position is pleasing to the enemies of mankind.

The forces which made man, alone of all animals, erect, love to see him thank Them for that independence by refusing to surrender it.

The main plan of Dr. Vesquit's ceremony was simple; it was to invoke the spirit of a demon into the goat, and slaying the animal at that moment of possession upon the corpse of Gates, to endow that corpse with the demoniac power, in a kind of hideous marriage.

The object was then identical with that of spiritism, or "spiritualism", as it is commonly and illiterately called; but Dr. Vesquit was a serious student, determined to obtain results, and not to be duped; his methods were consequently more efficient than those of the common or parlour medium.

Arthwait opened the Grimoire and began his conjurations. It would be impossible to reproduce the hideous confusion and complexity of the manner, and undesirable to indicate the abomination of the matter. But every name of opposition to light was invoked in its own rite; the fearful deities of man's dawn, when nature was supposed to be a personal power of cruelty, delighting in murder, rape, and pillage, were called by their most secret names, and commemoration made of their deeds of infamy.

Such was the recital of horror that, cloaked even as it was in Arthwait's unintelligible style, the meaning was salient by virtue of the tone of the enchanter, and the gestures with which Vesquit accompanied him, going in dumb show through all the gamut of infernal discord, the music of the pit. He showed how children were cast into the fire, or thrown to bears, or offered up in sacrifice on bloody altars; how peaceful nations were uprooted by savage tribes in the name of their demon, their men slain or mutilated and enslaved, their women butchered, their virgins ravished; how miracle testified to the power of the evil ones, the earth opening to swallow heretic priests, the sun stopped in the sky that the hours of massacre might be prolonged.

It was in short one interminable recital of treachery and murder and revenge; never a thought of pity or of kindliness, of common decency or common humanity, struck a false note in that record of vileness; and it culminated in the ghastliest atrocity of human history, when the one man in all that cut-throat race who now and then showed gleams of a nobler mind was chosen for torture and death as a final offering to the blood-lust of the fiend.

With a sort of hellish laughter, the second conjuration continued the recital; how the demon had brought the corpse of his victim to life, and mocked and profaned his humanity by concealing himself in that man-shape, thence to continue his reign, and extend his empire, under the cloak of hypocrisy. The crimes that had been done openly in the fiend's name, were now to be carried on with fresh device of shame and horror, by those who called themselves the priests of his victim.

By this commemoration was concluded the first part of the ceremony; the atmosphere of the fiend, so to speak, was brought into the circle; in the second part the demon was to be identified with the goat; in the third part the two first were joined, and the goat as he died was to repeat the miracle wrought in long ages past upon that other victim, by coming to life again humanised by the contact of the ghost of the sorcerer.

It is not permissible to describe this ritual in detail; it is too execrably efficient; but the Turk, brought up in a merciful and cleanly religion, with but few stains of savagery upon it, faltered and nigh fainted; only his desire for Lisa, which had become a soul-tempest, held him to the circle.

And indeed the brains of them all were awhirl. As Eliphaz Levi says, evil ceremonies are a true intellectual poison; they do invoke the powers of hallucination and madness as surely as does hashish. And who dare call the phantoms of delirium "unreal"? They are real enough to kill a man, to ruin a life, to push a soul to every kind of crime; and there are not many "real" "material" things that have such weight in work.

Phantoms, then, were apparent to the necromancers; and there was no doubt in any of their minds that they were dealing with actual and malignant entities.

The hideous cries of the tortured cats mingled with the triumphant bleating of the goat and the nasal monotone of Arthwait as he mouthed the words of the Grimoire. And it seemed to all of them as though the air grew thick and greasy; that of that slime were bred innumerable creeping things, monsters misshapen, abortions of dead paths of evolution, creatures which had not been found fit to live upon the earth and so had been cast off by her as excrement. It seemed as if the goat were conscious of the phantoms; as if he understood himself as demon-king of those regions; for he bounded under the manipulations of Vesquit with such rage and pride that Abdul Bey was forced to use all his strength to hold him. It was taken as a sign of success by all the necromancers; and as Vesquit made the final gesture, Arthwait turned his page, and Abdul struck home with a great knife to the brute's heart.

Now, as the blood stained their grave-clothes, the hearts of the three sorcerers beat heavily. A foul sweat broke out upon them. The sudden change – psychological or magical? – from the turgid drone of Arthwait to the grimness of that silence in which the howls of the agonising cats rose hideous, struck them with a deadly fear. Or was it that they realised for the first time on what a ship they had embarked?

Suppose the corpse did move? Suppose Gates rose in the power of the devil, and strangled them? Their sweat ran down, and mingled with the blood. The stench of the slain goat was horrible, and the body of Gates had begun decomposition. The sulphur, burning in little patches here and there, where a candle had fallen and kindled it, added the reek of hell to that of death. Abdul Bey of a sudden was taken deathly sick; at the end he pitched forward, prone upon the corpses. Vesquit pulled him roughly back, and administered a violent stimulant, which made him master of himself.

Now Arthwait started the final conjuration. It can hardly be called language; it was like the jabber of a monkey-house, and like the yells of a thousand savages, and like the moaning of damned souls.

Meanwhile Vesquit proceeded to the last stage of his task. With his knife he hacked off the goat's head, and thrust it into a cavity slashed in the abdomen of the other body. Other parts of the goat he thrust into the mouth of Gates, while the obscene clamour of the cats mingled with the maniac howls of his colleague.

And then the one thing happened which they none of them expected. Abdul Bey flung himself down upon the carcasses, and began to tear them with his teeth, and lap the blood with his tongue. Arthwait shrieked out in terror that the Turk had gone mad: but Vesquit understood the truth. Abdul was the most sensitive of the party, and the least developed; it was in him that the spirit of Gates, demon-inspired, would manifest.

A few minutes of that scene, and then the Turk sat up. His face expressed the most extreme pleasure. It was the release of a soul from agony that showed itself. But he must have known that his time was short, for he spoke rapidly and earnestly, with febrile energy. And his words were commanding and convincing: Vesquit had no doubt that they were in presence of knowledge vastly superior to anything that he had yet found.

He wrote down the speech upon the tablets that he had prepared for the purpose.

"They are working by the moon towards the Sun.

"Hecate will come to help you. Attack from within, not from without.

"An old woman and a young man bring victory.

"All the powers are at your service; but they are stronger. Treachery shall save you.

"Abandon the direct attack; for even now you have called down your death upon you. Quick! snap the cord. Conceal yourselves awhile. Even so, you are nigh death. Oh haste! Look yonder who is standing ready to smite!"

The voice dropped. Well was it for Vesquit that he kept his presence of mind. The necromancers looked round over their shoulders, and in the East was a blue mist shaped like an egg. In the midst of it, standing upon two crocodiles, was the image of Brother Onofrio, smiling, with his finger upon his lips. Vesquit realised that he was in contact with a force a thousand times greater than any at his disposal. He obeyed instantly the command spoken through Abdul Bey. "I swear," he cried, raising his right hand to heaven, "I swear that we intend you no manner of hurt." He flushed inwardly, knowing it for a lie, and therefore useless to avert the blow which he felt poised above him. He sought a new form of words. "I swear that we will not seek to break through your defences." This, he thought, should satisfy the captain of the gate, and yet permit him to do as he intended in the matter of trying to attack from within. Abdul Bey gasped out that it was well, that no more could be done, that the link with the White Lodge was broken. "But now our own blow strikes us to the earth." He fell backwards, as one dead. In another moment Arthwait, with a yell, a last invocation of that fiend whom he really believed to be omnipotent, entered into spasmodic convulsions, like a man poisoned with strychnine, or dying of tetanus. Vesquit, appalled at the fate of his companions, gazed on the figure of Brother Onofrio in an agony of fear and horror. It retained the infant smile, and Vesquit reached his arms toward it. "Mercy!" he cried, "oh, my lord, mercy!"

Arthwait was writhing upon the corpses, horribly twisting, foaming black blood from his lungs.

And the old man saw that his life had been an imbecility, that he had taken the wrong path.

Brother Onofrio still smiled. "Oh my lord!" cried Vesquit, rising to his feet, "'twere better I should die."

The formula of humanity is the willing acceptance of death; and as love, in the male, is itself of the nature of a voluntary death, and therefore a sacrament, so that he who loves slays himself, therefore he who slays himself that life may live becomes a lover. Vesquit stretched out his arms in the sign of the cross, the symbol of Him who gives life through his own death, or of the instrument of that life and of that death, of the Holy One appointed from the foundation of the world as its redeemer.

It was as if there had come to him a flash of that most secret Word of all initiated knowledge, so secret and so simple that it may be declared openly in the market-place, and no man hear it. At

least he realised himself as a silly old man, whose weakness and pliability in the hands of evil men had made him their accomplice. And he saw that death, grasped now, might save him.

Brother Onofrio still smiled.

"I invoke the return of the current!" cried Vesquit aloud; and thus, uniting justice with self-sacrifice, he died the death of the righteous.

The image of Brother Onofrio faded away.

The great operation of necromancy had come to naught.

Yet the writing remained; and, nearly a day later, when Abdul Bey came to himself, it was the first thing that caught his eye. He thrust it into his shroud, automatically; then stumbled to his feet, and sought his colleagues. At his feet the old coroner lay dead; Arthwait, his convulsions terminated by exhaustion approximating coma, lay with his head upon the carrion, his tongue, lolling from his mouth, chewed to a bloody pulp.

The Turk carried him from the chapel to the villa. His high connexions made it easy for him to secure a silent doctor to certify the death of Vesquit, and to attend to Arthwait, who passed from one convulsion to another at frequent intervals. It was almost a month before he could be considered out of danger, but a week after that he was his own man again. They repaired immediately to Paris to lay the case before Douglas; for even Arthwait was compelled to recognise some elements in the business which were not satisfactory, incidents which he could not but regard as indicating that he had fallen appreciably short of his high standard of success.

The day succeeding the exploit of the necromancers dawned gay and bright. The earth dried up again, but breathed refreshment. A light mist hung over the walled garden where Iliel stood upon her terrace.

The moon sank large and pale over the ocean as sunrise awoke the waves, and Iliel, her vigil almost ended, prepared for the ceremony that ended her day.

But no sooner had she gone to the care of her hand-maidens than Cyril Grey came down the garden with Brother Onofrio. Their arms were crossed upon their breasts in the stately fashion of the Order; and Brother Onofrio's scarlet robe contrasted magnificently with the soft green silk of Brother Cyril's.

In the eyes of the Italian was a passionate reverence for the younger, but more gifted, man, coupled with a human affection which was almost more than friendship; there was in it the devotion, selfless and unsleeping, which is only possible to those of immense singleness of heart. He understood that Brother Cyril was of a finer mould than himself; he seemed to be rather a flame of fire than a man, so subtle and so keen was he. For in every talk, whenever he thought that he had sounded Cyril's guard, he suddenly found, on the riposte, that he had lost touch of his blade without knowing it. But he burned with constant ardour to know more of his idol; and this morning the young man had awakened him softly with a whisper, smiling, with a finger pointed to the terrace: "Let's go over there, where the Chancellor of the Exchequer can't hear us." So they had risen and come down to the lily-pool, after the morning adoration of the Sun, and their daily exercise of meditation.

Brother Cyril proved to be in his airiest mood, "Do you remember who said '*Surtout, pas de zèle?*'" he began.

"Whoever it was then, I'm saying it now. Brother Onofrio, big brother, strong brother, clever brother, it won't do. You're doing much too well. Think you're a Russian General, if that will assist your feeble intelligence; but what you think doesn't matter, so long as you understand that to win too many victories is as bad as to eat *toujours perdrix*. You have not merely defended this excellent citadel, for which I formally tender you the thanks of the Republic. You may kiss my hand. But you have pursued the defeated enemy; you have annihilated their strongest regiments; and, after last night, I am afraid that they will abandon the attack altogether. The situation is lamentable."

"But they invoked the death-current themselves," objected Brother Onofrio. "How could I tell that they would send for poor old Vesquit, and prepare an operation so formidable that something definite was bound to happen, one way or the other?"

"But you failed to deal gently with the young man Gates!"

"I know I'm liable to be carried away by a Tarot divination; but he was himself attempting a magical murder. You can't work things except on their own plane. He who taketh the sword shall perish by the sword."

"I dare say you're right; but I'm terribly afraid you've scared the game. I wanted to have Douglas and Balloch down here; then was the moment to turn loose those engines of destruction."

"You might have told me."

"Ah, if I had only known!"

Brother Onofrio gave a savage gesture. Once again he was being eluded.

"I only realised just now how fit and final were your labours. And now we are going to eat our hearts out in enervating peace and Capuan luxury. Alas! Think of the fate of Hannibal and of Napoleon. Always the same story – too much victory!"

Brother Onofrio bounded again in his amazement. "Peace! Luxury!" he cried. "Haven't we got the Great Experiment?"

"Have we?" sighed Cyril, languidly.

"Isn't the crisis in a month?"

"There are twelve months in a year."

Brother Onofrio rose in indignation. He hated to be played with in this manner; he could see no point in the jest, if it were one; or excuse for the rudeness, in the alternative.

"Sit down, sit down!" said Cyril dreamily. "You say yourself the crisis is not for a month. What a wonderful way is Ocean, girdling the five continents like a mother with her children. I should like to sail out westward, past the Pillars of Hercules, and up into the stormy reaches of the Bay, and – ah well! it may not be. We are held here by our stern duty; we are the chosen warriors of the Final Battle to decide whether men shall mould their own destiny, or remain the toys of Fate; we are the pioneers of the Great Experiment. To arms, Brother Onofrio! Be diligent! Be courageous! The crisis is upon us – a month, no more! Return to me with your shield, or upon it!

"*Dulce et decorum est pro patria mori.*"

"Ah! now I understand you!" cried Onofrio warmly, clasping him in the impulsive Italian fashion.

"That's splendid of you," he said brightly. "I do appreciate that."

Brother Onofrio wriggled again.

"I half think," he said "that you know the Great Experiment will be a failure, and that for some reason you don't care!"

"The bluntness of the British diplomat was no match for the subtlety of the ambitious, wily, and astute Italian."

"Confound it! Is there anything real or true to you?"

"Wine, spirits, and cigars."

"You won't be serious. You jest about everything most vital; and you make solemnities of merest wisps of fancy. You would make drumsticks of your father's bones, and choose a wife by blowing a puff-ball!"

"While you would go without music for fear of disturbing your father, and choose a wife by the smell of a powder-puff."

"Oh, how can you do it?"

Brother Cyril shook his head

"I must explain myself more carefully," he said. "Let me ask you, in the first place, what is the most serious thing in the world."

"Religion."

"Exactly. Now, what is religion? The consummation of the soul by itself in divine ecstasy. What is life but love, and what is love but laughter? In other words, religion is a joke. There is the spirit of Dionysus and there is the spirit of Pan; but they are twin phases of laughter. Religion is a joke. Now what is the most absurd thing in the world?"

"Woman."

"Right again. And therefore she is the only serious island in this ocean of laughter. While we hunt and fish, and fight, and otherwise take our pleasure, she is toiling in the fields and cooking, and bearing children. So, all the serious words are jests, and all the jokes are earnest. This, oh my brother, is the key to my light and sparkling conversation."

"But –"

"I know what you are going to say. You can reverse it again. That is precisely the idea. You keep on reversing it; and it gets funnier and more serious every time, and it spins faster and faster until you cannot follow it, and your brain begins to whirl, and presently you become That Spiral Force which is of the Quintessence of the Absolute. So it is all a simple and easy method of attaining the summit of perfections, the stone of the Wise, True Wisdom and Perfect Happiness."

"Listening to you," reflected Brother Onofrio, with a whisk of the rapier, "produces something of this effect!"

"Then praise the Father of All for making me, and let us go to break our fast!"

In the refectory a telegram awaited Cyril Grey. He read it carefully, destroyed it, and, looking with quaint spieglish eyes at Brother Onofrio, refrained ostentatiously from a prolonged fit of

laughter. His face grew exceedingly grave, and he spoke with the weightiest deliberation. "I deeply regret to be obliged to inform you," he said at last, "that the exigencies of the situation combine to make it incumbent on me to proceed to instant action by asking you to pass the sugar."

With sullen grace Brother Onofrio complied.

"What saith the Scripture?" asked Cyril, still more portentous. "*Ornithi gluku* – a little bit of sugar for the bird!"

CHAPTER XVI

OF THE SPREADING
OF THE BUTTERFLY-NET

**WITH A DELECTABLE DISCOURSE CONCERNING
DIVERS ORDERS OF BEING; AND OF THE STATE OF
THE LADY ILIEL, AND HER DESIRES, AND OF THE
SECOND VISION THAT SHE HAD IN WAKING**

A GREAT peace brooded on the Villa. Daily sun gathered the strength; and the west wind told the flowers that a little bird had whispered to him that the spring was coming.

The results of the magical invocations began to peep through the veil of matter, like early crocuses. The atmosphere of house and garden was languid and romantic, so that a stranger could not have failed to feel it; yet with this was a timid yet vigorous purity, a concentration of the longing of the magicians.

The physical signs were equally unmistakable. By night a faint blue luminosity radiated from the whole enclosure, visible to the natural eye; and to one seated in the garden, darting scintillations, star-sparkles, would appear, flitting from flower to flower, or tree to stone, if he kept as still and sensitive as one should in such a garden. And on the rightly tuned and tempered ear might fall, now and again, vague snatches of some far-off music. Then there were pallid perfumes in the air, like suggestions of things cool, and voluptuous, and chaste and delicate, and lazy, of those soft tropical loves which satisfy themselves with dreams.

All these phenomena were of a peculiar quality. It will be well to recite the fact, and to suggest an explanation.

These sights and sounds are conveyed clearly enough; but they disappear the moment the full attention is turned upon them. They will not bear inspection; and the fact has been used by shallow thinkers as an argument against their reality. It is a foolish point to take, as will now be proved.

The range of our senses is extremely limited. Our sensorial apparatus only works properly with reference to a very few of very many things. Every child knows how narrow is the spectrum, how confined the range of musical tone. He has not yet been drilled properly to an understanding of what this may mean, and he has not been told with equal emphasis many similar facts relating to other forms of perception. In particular, he has not learnt the meaning of diluted impression, in spite of an admirable story called *The New Accelerator* by Mr. H. G. Wells.

Our vision of things depends upon their speed; for instance, a four-bladed electric fan in motion appears as a diaphanous and shining film. Again, one may see the wheels of automobiles moving backwards in a cinematograph; and, at certain distances, the report of a cannon may be heard before the order to fire is given. Physics is packed with such paradoxes. Now we know of living beings whose time-world is quite different to ours, only touching it over a short common section. Thus, a fly lives in a world which moves so fast that he cannot perceive motion in anything with a speed of less than about a yard a second, so that a man may put his hand upon it if he can restrain the impulse to slap. To this fly, then, the whirling fan would look quite different; he would be able to distinguish the four blades.

We have thus direct evidence that there are "real" "material" beings whose senses are on a different range to ours.

We also have reason to believe that this total range is almost inconceivably great. It is not merely a question of the worlds of the microscope and the telescope; these are mere extensions of our gamut. But we now think that a molecule of matter is a universe in most rapid whirl, a cosmos comparable to that of the heavens, its electrons as widely separated from each other, in proportion to their size, as the stars in space. Our universe, then, in its unmeasured vastness, is precisely similar in constitution to one molecule of hydrogen; and we may suppose that it is itself only a molecule of some larger body; also that what we call an electron may itself be a universe – and so on for ever. This suggestion is supported by the singular fact, that the proportion in size of electron to molecule is about the same as that of sun to cosmos, the ratio in each case being as 1 to 10,000,000,000,000,000,000,000,000.

Suppose a drop of water, ⅛ inch in diameter, to be magnified to the size of the earth, there would be about 30 molecules in every cubic foot of it, each molecule being about the size of a golf ball, or a little more.

However, the point involved is a simpler one, so far as our argument is concerned; it is this – that there is no question of "illusion" about any of these things. Electrons are quite as elusive as ghosts; we are only aware of them as the conclusion to a colossal sorites. The evidence for ghosts is as strong as that for any other phenomenon in nature; and the only argument, for a horse-laugh is not argument, which has been adduced against their existence is that you cannot catch them. But, just as one can catch the fly by accommodating oneself to the conditions of its world, one might (conceivably) catch the ghost by conforming with its conditions.

It is one magical hypothesis that all things are made up of ten different sorts of vibrations, each with a different gamut, and each corresponding to a "planet". Our own senses being built up similarly, they only register these when they are combined. Hence, a "lunar" being, purified of other elements, would be imperceptible. And if one, by emphasising the lunar quality in oneself, began to acquire the power of perceiving similar beings, one would begin by perceiving them as tenuous and elusive; just, in fact, as is observed to be the case.

We are therefore justified in regarding the phenomena of the magicians as in all respects "real", in the same sense as our own bodies; and all doubt on the subject is removed by consideration of the fact, to which all magicians testify, that these phenomena can be produced at will, by using proper means.

It is no criticism to reply that it should be possible to show them "in the laboratory", because laboratory conditions happen not to suit their production. One does not doubt the reality of electrical phenomena either, because electricity is not perceptible directly by any of the senses, or because its ultimate nature is unknown, or because the electrician refuses to comply with your "test conditions" by his irrational and evidently felonious habit of insulating his wires.

So far as Iliel was concerned, the result of the operation was almost too evident. Simon Iff might have thought that things were being overdone. For she had become extremely fat; her skin was of a white and heavy pallor; her eyes were almost closed by their perpetual droop. Her habit of life had become infinitely sensuous and languid; when she rose from recumbency she lolled rather than walked; her lassitude was such that she hardly cared to feed herself; yet she managed to consume five or six times a normal diet. She seemed always half asleep. A cradle, shaped like a canoe, had been arranged for her on the Terrace of the Moon; and most of her waking hours were spent there, drinking milk, and munching creams flavoured with angelica. Her soul seemed utterly attracted to the moon. She held out her body to it like an offering.

Just before the new moon of February, Abdul Bey, before leaving Naples, determined to seek a last sight of his adored Lisa. He had found her easily, and was amazed at the physical changes in her. They increased his passion beyond all measure, for she was now the very ideal of any Turkish lover. She appeared hardly conscious of his presence upon the wall beyond the little lane that wound below the Terrace of the Moon, but in reality she absorbed his devotion with a lazy hunger, like a sponge. For her activity and resistance had been reduced to zero; she reflected any impression, feeling it to the utmost, but incapable of response. He understood that she could not have repulsed him, yet could have taken no step towards him; and he cursed the vigilance of the patrol. Help he must have; and though it was agony to drag himself from Naples, he knew that without Douglas he could do nothing more.

From the new moon of February, the invocations of Artemis had become continuous. Brother Onofrio and his two henchmen devoted their time and energy to the rituals which banish all other ideas than the one desired; but the boys had joined Sister Clara and her maidens in an elaborate ceremony in which the four represented the four phases of the moon. This ceremony was performed thrice daily; but the intervals were fully occupied. During the whole of the twenty-five hours one or the other of the enchanters kept up their conjurations by spells, by music, and

by dances. Every day witnessed some new phenomenon, ever more vivid and persistent, as the imminence of the lunar world increased, and as the natures of the celebrants became more and more capable of appreciating those silvern vibrations.

Cyril Grey alone took no active part. He represented the solar force, the final energy creatrix of all subordinate orbs; his work had been done when he had set the system in motion. But since Brother Onofrio represented so active a force as Mars, he made himself a silent partner to the Italian, an elasticity to buffer the reactions of his vehemence. Thus he became a shadow to the warrior, giving him the graceful ease which was the due reward of fatigues so exhausting as were involved in the Keeping of the Circle. For the labour of banishing became daily more arduous; the preponderance of lunar force within the circle created a high potential. All the other forces of Nature wished to enter and redress the balance. It is the same effect as would be seen were one to plunge a globe full of water beneath the sea, and gradually withdraw the water from the globe. The strain upon the surface of the globe would constantly increase. It may be remarked in parenthesis that the Laws of Magick are always exactly like those of the other natural forces. All that magick lacks to put it on a footing with hydrostatics or electricity is a method of quantitative estimation. The qualitative work is admirably accomplished.

The moon was waxen beyond her first phase; she set well after midnight. The nights were yet cold; but Iliel's cradle had been made like a nest in cloudland with fleece of camels – for they are sacred to the moon; and she was covered with a quilt of silver fox. Thus she could lie in the open without discomfort, and yearn toward her goddess as she moved majestically across heaven.

Now that the climax of the Experiment was upon her, the exaltation of wonder seized her wholly; she was in precisely the state necessary to the magical plan. She remained in a continuous reverie of longing and expectancy for the marvel which was to come to her.

It was now the night of the full moon. She rose over the crest of Posilippo soon after sunset, and Iliel greeted her from her cradle on the Terrace with a hushed song of adoration.

She was more languid than ever before, that night. It seemed to her as if her body were altogether too heavy for her; she had the feeling so well known to opium-smokers, which they call "*cloué à terre*". It is as if the body clung desperately to the earth, by its own weight, and yet in the same way as a tired child nestles to its mother's breast. In this sensation there is a perfect lassitude mingled with a perfect longing. It may be that it is the counterpart of the freedom of the soul of which it is the herald and companion. In the Burial Service of the Church, we read "earth to earth, dust to dust", coupled with the idea of the return of the spirit to the God that gave it. And there is in this state some sister-similarity to death, one would not say sleep, for the soul of the sleeper is usually earth-bound by his gross desires, or the memory of them, or of his recent impressions. But the smoker of opium, and the saint, self-conscious of their nature celestial, heed earth no more, and on the pinions of imagination or of faith seek mountain-tops of being.

It was in this state or one akin to it that Iliel found herself. And gradually, as comes also to the smoker of opium, the process of bodily repose became complete; the earth was one with earth, and no longer troubled or trammelled her truer self.

She became acutely conscious that she was not the body that lay supine in the cradle, with the moon gleaming upon its bloodless countenance. No; she was rather the blue mist of the whole circle of enchantment, and her thoughts the sparkling dew-spirits that darted hither and thither like silvery fire-flies. And, as if they were parts of herself, she saw Sister Clara and her pages and her hand-maidens under the image of stars. For each was a radiant world of glory, thrilling with most divine activities, yet all in azure orbits curling celestially, their wake of light like comets' tails, wrapping her in a motion that was music.

A flaming boundary to her sphere, the fires of the circle blazed far into the night, forked swords of scarlet light in everlasting motion, snakes of visible force extended every way to keep the gates of her garden. She saw the forms of Brother Onofrio and his captains, of the same shape as those of Sister Clara and her companions, but blazing with a fierce and indomitable heat, throwing off coruscations into the surrounding blackness. She was reminded of a visit that yonder idle carcass in the cradle had once made to an observatory, where she had been shown the corona of the sun.

And then, instinctively, she looked for Cyril Grey. But all that she could find of him was the green-veiled glory that surrounded the sphere of Brother Onofrio; and she understood that this was a mere projection of part of his personality. Himself she could not find. He should have been the core of all, the axis on which all swung; but she could feel nothing. Her intuition told her, in a voice of cogency beyond contradiction, that he was not there.

She began to argue with herself, to affirm that she held a part of him by right of gift; but, looking on it, she beheld only an impenetrable veil. She knew and understood that not yet was the Butterfly in the Net, and in that she acquiesced; but the absence of her lover himself from her, at this moment of all moments, was mystery of horror so chill that she doubted for a time of her own being. She thought of the moon as a dead soul – and wondered – and wondered –

She would have striven to seek him out, to course the universe in his pursuit; but she was incapable of any effort. She sank again into the receptive phase, in which impressions came to her, like bees to a flower, without eliciting conscious response.

And it was then that her bodily eyes opened. The action drew her back into her body; but the material universe held her only for a second. She saw the moon, indeed, but in its centre was a shape of minute size, but infinite brightness. With the speed of a huntress the shape neared her, hid the moon from her, and she perceived the buskined Artemis, silver-sandalled, with her bright bow and her quiver of light. Leaping behind her came her hounds, and she thought that she could hear their eager baying.

Between heaven and earth stood the goddess, and looked about her, her eyes a-sparkle with keen joy. She unslung her baldric, and put her silver bugle to her lips.

Through all the vastness of heaven that call rang loud; and, in obedience, the stars rushed from their thrones, and made obeisance to their mistress. It was a gallant hunting-party. For she perceived that these were no longer stars, but souls. Had not Simon Iff once said to her: "Every man and every woman is a star"? And even as she understood that, she saw that Artemis regarded them with reverence, with awe even. This was no pleasure chase; he who won the victory was himself the quarry. Every soul was stamped with absolute heroism; it offered itself to itself, like

Odin, when nine windy nights he hung in space, his own spear thrust into his side. What gain might be she could not understand; but it was clear enough that every act of incarnation is a crucifixion. She saw that she had been mistaken in thinking of these souls as hunters at all; and at that instant it seemed to her as though she herself were the huntress. For a flash she saw the fabled loadstone rock which draws ships to it, and, flashing forth their bolts by the might of its magnetism, loosens their timbers so that they are but waifs of flotsam. It was only a glimpse; for now the souls drew near her. She could distinguish their differences by the colour of the predominating rays. And as they approached, she saw that only those whose nature was lunar might pass into the garden. The others started back, and it seemed to her that they trembled with surprise, as if it were a new thing to them to be repelled.

And now she was standing on the Terrace of the Moon with Artemis, watching the body of Lisa la Giuffria, that lay there in its cradle. And she saw that the body was a dead thing, as dead as the cradle itself; it was unreal; all "material" things were unreal, shells void of meaning, geometrical abstractions, as Simon Iff had explained to her on their first meeting. But this body was different to the other husks in one respect, that it was the focus of a most startling electrical phenomenon. (She could not think of it but as electrical.) An incandescent cone was scintillating before her. She could see but the tip of it, but she knew intuitively that the base of it was in the sun itself. About this cone played curious figures, dancers wreathed with vine leaves, having all sorts of images in their hands, like toys, houses, and dolls, and ships and fields, and woods, little soldiers in their uniforms, little lawyers in their wigs and gowns, an innumerable multitude of replicas of everyday things. And Iliel watched the souls as they came into the glow of the cone. They took human shape, and she was amazed to see among them the faces of many of the great men of the race.

There was one very curious feature about the space in which this vision took place: this, that innumerable beings could occupy it at once, yet each one remain distinct from all the rest as the attention happened to focus it. But it was no question of dissolving views; for each soul was present equally all the time.

With most of the faces there was little attachment, scarce more than a vague wreath of a mist that swirled purposelessly about them. Some, however, were more developed; and it seemed as if more or less definite shapes had been formulated by them as adjuncts to their original personalities. When it came to such men as Iliel remembered through history, there was already a symbolic or pictorial representation of the nature of the man, and of the trend of his life, about him. She could see the unhappy Maximilian, once Emperor of Mexico, a frail thing struggling in an environment far too intense for him. He was stifled in his own web, and seemed afraid either to stay where he was, or to attempt to approach the cone.

Less hampered, but almost equally the prey of hideous vacillation, lack of decision, was General Boulanger, whose white horse charged again and again through space toward the cone, only to be caught up each time by the quick nervous snatch at his rein.

Next him, a gracious girlish figure was the centre of sparkling waves of music, many-hued; but one could see that they were not issuing from her, but only through her. A man of short stature,

with a pale face, stood before her, very similar in the character of his radiations; but they were colder, and duller, and less clear and energetic.

And now all gave way to a most enigmatic figure. It was an insignificant face and form; but the attributions of him filled all heaven. In his sphere was primarily a mist which Iliel instinctively recognised as malarious; and she got an impression, rather than a vision, of an immense muddy river rushing through swamps. And then she saw that from this man's brain issued phantoms like pigeons. They were neither Red Indians nor Israelites, yet they had something of each in their bearing. And these poured like smoke from the head of this little man. In his hand was a book, and he held it over his head. And the book itself was guarded by an angelic figure whose face was extraordinarily stern and unbeautiful, but who scattered with wide hands the wealth of life, children, and corn, and gold. And behind all these things was a great multitude; and about them were the symbolic forms of exile and death and every persecution, and the hideous laughter of triumphant enemies. All this seemed to weigh heavily upon the little man that had created it; Iliel thought that he was seeking incarnation for the sake of its forgetfulness. Yet the light in his eyes was so pure and noble and magnetic that it might have been that he saw in a new birth the chance to repair his error.

And now her attention was drawn to a yet nobler and still more fantastic formal. It was a kingly figure, and its eyes blazed bright with an enthusiasm that was tinged almost with madness. His creations, like those of the last seen, were something vague and unsubstantial. They lacked clear draughtsmanship. But they made up for this by their extravagance and brilliance. It was a gorgeous play of dream; yet Iliel could see that it was only dream. Last of this company came a woman proud, melancholy, and sweet. Her face was noble and intelligent; but there was a red line about her throat, and the eyes were suffused with horror, and about her heaved rolling mists of blood. And then the greater pageant spread its peacockry.

In this great group not only the men but all their spheres were clean-cut and radiant; for here was direct creation, no longer the derivative play of fancy upon existing themes. And first came one "with branded and ensanguined brow", a mighty figure, although suffering from a deformity of one foot, virile, Herculean, intense but with a fierce sadness upon him. He came with a rush and roar as of many waters, and about him were a great company of men and women, almost as real as he was himself. And the waves (which Iliel recognised as music) surged about him, a stormy sea; and there were lightnings, and thunders, and desolations!

Behind him came another not unlike him, but with less vehemence; and instead of music were soft rays of light, rosy and harmonious; and his arms were folded upon his heart and his head bowed. It was clear that he understood his act as a sacrament.

Then came a strange paradox of a man – utter violence and extreme gentleness. A man at war within himself! And in his ecstasy of rage he peopled space with thousands of bright and vigorous phantasms. They were more real than those of all the others; for he fed them constantly with his own blood. Stern savagery, and lofty genius, hideous cruelty and meanness inexplicable, beauty, and madness, and holiness, and loving-kindness; these followed him, crying aloud with the exultation and the passion of their fullness of life.

Close upon him came one who was all music, fierce, wild, mystical, and most melancholy. The waves of his music were like pines in the vast forest, and like the undulations of frozen steppes; but his own face was full of a calm glory touched with pity.

Behind him, frowning, came a hectic, ape-like dwarf. But in his train were many people of all climes, soft Indians, fierce Malays and Pathans and Sikhs, proud Normans, humble Saxons, and many a frail figure of woman. These were too self-assertive, Iliel thought, to be as real as those of the other man. And the figure himself was strained, even in his pride.

Now came a marvellous person – almost a god, she thought. For about him were a multitude of bones that built themselves up constantly into the loveliest living forms, that changed from one into another, ever increasing in stature and in glory. And in his broad brow she read the knowledge of the Unity of Things, and in these eyes the joy unspeakable which that knowledge gives. Yet they were insatiable as death itself; she could see that every ounce of the man's giant strength was strained toward some new attainment.

And now came another of the sons of music. But this man's waves were fiery flames like snakes contorted and terrible. It seemed to Iliel as if all heaven were torn asunder by those pangs. Wave strove with wave, and the battle was eaten up by fresh swords of fire that burst from him as he waved onward those battalions to fresh wrath. These waves moreover were peopled with immense and tragic figures; Iliel thought that she could recognise Electra, and Salome, daughter of Herodias.

Next, amid a cloud of angels bearing silver trumpets, came one with great height of brow, and eyes of golden flashes. In him the whole heaven rocked with harmonious music, and faint shapes formed up among the waves, like Venus born of ocean foam. They had not substance, like so many Iliel had seen; they were too great, too godlike, to be human. Not one was there of whom it could not be said "Half a woman made with half a god". And these, enormous and tragic, fiery, with wings and sandals of pure light, encompassed him and wooed him.

Last of this company – only a few of the visions are recorded here – came the greatest of them all. His face was abrupt and vehement; but a veil was woven over it, because of the glory of his eyes, and a thick scarf, like a cloud, held over his mouth, lest the thunder of it destroy men's hearing. This man was so enormous that his stature spanned all heaven; and his creatures, that moved about him, were all godlike – immensely greater than the human. Yet were they human; but so patriarchal, so intense, that they almost overwhelmed Iliel.

On him she dared not look. He had the gift of making every thing a thousand times larger than its natural size. She heard one word of his, a mere call to a pet: "Tiger, tiger!" But the beast that broke through the mazes of heaven was so vast that its claws spanned star and star. And with all that he smiled, and a million babe-children blossomed before him like new-budded flowers. And this man quickened as he came nigh to Iliel; he seemed to understand wholly the nature of the Great Experiment.

But every soul in all that glorious cohort of immortals, as it touched the cone, was whirled away like a pellet thrown upon a swiftly moving fly-wheel. And presently she perceived the cause of this.

The tip of the cone was sheathed in silver. So white and glittering with fierce heat was that corselot, and so mighty its pulse of vibration that she had thought it part of the cone. She understood this to be the formula of the circle, and realised with a great ache, and then a sudden anger, that it was by this that she was to be prevented from what might have been her fortune, the gaining of the wardenship of a Chopin or of a Paul Verlaine.

But upon the face of Artemis was gaiety of triumph. The last of the souls whirled away into the darkness. Humanity had tried and failed; it was its right to try; it was its fate to fail; now came the turn of the chosen spirits, proved worthy of the fitted fastness.

They came upon the Terrace in their legions, Valkyrie-brave in silver arms, or like priestesses in white vestments, their hair close bound upon their brows, or like queens of the woodland, swift for the chase, with loose locks and bright eyes, or like little children, timid and gracious.

But amid their ranks were the black hideous forms of hags, bent and wrinkled; and these fled instantly in fear at the vision of the blazing cone. There were many other animal shapes; but these, seeing the cone, turned away indifferent, as not understanding. Only the highest human-seeming forms remained; and these appeared as if in some perplexity. Constantly they looked from Artemis to the cone, and back again to Artemis. Iliel could feel their thought; it was a child-like bewilderment, "But don't you understand? This is a most dangerous place. Why did you bring us here? Surely you know that to touch the cone is certain death to us?"

Iliel understood. The human souls had long since made themselves perfect, true images of the cosmos, by accepting the formula of Love and Death; they had made the great sacrifice again and again; they were veterans of the spiritual world-war, and asked nothing better than to go back to the trenches. But these others were partial souls; they had not yet attained humanity; they had not understood that in order to grow one must assimilate oneself with another being, the death of two to create the life of one, in whom the two live once more, transmuted and glorified, the corruptible having put on incorruption. To them incarnation was death; and they did not know that death was life. They were not ready for the Great Adventure.

So they stood like tall lilies about the coruscating cone of Light, wondering, doubting, drooping. But at the last came one taller than all the rest, sadder of mien, and lovelier of features; her robes were stained and soiled, as if by contact with other colours. Artemis drew back with quick repulsion.

For the first time the maiden goddess spoke.

"What is thy name?" she cried.

"I am Malkah of the tribe of the Sickles."

"And thy crime?"

"I love a mortal."

Artemis drew back once more.

"Thou, too, hast loved," said Malkah. "I drew my mortal lovers unto me; I did not sully my life with theirs; I am virgin unto Pan!"

"I also am virgin; for whom I loved is dead. He was a poet, and he loved thee above women, 'And haply the Queen-Moon is on her throne clustered around by all her starry fays', whereof I

being one, loved him that he loved Thee! But he died in the city of Mars and the Wolf, before I could make him even aware of me. I am come hither to seek immolation; I am weary of the pale beauty of Levanah; I will seek him, at the price of death. I deny our life; I crucify myself unto the God we dare not name. I go. Hail and farewell!"

She flung up her arm in a wild gesture of renunciation, and came closer to the Cone. She would not haste, lest her will prove but impulse; she poised her breast deliberately over the Cone. Then, with fierce zest, so that the one blow might end all, she thrust herself vehemently down upon the blazing spike.

At that moment Iliel swooned. She felt that something had happened to her, something tremendous; and her brain turned crazily in her. But as she lost consciousness she was still aware of the last phase of the vision: that the sacrifice of Malkah had created a void in the ranks of the Amazon armies of the Moon; and she saw them and their mist of blue, licked up in the swirl of the vortex. The whole of the invoked forces were sucked up into her as Malkah in her death-agony took possession of that basis of materialisation. Heroic – and presumptuous; for of all the qualities that go to make humanity she had but one, and she would have to shift, for the rest, with orts of inheritance. Among mankind she would be a stranger, a being without conscious race-experience, liable to every error that a partial view of life can make. Ill indeed for such a one who is without the wardenship of high initiates! It was for Cyril Grey to keep her unspotted from the world, to utilise those powers which she wielded in pre-eminence from her inheritance in the white sphere of Levanah!

When Sister Clara came to summon Iliel, she found her still in swoon. They carried her to her room. At noon she recovered consciousness.

Cyril Grey was seated by her bed. To her surprise, he was dressed in mundane attire, an elegant lounge suit of lavender.

"Have you seen the papers?" he cried gaily. "Neapolitan Entomologists capture rare butterfly, genus Schedbarshamoth Scharthathan, species Malkah be-Tharshishim ve-Ruachoth ha-Sche-halim!"

"Don't talk nonsense, Cyril!" she said, lazily, a little uncertain whether this unexpected apparition were not a dream.

"Perfect sense, I assure you, my child. The trick is turned. We have caught our Butterfly!"

"Yes, yes," she murmured; "but how did you know?"

"Why, use your eyes!" he cried. "Use your br – I should say your sensory organs! Look!"

He waved at the window, and Iliel idly followed with her eyes.

There could be no mistake. The garden was normal. Every vestige of magical force had disappeared.

"Couldn't have gone better," he said. "We don't know where we're going, but we know we're on the way. And, whatever we've got, we've got it."

Suddenly her mind ran back to her vision. "Where were you last night, Cyril?"

He looked at her for a moment before replying.

"I was where I always am," he said slowly.

"I looked for you all over the house and the garden." "Ah! you should have sought me in the House of my Father."

"Your father?"

"Colonel Sir Grant Ponsonby Grey, K.C.M.G., K.C.S.I., G.C.I.E. Born in 1846 at the Round Tower, Co. Cork; educ. Winchester and Balliol; Lieutenant Royal Artillery 1868; Indian Political Department 1873; in 1880 m. Adelaide, only d. of the late Rt. Hon. Lord Ashley Lovell, P.C.; one s., Cyril St. John, q.v. Residence, The Round Tower, Co. Cork; Bartland Barrows, Wilts.; 93, Arlington Street. W. Clubs. Carlton, Athenaeum, Travellers', Hemlock, etc. Amusements: Hunting, talking shop."

"You dear incorrigible boy!"

He took her hand and kissed it.

"And am I to see something of you now?"

"Oh, we're all penny plain humans from now on. It's merely a question of defending you from the malice of Douglas and Co.; a much simpler job than blocking out nine-tenths of the Universe! Apart from that, we are just a jolly set of friends; only I see less of you than anyone else does, naturally."

"Naturally!"

"Yes, naturally. You have to be saved from all worry and annoyance; and if there's one thing in the world more annoying and worrying than a wife, it's a husband! With the others, you have nothing to quarrel about; and if you try it on Brother Onofrio, in particular, he simply sets in motion a deadly and hostile current of will by which you would fall slain or paralysed, as if blasted by the lightning flash! Click!"

Iliel laughed; and then Sister Clara appeared with the rest of the garrison, the boys and maidens burdened with the means of breakfast; for this was a day of festival and triumph.

But, as he shook hands with her, Iliel discovered, with a shock, that she hated Brother Onofrio.

CHAPTER XVII

OF THE REPORT WHICH EDWIN ARTHWAIT MADE TO HIS CHIEF

AND OF THE DELIBERATIONS OF THE BLACK LODGE THEREUPON; AND OF THE CONSPIRACIES THERE-BY CONCERTED; WITH A DISCOURSE UPON SORCERY

"*E*XORDIUMATICALLY, *deponent precateth otity orient exaudient, dole basilical's assumpt. Pragmatics, ex Ventro Genesiaco ad umbilicum Apocalypticum, determinated logomachoepy's nodal puncts, genethliacally benedict, eschatologically --- kakoglaphy-rotopical! Ergmoiraetic, apert parthenorhododactylical, colophoned thanatoskianko-morphic!*"

Footnote Translation:
"Exordiumatically – First genethliaeally – at first
deponent precateth – I beg
benedict – fortunate
otity – hearing
esehatologically – later
orient – increasingly
kakoglaphyrotopical – in a bad hole
exaudient – favourable

erg – work

dole basilical's – a royal gift*

smoiractic – fatal

assumpt – assumption

apert – opened

Pregmatics – Facts

parthenorhododactylical – like the ex ventro Genesiaco ad umbilicum
    rosy fingers of a maid

Apocalypticum – from beginning

colophoned – closed to end

tbanatoskiankomorphic – in the determinate

mark shape of the valley of the shadow logomachoepy's – (my) story's
    of death

nodal puncts – limits

With these striking words the official Report of Douglas' chief commissioner began. It would be tedious to quote the 488 folio pages in full. Douglas himself did not read it; the transcript made by Vesquit of Abdul Bey's "inspiration", with a few practical questions to the latter, told him all that he needed.

Audience over, he dismissed Arthwait and his companion with orders to hold themselves in readiness for a renewal of the campaign. Douglas had many a moment of bitter contemplation; his hatred of Cyril Grey fed upon repulse; and it was evident that his assistants had met more than their match. He would have to act personally – yet he feared to expose himself in open battle. His plan hitherto had been to bribe or dupe some of the jackal journalists of London to attack him; but Grey had not so much as troubled to bring libel actions.

But he would not give in. He studied Vesquit's transcripts attentively, and with indecision. He did not know how far to trust the oracle, and he did not understand how Vesquit had come to die, since on that point even Arthwait had been silent. The demons whom he consulted were emphatic in favour of the document, but failed to explain how the fortress was to be reduced from the inside.

He was clear in his mind as to the nature of Grey's operation; he saw perfectly that Lisa herself was the weak point in it; but he did not see how to get at her.

He continued in his bitter mood until the early hours, and he was interrupted by the return of his wife from her miserable night's trudging. She put two francs on the table without a single word as soon as she entered.

"Is that all?" snarled Douglas. "You ought to be getting fives again now spring's coming. Though you're not as pretty as you were."

He garnished this greeting with garlic of low abuse. Rarely to any other person did he use even mild oaths; he affected the grand manner; but he knew that foulness of speech emphasised his wife's degradation. He had no need of the vile money that she earned; he had a thousand

better means of buying whisky; but he drove her to the streets as no professional *souteneur* would have dared do. By extreme refinement of cruelty he never struck or kicked her, lest she should think he loved her. To him, she was a toy; a means of exercising his passion for torture; to her, he was the man she loved.

Pitifully she pleaded that the cold rain of the night – she was wet through – had driven all Paris from the boulevard to the cafe; and she added an excuse for her unattractiveness which should have sent her husband to his pistol for very shame had a spark of manhood, or a memory of his mother, been alive within him.

Instead, he promised to change all that the next time Dr. Balloch came to Paris.

He had systematically degraded and humiliated her, corrupted her, branded her with infamy, for many a year; yet there was still in her a motion of revolt against the crime. But even as she made her gesture of repulsion, Douglas leapt to his feet, with the light of hell burning in his eyes. "I have it!" he shouted, "get to your straw, you stinking slut. And you may thank your stars that as you can't be ornamental, you're going to be useful."

It was dawn before Douglas turned into bed, for his great idea brought with it a flood of imagination, and a million problems of detail. The servant girl was already half dressed for the day's work; and he made her fetch him a final whisky before he slept.

Late in the following afternoon he woke, and sent Cremers, whom he had turned into a drudge, to telegraph to Balloch to come over, and to bring her friend Butcher to see him.

Douglas had previously refused to see this man, who was a Chicago semi-tough. He ran a fake Rosicrucian society in America, and thought that Douglas could give him power over the elusive dollar. But Douglas had found no use for him; he rather insisted on respectability in his neophytes; it was only in the higher grades that one found the disreputable. It was an obvious point of policy. But Douglas had now remembered one little fact about this person; he fitted the Great Idea so nicely that his presence in Paris seemed as apt as an answer to prayer.

It was a rare, if doubtful, privilege to visit Douglas in his home. He never allowed the visit of any but those high in his confidence; the locality was hardly inspiring to an inquiring duchess. He had two other places in Paris, which he used for two types of interviewer; for although he discouraged knowledge of his authority in the Black Lodge, he did a good deal of the fishing himself, especially with rich or highly placed people. For his subordinates had sticky fingers.

One of these places was a discreet apartment in the very best quarter of Paris. Here he was the Scottish Nobleman of the Old School. The decorations were rich but not gaudy; even the ancestors were not overdone. The place of honour was occupied by Rob Roy's claymore, alleged. One of his claims was that the Highland Cateran was his ancestor, owing to a liaison with a fairy. Another claim was that he himself was James IV of Scotland, that he had survived the Battle of Flodden Field, become an adept, and immortal. Despite what to a profane mind might seem the incompatibility of these two legends – to say nothing of the improbability of either – they were greedily swallowed by the Theosophist section of his following.

In this apartment he received the credulous type of person who is impressed by rank; and no man could play the part of stateliness better than this old reprobate.

His other place was of the hermit's cell model, a tiny cottage with its well-kept garden; such abound all over Paris in the most unexpected spots.

He actually imposed upon the old lady who kept this house for him. Here he was the simple old man of utter holiness, the lonely recluse, the saintly anchorite, his only food bruised herbs or pulse, his only drink the same as quenched the thirst of Father Adam. His long absences from this sacrosanct abode were explained by the fact of his absorption in trance, in which he was supposed to indulge underground. Of course he only visited the place when he had to receive a certain type of visitor, that loftier type which has enough rank and wealth to know that they are not necessary to a search after Truth, and is impressed by simplicity and saintliness.

It was at the former address that the Count received Mr. Butcher. He was dressed in severe and refined broadcloth, with the rosette of the Legion of Honour – to which he was well entitled – in his buttonhole.

In presence of this splendour the American was ill at ease; but Douglas knew how to make a man his own by giving him a good conceit of himself.

"I am proud to meet you, Mr. Butcher," he began, affably. "May I beg of you to take the trouble to be seated! The chair is worthy of you," he added, with a smile; "it was at one time the property of Frederick the Great."

The servant, who was dressed as a Highland Gillie in gala costume, offered cigars and whisky.

"Say, this is sure some whisky, Count! This is where I fall off the wagon, one time, John. You watch my batting average!" observed Mr. Butcher, settling himself by placing his legs upon the table.

"It is from the private stock of the Duke of Argyll," returned Douglas. "And you, Mr. Butcher? I knew a Count Butcher many years ago. You are a relation?"

Mr. Butcher had only the vaguest notion as to his ancestry. His mother had broken down under cross-examination.

"Search me!" he replied, biting the end off his cigar, and spitting it out. "We Rosicrucians are out for the Hundred Years Club Dope, and the Long Green Stone; we should worry. We're short on ancestors in Illinois."

"But these matters are important in magic," urged Douglas. "Heredity goes for much. I should be glad indeed to hear that you were one of the Dorsetshire Butchers, for example, or even the Shropshire branch. In both families second sight is an appanage."

Here the conversation was interrupted by the gillie. "I crave your pardon, my lord," he said, bowing; "but his Grace the Duke of Hants is at the door to beg your aid in a most urgent matter which concerns his family honour."

"I am engaged," said Douglas. "He may write." The man withdrew with a solemn bow.

"I must apologise for this disturbance," continued Douglas. "The importunity of one's clients is exceedingly distressing. It is one of our penalties. I venture to suppose that you are yourself much annoyed in similar ways."

Butcher would have liked to boast that J. P. Morgan was always trying to borrow money from him, but he dared not attempt to bluff his host. Nor did he suspect that Douglas was himself engaged in that diverting and profitable pastime.

"To come to business," went on Douglas, eyeing his guest narrowly, and assuring himself that his scheme had borne fruit in due season, "What is it that you require of me? Frankly, I like you; and I have long admired your noble career. All that I can do for you – in – honour – pray count it done!"

"Why, Count," said Mr. Butcher, spitting on the floor; "Buttinsky's in Kalamazoo. But to come down to brass tacks, I guess I'd like to sit into the game."

"I pray you to excuse me," replied Douglas, "but my long residence in Paris has almost deprived me of the comprehension of my mother tongue. Could you explain yourself further?"

"Why, this Black Lodge stunt, Count. It's a humdinger. I guess it's a hell of a favour, but I see a dollar at the end of it, and old Doc. Butcher buys a one-way ticket."

Douglas grew portentous. "Are you aware of what you ask?" he thundered. "Do you understand that the ineffable and Sacrosanct Arcanum is not to be touched by profane hands? Must I inform you that Those who may not be named are even now at the Gate of the Abyss, whetting their fangs upon the Cubical Stone of the Unutterable? Oh ye magistral ministrants of the Shrine of the Unspeakable Abomination! Hear ye the Word of Blasphemy!" He spoke rapidly and thickly in a tongue unknown to Butcher, who became alarmed, and even took his legs off the table.

"Say!" he cried. "Have a heart! Can the rough dope, Count! This is a straight proposition, honest to God!"

"I am already aware of your sincerity," answered the other. "But infinite courage is required to confront those formidable Entities that lie in wait for the seeker even at the first Portal of the Descending Staircase!"

"Oh, I'm wise to Old Dog Cerberus. Ish Kabibble. Gimme an upper berth in the Chicawgo, Saint Lewis, and Hell Limited, if it busts the roll. Do you get me, Steve?"

"I understand you to say that you persist in your application."

"Sure. Andrew P. Satan for mine."

"I shall be pleased to place your name before the Watchers of the Gate."

"How deep do I have to dig?"

"Dig? I did not quite catch your remark."

"In the wad. Weigh the dough! What does it set me back? Me for the bread-line?"

"The initiation fee is one thousand francs."

"I guess I can skin that off without having to eat at Childs."

"You will remit the amount to the Comptroller of my Privy Purse. Here is the address. Now be so good as to sign the preliminary application-form."

They went over to the bureau (Douglas was prepared to derive it from the library of Louis XIV), on which lay a private letter from the Kaiser, if one might believe the embossed arms and address, and a note asking President Poincaré to dinner, "quite informally, my dear friend", which Butcher could not fail to see. The preliminary application form was a document which might have served for an exceptionally solemn treaty. But Douglas was above the charlatanism of requiring a signature in blood: Butcher signed it with an ordinary fountain pen.

"And now, Mr. Butcher," said Douglas, "I will ask you in your turn to render me a small service."

"Bat it up!" said Mr. Butcher. "I would buy an Illustrated Edition of O. Henry in nineteen parts."

Douglas did not know that Americans dread book agents more than rattlesnakes; but he gathered that his guest would acquiesce in any reasonable suggestion.

"I am informed that you are – or were – a Priest of the Roman Church."

"Peter is my middle name," admitted the "Rosicrucian", "and that's no jolly."

"But – apart from questions of nomenclature for the moment, if you will pardon me – you are a priest of the Roman Church?"

"Yep: I took a chance on Pop Dago Benedict. But it's a con game; I'm from Missouri. Four-flushing gold brick merchants! Believe me, some bull! I took it like playing three days in Bumville. Them boobs got my goat for fair, babe. No pipe!"

"You were interdicted in consequence of some scandal?"

"I ran a sporting house on the side, and I guess they endorsed my license for speeding."

"Your Bishop took umbrage at some business activity which he judged incompatible with your vows?"

"Like Kelly did."

"Oh, Bishop Kelly. Far too severe a disciplinarian, in my judgment. But you are still a priest? Your orders are still valid? A baptism or a marriage performed by you would hold good?"

"It's a cinch. The Hallelujah Guarantee and Trust Company, St. Paul. Offices in the James D. Athanasius Building."

"Then, sir, I shall ask of you the favour to hold yourself in readiness to baptise two persons at nine of the evening precisely, the day after tomorrow. That ceremony will be followed by another, in which you will marry them."

"I swan."

"I may rely on your good offices?"

"I'll come in a wheelbarrow."

"Suit yourself, Mr. Butcher, as to the mode of transit; but pray be careful to attend punctually, and in canonical costume."

"I'll dig the biretta out of the ice-box."

After a further exchange of courtesies the new disciple took his leave.

The same evening witnessed a very different interview.

Lord Antony Bowling was being entertained at dinner by Simon Iff, and their conversation turned upon the favourite subject of the old mystic – the Way of the Tao.

"In view of what you have been saying about the necessity of dealing with mediums on their own ground," remarked the host, "let me tell you of a paradox in magick. Do you remember a certain chapter in the Bible which tells one, almost in consecutive verses, firstly to answer a fool according to his folly, and secondly, not so to answer him? This is the Scriptural version of a truth which we phrase otherwise. There are two ways of dealing with an opponent; one by beating him on his own ground, the other by withdrawing to a higher plane. You can fight fire with fire, or you can fight fire with water.

"It is, roughly speaking, legitimate magick to resolve a difficult situation in either of these two ways. Alter it, or withdraw to higher ground. The black magician, or as I prefer to call him, sorcerer, for the word magick should not be profaned, invariably withdraws to lower planes. Let us seek an analogy in the perfectly concrete case of the bank cashier.

"This gentleman, we will assume, finds his salary inadequate to his outgoings. Now he may economise, that is, withdraw himself to a kind of life where money is no longer needed in such quantity, or he may devote himself day and night to his business, and so increase his salary. But there is no third course open to a man of self-respect. The sorcerer type of man appeals to lower planes of money-making. He begins by gambling; beaten there, he resorts to the still viler means of embezzlement; perhaps, finally, he attempts to cover his thefts by murdering his mother for the insurance money.

"Notice how, as his plane becomes debased, his fears grow greater. At first, he is merely annoyed about his creditors; in the next stage, he fears being sharped by his fellow-gamblers; then, it is the police who loom terrible in his mind; and lastly the grim form of the executioner threatens him."

"Very nicely Hogarthed," said Lord Antony. "Reminds me of how the habit of lying degenerates into unintelligible stupidity. We had a case in the War Office last month, a matter of supplying certain furs. As you know, the seal furnishes a valuable fur. Less valuable, though superficially similar, is that of the rabbit. Now in trade, so it appears, it is impolitic to say rabbit, which sounds cheap and nasty, so the Scriptural equivalent, coney, is employed, thus combining Piety with Profit. Having caught your coney, you proceed to cook him, until he resembles seal. So you have a dyed rabbit-skin, and you call it seal coney. But there are by-ways that stray further yet from the narrow lane of truth. The increasing demand for rabbits has reduced the profit on seal coney, and it becomes desirable to find a cheaper substitute. Reckless of the susceptibilities of the ancient Egyptians, this is found in that domesticated representative of the lion family which consoles our spinsters. Having disguised the skin as far as may be, they next disguise the name; some buyer must be made to pay the price of seal coney, and think that he is getting it; so 'cat' becomes 'trade seal coney' – and unless one has the whole story there is no possibility of derivation. The lie has become mere misnomer."

"It is the general case of Anglo-Saxon hypocrisy," returned Simon Iff. "I had an amusing example the other day in an article that I wrote for the *Review* – rather prudish people. My little essay ended: 'So Science offers her virgin head to the caress of magick.' The editor thought 'virgin' rather a 'suggestive' word, and replaced it by 'maiden.'"

"You remind me of a curate we had over at Grimthorpe Ambrose. 'Leg' has for many years been a not quite proper word; when the terrible necessity of referring to it arose, the polite ass replaced it by 'limb'.

"The refined sensibility of our curate perceived the indelicacy of saying 'limb', since every one knew that it meant 'leg'; so he wrapped it up in the decent obscurity of the Latin language, and declined to play croquet one afternoon on the ground that, the day before, in visiting old Mrs. Postlethwaite, he had severely strained his member."

"The wicked fall into the pit that they have digged," said Iff. "All this applies to the question of magick. It is a question of debasing coinage. I have great sympathy with the ascetics of India and their monkish imitators in Europe. They held spiritual gifts to be of supreme value, and devoted their lower powers to the development of the higher. Of course mistakes were made; the principle was carried too far; they were silly enough to injure their lower powers by undue fasting, flagellation, and even mutilation. They got the false idea that the body was an enemy, whereas it is a servant – the only servant available. But the idea was right; they wanted to exchange dross for gold. Now the sorcerer offers his gold for dross, tries to exchange his highest powers for money or the gratification of envy or revenge. The Christian Scientist, absurdly so-called, is a sorcerer of the basest type, for he devotes the whole wealth of religion to the securing of his bodily health. It is somewhat stupid, too, as his main claim is that the body is only an illusion!"

"Am I right in suggesting that ordinary life is a mean between these extremes, that the noble man devotes his material wealth to lofty ends, the advancement of science, or art, or some such true ideal; and that the base man does the opposite by concentrating all his abilities on the amassing of wealth?"

"Exactly; that is the real distinction between the artist and the bourgeois, or, if you prefer it, between the gentleman and the cad. Money, and the things money can buy, have no value, for there is no question of creation, but only of exchange. Houses, lands, gold, jewels, even existing works of art, may be tossed about from one hand to another; they are so, constantly. But neither you nor I can write a sonnet; and what we have, our appreciation of art, we did not buy. We inherited the germ of it, and we developed it by the sweat of our brows. The possession of money helped us, but only by giving us timse and opportunity and the means of travel. Anyhow, the principle is clear; one must sacrifice the lower to the higher, and, as the Greeks did with their oxen, one must fatten and bedeck the lower, so that it may be the worthier offering."

"And what happens when you go on the other tack?"

"When you trade your gold for pewter you impoverish yourself. The sorcerer sells his soul for money; spends the money, and finds he has nothing else to sell. Have you noticed that Christian Scientists are hardly ever in robust health? They have given up their spiritual forces for a quite imaginary standard of well-being; and those forces, which were supporting the body quite well enough without their stupid interference, are debilitated and frittered away. I pray daily for a great war, that may root out the coward fear of death and poverty in the minds of these degenerate wretches. Death should be, as it used to be in the middle ages, even, and yet more in pagan times, the fit reward and climax of a life well spent in risking it for noble causes; and poverty should be a holy and blessed state, worthy of the highest minds and the happiest, and of them alone.

"To return to our sheep – I mean our sorcerer. He has not much against him to begin with, but he chooses to trade his sword for gold. The barbarian, having the sword, naturally uses it to recover the gold. In other words, the devil, having bought the soul, regains the price, for the sorcerer spends it in the devil's service. The next stage is that the sorcerer resorts to crime, declares war on all humanity. He uses vulgar means to attain his ends, and the price may be his liberty. Ultimately, he may lose life itself in some last desperate effort to retrieve all at a blow.

When I was young and had less experience, I had many a fight with sorcerers; and it was always the end of the fight when Mr. Sorcerer broke the law. He was no longer fighting me, but the consolidated will of humanity; and he had no time to attack me when he was busy building breakwaters.

"And that reminds me. We have a young friend at bay – with the worst pack of devils in the world at him. I wonder if I have done wrong to leave him so much to himself. But I wanted the boy to gain all the laurels; he's young enough to like them."

"I think I know who you mean," said Lord Antony, smiling; "and I don't think you need be very much afraid. I never saw any one much better fitted to take care of himself."

"For all that, he's in urgent danger at this very moment. He has incurred the greatest possible risk; he has gained a victory. But it has been only a clash of outposts; the enemy is coming up now, horse, foot, and artillery, with lust of revenge and desperate fear to enflame the original hatred; and, unfortunately, the boy made some fundamental errors in his plan of campaign."

"Ah, well, Napoleon did that. Jena was the result of his own blundering miscalculations; so, to a certain extent, was Austerlitz. Don't fret! The bigger they are, the harder they fall, as my father's pet pugilist used to say. And now I must run away; there is a seance with a lady who materialises demon slugs. Do not forget to inscribe my name among the martyrs!"

CHAPTER XVIII

THE DARK SIDE OF THE MOON

THE spring gathered her garments together, then flung them wide over the Bay of Naples. Hers is the greatest force in Nature, because her clarion sounds the summons of creation. It is she that is the Vicegerent of the All-Father, and of His spirit hath He dowered her with a triple essence.

In southern lands, even before the Equinox opens its gates before her conquering armies, one feels her imminent. Her light-armed troops swarm over the breached ramparts of the winter, and their cry is echoed in the dungeons of the soul by those whom she has come to save.

Yet in her hands is nothing but a sword. It is a disturbance of the equilibrium to which the dying year has attained after its long joy and agony; and so to the soul which is at ease she comes with alarum and tocsin. A soul like Iliel's, naturally apt to receive every impulse, to multiply it, and to transform it into action, is peculiarly sensitive, without knowing it, to cosmic forces so akin to its own inborn turbulence.

In her idlest moods, Lisa la Giuffria would have started for China at the least provocation, provided that she could start within the hour.

She could take a lover, or throw one away, a dozen times in a year, and would have been indignant and amazed if any one had called her fickle. She was not insincere; but she believed with her whole soul that her immediate impulse was the true Will of her whole Self. One night at the Savoy Hotel with Lavinia King, just before Christmas, the talk had turned on the distress then prevailing in London. Instantly she had dragged the whole party downstairs, provided it with the entire supply of silver money that the hotel happened to have on hand, and rushed it to the Embankment to rescue the unemployed. That night she was a super-Shaftsbury; she formulated a dozen plans to solve the problem of poverty, root, branch, and leaf; and the next morning her dressmaker found her amid a sheaf of calculations.

But a new style of costume being displayed, she had plunged with equal ardour into a cosmopolitan scheme of dress reform.

To such an one a thwarted impulse involves almost a wreckage of the soul. Iliel began openly to chafe at the restrictions to which her own act had bound her. She had never been a mother, and the mere physical disabilities of her condition were all the more irritating because they were so unfamiliar.

The excitement of the Butterfly-chase had kept her toe to the mark, and the strange circumstances with which she was surrounded had aided to make it easy for her. It flattered her vanity that she was the keystone of so great an arch, destined to span earth and heaven. Her new conditions, the relaxation of the tension, threw down her exaltation. The experiment was over; well, then, it ought to *be* over – and she had months of boredom before her which must be endured with no stimulus but that of normal human duty. She was one of those people who will make any sacrifice at the moment, beggar themselves to help a friend, but who are quite incapable of drawing a weekly cheque for a trifling sum for no matter how important a purpose.

In this March and April she was one mass of thwarted impulse. The mere necessity, demanded by safety, of remaining within the circle, was abhorrent to her. But, though she did not know it, she was held in subjection by the wills of her guardians.

In Astrology, the moon, among its other meanings, has that of "the common people", who submit (they know not why) to any independent will that can express itself with sufficient energy. The people who guillotined the mild Louis XVI died gladly for Napoleon. The impossibility of an actual democracy is due to this fact of mob-psychology. As soon as you group men, they lose their personalities. A parliament of the wisest and strongest men in the nation is liable to behave like a set of schoolboys, tearing up their desks and throwing their inkpots at each other. The only possibility of co-operation lies in discipline and autocracy, which men have sometimes established in the name of equal rights.

Now Iliel was at present a microcosm of the Moon, and her resentments were either changed into enthusiasms by a timely word from Sister Clara or one of the others, or else ignored. The public is a long-suffering dumb beast, an ass crouching beneath heavy burdens, and it needs not only unendurable ill-treatment, but leadership, before it will revolt. All Iliel's impulses were purposeless, negative things, ideas rather of escape than of any definite programme. She wanted to jump out of the frying-pan, neither fearing the fire nor having any clear idea of how to act when she got there. She lacked so much as a day-dream of any alternative Future; hers was the restless wretchedness of a *morphineuse* deprived of the drug.

She was, as it were, the place where four winds met; and such a place is dangerous for a ship that is without internal means of propulsion. She sagged, a dismasted derelict, in tow of Cyril Grey; and the rope of love which held her to him strained her creaking timbers.

The first evidence of these very indefinite feelings was shown by her unreasonableness. Under the rigid discipline of the ceremonies, she had been too well schooled, too absorbed, too directly under the influence of the forces invoked, to feel or express constraint; the mere human hygiene of her present position served only to make her more discontented. A similar phenomenon has been observed also with democracies; they are happiest when most thoroughly cowed and bullied.

Once or twice she treated Cyril to an outburst of temper; but he was very young, so he was tactless enough to refuse to be angry, and made every allowance for her. Such treatment insults women like Lisa; their rage smoulders in them. A blow and a caress would have tripled her passion for him. "What is the use of being a Chinese god," she might have asked, "if you do not gratify your worshippers by inflicting Chinese tortures?"

But the principal manifestation of her moral instability was in her whims.

These were in some degree, no doubt, due to her physical condition; but the mental stress exaggerated them to an abnormal height, like a glacier cramped between two mountain chains. It is necessary, in this world, to be made of harder stuff than one's environment. But Iliel had no ambition to any action; she was reflex; simple reaction to impression was what she thought her will. And so she inflicted phantasies upon the patient fold about her; one day she was all for dressing herself strangely; another day she would insist upon a masque or a charade; but she took no true pleasure in any of these things. Cyril Grey was assiduous in meeting her desires; there were but two prohibitions left of all the elaborate restrictions of the second stage of the experiment; she might not be unduly intimate with him, and she might not in any way communicate with the outside world. In other words, the citadel and the ramparts must be kept intact; between these was a wide range for whim. Yet she was not content; it was just those two forbidden things that haunted her. (The serpent is a later invention in the story of the Fall!) Her unconscious wish to violate these rules led to a dislike for those who personified their rigidity; namely Cyril Grey and Brother Onofrio. And her febrile mind began to join these separate objects in a common detestation.

This shewed itself in a quite insane jealousy of their perfectly natural and necessary intimacy. Sometimes, as they sat sunning themselves upon the wall of one of the terraces she would come flaming down the garden with some foolish tale, and Brother Onofrio at least could not wholly hide his annoyance. He was naturally anxious to make all he could out of the presence of the more advanced adept; and his inborn ecclesiastical contempt for women showed through the tissue of his good manners. Cyril's most admirable patience tried her even more sorely. "Are you my lover or my grandfather?" she screamed at him one night, when he had been more than usually tactful.

Had the matter rested there, it had been ill enough with her. But the mind of man is a strange instrument. "Satan finds some mischief still for idle hands to do" is a rattling good piece of psychology. Iliel had nothing to occupy her mind, because she had never trained herself to concentrate the current of her thoughts on one thing, and off all others. A passion for crochet-work has saved many a woman from the streets or the river. And as on marshes methane forms, and Will o' th' Wisp lures peasants to their oozy doom, so in the idle mind monsters are bred. She began to suffer from a real insanity of the type of persecution-mania. She began to imagine that Cyril and Brother Onofrio were engaged in some mysterious plot against her. It was lucky that every one in the house possessed medical knowledge and training, with specialisation in psychology, so that they knew precisely how to treat her.

Yet in the long run that very knowledge became a danger. The extraordinary powers of mind – in certain limited directions – which insanity often temporarily confers, enabled her to see

that she was regarded as in a critical mental state. She accepted the situation as a battle, instead of co-operating in frank friendship, and began to manoeuvre to outwit her guardians. Those who have any experience of madness, or its congeners, drug-neuroses, know how infernally easy was her task. Many's the woman who, with her pocket handkerchief to her face, and the tears pouring from her eyes, has confessed all to the specialist, and begged him to break her of the whisky habit, the while she absorbed a pint or so of the said whisky under cover of the said pocket handkerchief.

Iliel simply noted the states of mind which they thought favourable, and simulated them. Peaceful absorption in nature, particularly in the moon when she was shining, pleased them; and she cultivated these states, knowing that the others never disturbed her at such times; and, thus secured, she gave herself over to the most hideous thoughts.

They were in fact the thoughts of madness. It is a strange fact that the most harmless states of mind, the most correct trains of idea, may accompany a dangerous lunacy. The difference is that the madman makes a secret of his fancies. Lord Dunsany's stories are the perfect prose jewels of a master cutter and polisher, lit by the rays of an imagination that is the godlike son of the Father of All Truth and Light; but if he kept them to himself, they would be the symptoms of an incurable lesion of the brain. A madman will conceal the Terrible Secret that "today is Wednesday", perhaps "because the devil told him to do so". "I am He who is Truth" was the boast of a great mystic, Mansur, and they stoned him for it, as they stone all men who speak truth; but had he said: "Hush! I am God!" he would have been merely a maniac.

So Iliel acquired the habit of spending a great part of the day in her cradle, and there indulging her mind in every possible morbidity. The very fact that she could not go on to action served to make the matter worse. It is a terrible error to let any natural impulse, physical or mental, stagnate. Crush it out, if you will, and be done with it; or fulfil it, and get it out of the system; but do not allow it to remain there and putrefy. The suppression of the normal sex instinct, for example, is responsible for a thousand ills. In Puritan countries one inevitably finds a morbid preoccupation with sex coupled with every form of perversion and degeneracy. Addiction to excess of drink, and to the drug habits, which are practically unknown in Latin countries, increase one's admiration at the Anglo-Saxon temperament.

Thus also Iliel's stagnant mind bred fearsome things. Hour after hour, the pageant of diseased thoughts passed through the shadowy gulfs of her chaotic spirit. Actual phantoms took shape for her, some seductive, some menacing; but even the most hideous and cruel symbols had a fierce fascination for her. There was a stag-beetle, with flaming eyes, a creature as big as an elephant, with claws in constant motion, that threatened her continually. Horribly as this frightened her, she gloated on it, pictured its sudden plunge with those ghastly mandibles upon her flanks. Her own fatness was a source of curious perverse pleasure to her; one of her favourite reveries was to imagine herself the centre of a group of cannibals, watch them chop off great lumps from her body, and seethe them in the pot, or roast them on a spear, hissing and dripping blood and grease, upon the fire. In some insane or atavistic confusion of mind this dream was always recognised as being a dream of love. And she understood, in some sub-current of thought, why

Suffragettes forced men to use violence upon them; it is but a repressed sexual instinct breaking out in race-remembrance of marriage by capture.

But more dangerous even than such ideas were many which she learned to group under a name which one of them gave her. It was not a name that one can transcribe in any alphabet, but it was exactly like a very short slight cough, hardly more than a clearing of the throat, a quite voluntary cough of the apologetic type. She had only to make this little noise, and immediately a certain landscape opened before her. She was walking on a narrow ribbon of white path that wound up a very gentle slope. On either side of her were broad rough screes, with sparse grass and scrub peeping between the stones. The path led up to a pass between two hills, and near the crest of the ridge were two towers, one on either side of the path, as if for defence. These towers were squat and very ugly, with no windows, but mere slits for archery, and they had no sign of habitation. Yet she was quite sure that Something lived there, and she was conscious of the most passionate anxiety to visit whoever it might be. The moon, always in her wane, shone bright above the path, but little of her illumination extended beyond those narrow limits. Upon the screes she could see only faint shadows, apparently of some prowling beast of the jackal or hyena type, for she could hear howling and laughing, with now and again fierce snarls and cries as though a fight were in progress "in that fell cirque". But nothing ever crossed the path itself, and she would walk along it with a sense of the most curious lightness and pleasure. It was often her intention to go to the towers; but always she was deterred from doing so by the Old Lady.

It was at a sharp turn of the path round an immense boulder that this individual usually appeared, coming from a cleft in its face. On the first occasion she had herself greeted the Old Lady, asking if she could assist her. For the Old Lady was seated on the ground, working very hard.

"May I help you?" said Iliel, "in whatever you are doing?"

The Old Lady sighed very bitterly, and said that she was trying to make a fire.

"But you haven't got any sticks."

"We never use sticks to make a fire – in this country."

The last three words were in sing-song.

"Then what do you burn?"

"Anything round, and anything red, and anything ripe – in this country."

"And how do you kindle it? Have you matches, or do you rub sticks together, or do you use the sun's rays through a burning-glass?"

"Hush! there is no phosphorus, nor any sticks, nor any sun – in this country."

"Then how do you get fire?"

"There is no fire – in this country."

"But you said you were making a fire!"

"Trying to make a fire, my dear; we are always trying, and never succeeding – in this country."

"And how long have you been trying?"

"There is no time – in this country."

Iliel was half hypnotised by the reiteration of that negation, and that final phrase. She began to play a game.

"Well, Old Lady, I've something round, and something red, and something ripe to make your fire with. I'll give it to you if you can guess what it is."

The Old Lady shook her head. "There's nothing round, and there's nothing red, and nothing ripe – in this country."

"Well, I'll tell you: it's an apple. If you want it, you may have it."

"We never want anything – in this country."

"Well, I'll go on."

"There's no going on – in this country."

"Oh, but there is, and I'm off."

"Don't you know what a treasure we have – in this country?"

"No – what is it?"

The Old Lady dived into the cleft of the rock, and came out again in a moment with a monkey, and a mouse-trap, and a mandolin.

"I began," she explained, "with an arrow, and an adder, and an arquebus; for there are terrible dangers in the beginning – in this country."

"But what are they good for?"

"Nothing at all – in this country. But I'm changing them for a newt, and a narwhal, and a net, hoping that one day I may get to the end, where one needs a zebra, a zither, and a zarape, and one can always exchange those for something round, and red, and ripe – in this country."

It was really a sort of child's fairy story that Iliel was telling herself; but the teller was independent of her conscious mind, so that she did not know what was coming next. And really the Old Lady was quite a personality. On the second occasion she showed Iliel how to use her treasure. She made the monkey play the mandolin, and set the mouse-trap; and sure enough the newt and the narwhal, attracted by the music swam up and were duly caught. As for the net, the Old Lady bartered her three treasures for Iliel's hair-net.

"I'm afraid it isn't very strong to catch things with," she said.

"I only need an orange, and an oboe, and an octopus; and they are easy enough to catch – in this country."

Little by little the Old Lady beguiled Iliel, and one day, while they were setting a trap to catch a viper, and a vineyard, and a violin with their unicorn, and their umbrella, and their ukulele, she suddenly stopped short, and asked Iliel point-blank if she would like to attend the Sabbath on Walpurgis-night – the eve of May-day – for "there's a short cut to it, my dear, from this country."

Iliel revolted passionately against the idea, for she scented something abominable; but the Old Lady said:

"Of course we should disguise you; it would never do for you to be recognised by Cyril, and Brother Onofrio, and Sister Clara; they wouldn't like to know you live – in this country."

"I don't," said Iliel, rather angrily, "I only come out here for a walk."

"Ah, my dear," chuckled the Old Lady, "but a walk's as good as a whale – in this country. And

you remember that the whale didn't put out Jonah where he wanted to go, but where somebody else wanted him. And that's the breed of whale we have – in this country."

"How do you know they'll be there on Walpurgis-night?"

"A how's as good as a hen – in this country. And what a hen doesn't know you may ask of a hog, and what a hog doesn't know you may ask of a horse, and what a horse doesn't know isn't worth knowing – in this country."

Iliel was in a black rage against her friends – why had they not asked her to come with them? And she went back that day in a vile temper.

This adventure of the Old Lady was only one of many; but it was the most vital, because the most coherent. Indeed, it led in the end to results of importance. For Iliel agreed to go to the Sabbath on Walpurgis-night. The Old Lady was very mysterious as to the method of travel. Iliel had expected conventionality on that point; but the Old Lady said:

"There are no goats, and no broomsticks – in this country."

Most of her visions were simply formless and incoherent horrors. Her foolish thoughts and senseless impulses took shape, usually in some distortion of an animal form, with that power of viscosity which is to vertebrates the most loathsome of all possibilities of life, since it represents the line of development which they have themselves avoided, and is therefore to them excremental in character. But to Iliel's morbidity the fascination of these things was overpowering. She took an unnatural and morose delight in watching the cuttle-fish squeeze itself slowly into a slime as black and oozy as the slug, and that again send trickling feelers as of leaking motor-oil, greasy and repulsive, with a foul scum upon its surface, until the beast looked like some parody of a tarantula; then this again would collapse, as if by mere weariness of struggle against gravitation, and spread itself slowly as a pool of putrefaction, which was yet intensely vital and personal by reason of its power to suck up everything within its sphere of sensation. It struck her that such creatures were images of Desire, a cruel and insatiable craving deprived of any will or power to take a single step towards gratification; and she understood that this condition was the most hideous and continual torture, agony with no ray of hope, impotence so complete as even to inhibit an issue in death. And she knew, too, that these shapes were born of her own weaknesses; yet, so far from rousing herself to stamp them out in her mind, she gloated upon their monstrosity and misery, took pleasure in their anguish, which was her own, and fed them with the substance of her own personality and will. It was this, a spiritual *Nostalgie de la boue*, which grew upon her like a cancer or a gangrene; treacheries of the body itself, so that the only possible remedy is instant extirpation; for once the flesh abandons its will to firmness, to organisation, and to specialised development, its degeneration into formless putrefaction becomes an accelerating rush upon a steepening slope.

How tenuous is the thread by which man climbs to the stars! What concentration of the sub-conscious will of the race, through a thousand generations, has determined his indomitable ascent! A single slackness, a single false step, and he topples into the morass wherein his feet still plash! Degeneration is the most fatally easy of all human possibilities; for the fell tug of cosmic inertia, that pressure of the entire universe which tends to the homogeneous, is upon

man continuously; and becomes constantly more urgent the more he advances upon his path of differentiation. It is more than a fable, Atlas who supports the Universe upon his shoulders, and Hercules, the type of the man, divinely born indeed, who must yet regain Olympus by his own fierce toil, taking upon himself that infinite load.

The price of every step of progress is uncounted, even in myriads of lives self-sacrificed; and every man who is unfaithful to himself is not only at war with the sum of things, but his own comrades turn upon him to destroy him, to crush out his individuality and energy, to assimilate him to their own pullulating mass. It is indeed the power of the Roman Empire which erects the Cross on Calvary; but there must needs be Caiaphas and Herod, so blind that they crush out their own one hope of salvation from that iron tyranny; and also a traitor among those who once "left all and followed" the Son of Man.

And who shall deny true Godhead to humanity, seeing that no generation of mankind has been without a Saviour, conscious of his necessary doom, and resolute to meet it, his face set as a flint towards Jerusalem?

CHAPTER XIX

THE GRAND BEWITCHMENT

THE Operation planned by the Black Lodge was simple and colossal both in theory and in practice. It was based on the prime principle of Sympathetic Magic, which is that if you destroy anything which is bound up with anybody by an identifying link, that person also perishes. Douglas had adroitly taken advantage of the fact of the analogy between his own domestic situation and that of Cyril Grey. He had no need to attack the young magician directly, or even Lisa; he preferred to strike at the weakest point of all, that being whose existence was as yet but tentative. He had no need to go beyond this; for if he could bring Cyril's magick to naught, that exorcist would be destroyed by the recoil of his own exorcism. The laws of force take no account of human prejudices about "good" or "evil"; if one is run over by a railway engine, it matters nothing, physically, whether one is trying to commit suicide or to save a child. The difference in the result lies wholly on a superior plane.

It is one mark of the short-sightedness of the sorcerer that he is content with his own sorceries; and if he should think that he can escape the operation of that superior law which does take account of spiritual and moral causes, he is the greater fool. Douglas might indeed wipe his enemy off the planet, but only with the result of fortifying the immortal and divine self which was within his victim, so that he would return with added power and wisdom; while all his success in aggrandising himself – as he foolishly called it – would leave his better part exhausted and disintegrated beyond refreshment or repair. He was like a man who should collect all his goods about him, and set fire to his house; while the true adepts beggar themselves (to all appearances) by transforming all their wealth into a shape that fire cannot touch.

The sorcerer never sees thus clearly. He hopes that at the last his accumulation of corruptible things will outweigh the laws of Nature; much as a thief might argue that if he can only steal enough, he can corrupt the judges and bribe the legislature, as is done in America. But the laws of nature were not made by man, nor can they be set aside by man; they were not made at all. There are no laws of Nature in the usual sense of the word "law"; they are but statements, reduced to a

generalised form in accordance with reason, of the facts observed in nature; they are formulae of the inherent properties of substance. It is impossible to evade them, or to suspend them, or to counteract them; for the effort to do so is itself in accordance with those laws themselves, and the compensation, though it be invisible for a time, is adjusted with an exactitude absolute because independent of every source of error. No trickery, no manipulation, can alter by the millionth of a milligramme the amount of oxygen in a billion tons of water. No existing thing is ever destroyed or magnified or lessened, though it change its form as it passes from one complexity to another. And if this be true of an atom of carbon, which is but one of the ideas in our minds, how much more is it true of that supremely simple thing which stands behind all thought, the soul of man? Doubt that? The answer comes: Who doubts?

The sorcerer is perhaps – at best – trying to create a permanence of his complexities, as who should try to fashion gold from the dust-heap. But most sorcerers do not go so deeply into things; they are set upon the advantage of the moment. Douglas probably did not care a snap of the fingers for his ultimate destiny; it may be that he deliberately avoided thinking of it; but however that may be, there is no doubt that at this moment he was ruthlessly pursuing his hate of Cyril Grey.

For great operations – the "set pieces" of his diabolical pyrotechnics – the sorcerer had a place set apart and prepared. This was an old wine-cellar in a street between the Seine and the Boulevard St. Germain. The entrance was comparatively reputable, being a house of cheap prostitution which Douglas and Balloch – screened behind a woman – owned between them. Below this house was a cellar where the apaches of Paris gathered to dance and plot against society; so ran the legend, and two burly *sergents de ville*, with fixed bayonets and cocked revolvers lying on the table before them, superintended the revels. For in fact Douglas had perceived that the apache spent no money, and that it would pay better to run the cellar as a show place for Americans, Cockneys, Germans, and country cousins from the provinces on a jaunt to Paris, on the hunt for thrills. No one more dangerous than a greengrocer had crossed that threshold for many a long year, and the visible apaches, drinking and swearing, dancing an alleged can-can and occasionally throwing bottles and knives at each other, were honest folk painfully earning the exiguous salary which the "long firm" paid them.

But beneath this cellar, unknown even to the police, was a vault which had once served for storing spirits. It was below the level of the river; rats, damp, and stale alcohol gave it an atmosphere happily peculiar to such abodes. There is no place in the world more law-abiding than a house of ill-fame, with the light of police supervision constantly upon it; and the astuteness of the sorcerer in choosing this for his place of evocation was rewarded by complete freedom from disturbance or suspicion. Any one could enter at any hour of day or night, with every precaution of secrecy, without drawing more than a laugh from the police on guard.

The entrance to the sorcerer's den was similarly concealed – by cunning, not by more obvious methods.

A sort of cupboard-shelf, reached by a ladder from the dancing cellar and by a few steps from one of the bedrooms in the house above, was called "Troppman's refuge", it being said

that that celebrated murderer once had lain concealed there for some days. His autograph, and some bad verses (all contributed by an ingenious cabaret singer) were shown upon the walls. It was therefore quite natural and unsuspicious for any visitor to climb up into that room, which was so small that it would only hold one man of average size. His non-reappearance would not cause surprise; he might have gone out the other way; in fact, he would naturally do so. But in the moment of his finding himself alone, he could, if he knew the secret, press a hidden lever which caused the floor to descend bodily. Arrived below, a corridor with three right-angled turns – this could, incidentally, be flooded at need, in a few moments – led to the last of the defences, a regular door such as is fitted to a strong room. There was an emergency exit to the cellar, equally ingenious; it was a sort of torpedo-tube opening beneath the water of the Seine. It was fitted with a compressed air-chamber. Any one wishing to escape had merely to introduce himself into a shell made of thin cork, and shoot into the river. Even the worst of swimmers could be sure to reach the neighbouring quay. But the secret of this was known only to Douglas and one other.

The very earliest steps in such thoroughgoing sorcery as Douglas practised require the student to deform and mutilate his humanity by accustoming himself to such moral crimes as render their perpetrator callous and insensible to all such emotions as men naturally cherish; in particular, love. The Black Lodge put all its members through regular practices of cruelty and meanness. Guy de Maupassant wrote two of the most revolting stories ever told; one of a boy who hated a horse, the other of a family of peasants who tortured a blind relative that had been left to their charity. Such vileness as is written there by the divine hand of that great artist forbids emulation; the reverent reference must suffice.

Enough to say that stifling of all natural impulse was a preliminary of the system of the Black Lodge; in higher grades the pupil took on the manipulation of subtler forces. Douglas' own use of his wife's love to vitriolise her heart was considered by the best judges as likely to become a classic.

The inner circle, the fourteen men about Douglas himself and that still more mysterious person to whom even he was responsible, a woman known only as "Annie" or as "A. B.", were sealed to him by the direst of all bonds. Needless are oaths in the Black Lodge; honour being the first thing discarded, their only use is to frighten fools. But before joining the Fourteen, known as the Ghaaghaael, it was obligatory to commit a murder in cold blood, and to place the proofs of it in the hands of Douglas. Thus each step in sorcery is also a step in slavery; and that any man should put such power in the hands of another, no matter for what hope of gain, is one of the mysteries of perverse psychology. The highest rank in the Lodge was called Thaumiel-Qeretiel, and there were two of these, "Annie" and Douglas, who were alone in possession of the full secrets of the Lodge. Only they and the Fourteen had keys to the cellar and the secret of the combination.

Beginners were initiated there, and the method of introducing them was satisfactory and ingenious. They were taken to the house in an automobile, their eyes blinded by an ordinary pair of motor-goggles, behind whose glass was a steel plate.

The cellar itself was arranged as a permanent place of evocation. It was a far more complex device than that used by Vesquit in Naples, for in confusion lay the safety of the Lodge. The floor was covered with symbols which even the Fourteen did not wholly understand; any one of them, crossed inadvertently, might be a magical trap for a traitor; and as each of the Fourteen was exactly that, in fact, had to be so to qualify for supreme place, it was with abject fear that this Unholy of Unholies was guarded.

At the appointed hour Mr. Butcher presented himself at the Count's apartment, was furnished with the necessary spectacles, and conducted to the Beth Choi, or House of Horror, as the cellar was called in the jargon of the Sorcerers.

Balloch, Cremers, Abdul Bey and the wife of Douglas were already present.

The first part of the procedure consisted in the formal renunciation by Mrs. Douglas of the vows taken for her in her baptism, a ceremonial apostacy from Christianity. This was done in no spirit of hostility to that religion, but to permit of her being rebaptised into it under Lisa's maiden name. The Turk was next called upon to renounce Islam, and baptised by the name of the Marchese la Giuffria.

The American priest next proceeded to confirm them in the Christian religion, and to communicate the Sacrament.

Finally, they were married. In this long profanation of the mysteries of the Church the horror lay in the business-like simplicity of the procedure.

One can imagine the Charity of a devout Christian finding excuses for the Black Mass, when it is the expression of the revolt of an agonising soul, or of the hysteria of a half-crazed debauchee; he can conceive of repentance and of grace following upon enlightenment; but this cold-blooded abuse of the most sacred rites, their quite casual employment as the mere prelude to a crime which is tantamount to murder in the opinion of all right-minded men, must seem even to the Freethinker or the Pagan as an abomination not to be forgiven.

No pains had been spared by Douglas to make all secure. Balloch and Cremers had sponsored both "infants", and Douglas himself, as having most right, gave his wife in marriage to the Turk.

A brutally realistic touch was needed to consummate the sacrilege; it was not neglected.

Much of the pleasure taken by Douglas in this miserable and criminal farce was due to his enjoyment of the sufferings of his wife. Each new spurt of filth wrung her heart afresh; and withal she was aware that all these things were but the prelude to an act of fiendish violence more horrible than them all.

Mr. Butcher, Cremers, and Abdul Bey, their functions ended, were led out of the cellar. Balloch remained to perform the operation from which the bulk of his income was derived.

But there was yet much sorcery of the more secret sort to be accomplished. Douglas who, up to now, had confined himself to intense mental concentration upon the work, forcing himself to believe that the ceremonies he was witnessing were real instead of mockery, that his wife was really Lisa, and Abdul really the Marchese, now came forward as the heart and brain of the work. The difficulty – the crux of the whole art – had been to introduce Cyril Grey into the affair, and this had been overcome by the use of a specimen of his signature. But now it was necessary also

to dedicate the victim to Hecate, or rather, to her Hebrew equivalent, Nahema, the devourer of little children, because she also is one aspect of the moon, and Lisa having been adopted to that planet, her representative must needs undergo a similar ensorcelment.

In the art of evocation Douglas was profoundly skilled. His mind was of a material and practical order, and distrusted subtleties. He gladly endured the immense labour of compelling a spirit to visible appearance, when a less careful or more fine-minded sorcerer would have worked upon some other plane. He had so far mastered his art that in a place, such as he now had, long habitated to similar scenes, he could call up a visible image of almost any demon required in a period of not more than half an hour. For place-association is of great importance, possibly because it favours concentration of mind. Evidently, it is difficult not to feel religious in King's College Chapel, Cambridge, or otherwise than profoundly sceptical and Pagan in St. Peter's, at Rome, with its "East" in the West, its adaptation of a statue of Jupiter to represent its patron saint, and the emphasis of its entire architecture in bearing witness that its true name is Temporal Power. Gothic is the only mystic type; Templar and Byzantine are only religious through sexuality; Perpendicular is more moral than spiritual – and modern architecture means nothing at all.

In the Beth Choi there was always a bowl of fresh bull's blood burning over a charcoal brazier.

Science is gradually being forced round once more to the belief that there is something more in life than its mere chemistry and physics. Those who practise the occult arts have never been in doubt on the subject. The dynamic virtue of living substance does not depart from it immediately at death. Those ideas, therefore, which seek manifestation in life, must do so either by incarnation or by seizing some still living matter which the idea or soul in possession has abandoned. Sorcerers consequently employ the fumes of fresh blood as a vehicle for the manifestation of the demons whom they wish to evoke. The matter is easy enough; for fiends are always eager to take hold on the sensory life. Occasionally, such beings find people ignorant and foolish enough to offer themselves deliberately to obsession by sitting in a dark room without magical protection, and inviting any wandering ghost or demon to take hold of them, and use their bodies and minds. This loathsome folly is called Spiritualism, and successful practitioners can be recognised by the fact that their minds are no use for anything at all any more. They become incapable of mental concentration, or a connected train of thought; only too often the obsessing spirit gains power to take hold of them at will, and utters by their mouths foulness and imbecility when the whim takes him. True souls would never seek so ignoble a means of manifesting in earth-life; their ways are holy, and in accord with Nature.

While the true soul reincarnates as a renunciation, a sacrifice of its divine life and ecstasy for the sake of redeeming those who are not yet freed from mortal longings, the demon seeks incarnation as a means of gratifying unslaked lusts.

Like a dumb beast in pain, the wife of Douglas watched her husband go through his ghastly ritual, with averted face, as is prescribed; for none may look on Hecate, and remain sane. The proper conjurations of Hecate are curses against all renewal of life; her sacrament is deadly night-shade or henbane, and her due offering a black lamb torn ere its birth from a black ewe.

This, with sardonic subter-thought, pleasing to Hecate, the sorcerer promised her as she made her presence felt; whether they could have seen anything if they had dared to look, who can say? But through the cellar moved an icy sensation, as if some presence had indeed been called forth by the words and rites spoken and accomplished.

For Hecate is what Scripture calls "the second death". Natural death is to man the greatest of the Sacraments, of which all others are but symbols; for it is the final and absolute Union with the creator, and it is also the Pylon of the Temple of Life, even in the material world, for Death is Love.

Certainly the wife of Douglas felt the presence of that vile thing evoked from Tartarus. Its chill struck through to her bones. Nothing had so torn her breast as the constant refusal of her husband to allow her to fulfil her human destiny. Even her prostitution, since it was forced upon her by the one man she loved, might be endured – if only – if only –

But always the aid of Balloch had been summoned; always, in dire distress, and direr danger, she had been thwarted of her life's purpose. It was not so much a conscious wish, though that was strong, as an actual physical craving of her nature, as urgent and devouring as hunger or thirst.

Balloch, who had been all his life high-priest of Hecate, had never been present at an evocation of the force that he served. He shuddered – not a little – as the sorcerer recited his surgical exploits; the credentials of the faith of her servant then present before her. He had committed his dastardly crimes wholly for gain, and as a handle for blackmail; the magical significance of the business had not occurred to him at all. His magical work had been almost entirely directed to the gratification of sensuality in abnormal and extra-human channels. So, while a fierce pride now thrilled him, there was mingled with it a sinking of the spirit; for he realised that its mistress had been sterility and death. And it was of death that he was most afraid. The cynical calm of Douglas appalled him; he recognised the superiority of that great sorcerer; and his hope to supplant him died within his breast.

At that moment Hecate herself passed into him, and twined herself inextricably about his brain. He accepted his destiny as her high-priest; in future he would do murder for the joy of pleasing her! All other mistresses were tame to this one! The thrill of Thuggee caught him – and in a very spasm of maniacal exaltation, he vowed himself again and again to her services. She should be sole goddess of the Black Lodge – only let her show him how to be rid of Douglas! Instantly the plan came to him; he remembered that "Annie" was high-priestess of Hecate in a greater sense than himself; for she was notorious as an open advocate of this kind of murder; indeed, she had narrowly escaped prison on this charge; he would tempt Douglas to rid himself of "Annie" – and then betray him to her.

So powerful was the emotion that consumed him that he trembled with excitement and eagerness. Tonight was a great night: it was a step in his initiation to take part in so tremendous a ceremony. He became nervously exalted; he could have danced; Hecate, warming herself in his old bones, communicated a devilish glee to him.

The moment was at hand for his renewed activity.

"Hecate, mother only of death, devourer of all life!" cried Douglas, in his final adjuration; "as I devote to thy chill tooth this secret spring of man, so be it with all that are like unto it! Even as it is with that which I shall cast upon thine altar, so be it with all the offspring of Lisa la Giuffria!"

He ended with the thirteenth repetition of that appalling curse which begins *Epikaloume se ten en to keneo pnevmati, deinan, aoraton, Pontokratora, theropoian kai eremopoian, e misonta, oikian efstathousanfl!* calling upon "her that dwelleth in the void place, the inane, terrible, inexorable, maker of horror and desolation, hater of the house that prospereth", and devoting "the signified and sealed, named and unnamed" to destruction.

Then he turned to Balloch, and bade him act. Three minutes later the surgeon gave a curse, and blanched, as a scream, despite herself, burst from the bitten lips of the brave woman who lay upon the altar.

"Why couldn't you let me give an anaesthetic?" he said angrily.

"What's wrong? Is it bad?"

"It's damned ugly. Curse it; not a thing here that I need!"

But he needed nothing; he had done more even than he guessed.

Mrs. Douglas, her face suddenly drawn and white, lifted her head with infinite effort towards her husband.

"I've always loved you," she whispered, "and I love you now, as – I – die."

Her head dropped with a dull crack upon the slab. No one can say if she heard the reply of Douglas:

"You sow! you've bitched the whole show!"

For she had uttered the supreme name of Love, in love; and the spell dissolved more swiftly than a dream. There was no Hecate, no sorcerer even, for the moment; nothing but two murderers, and the corpse of a martyr between them.

Douglas did not waste a single word of abuse on Balloch.

"This is for you to clear up," he said, with a simplicity that cut deeper than sneer or snarl, and walked out of the cellar.

Balloch, left to himself, became hysterical. In his act he recognised the first-fruits of the divine possession; his offering to the goddess had been stupendous indeed. All his exaltation returned: now would Hecate favour him above all men.

Well, he had but to take the body upstairs. The old woman understood these things; he would certify the death; there would be no fuss made over a poor prostitute. He would return at once to London, and open up the negotiations with "A. B."

CHAPTER XX

WALPURGIS-NIGHT

THE spring in Naples had advanced with eager foot; in her gait she revealed the truth of her godhead; and by the end of April there was no wreath of snow on Apennine, or Alban, or Apulian Hill.

The last day of the month was hot and still as midsummer; the slopes of Posillippo begged a breath from Ocean, and were denied. So heavy a haze hung on the sea that not only Capri, not only the blue spur that stabs the sunset, but Vesuvius itself, were hidden from the Villa where Iliel and her friends were nested.

Sunset was sombre and splendid; the disc itself was but a vague intensity of angry Indian red. His agony spilt a murky saffron through the haze; and the edges of the storm-clouds on the horizon, fantastically shapen, cast up a veritable mirage, exaggerated and distorted images of their own scarred crests, that shifted and changed, so that one might have sworn that monsters – dragons, hippogriffs, chimaerae – were moving in the mist, a saturnalia of phantasms.

Iliel impatiently awaited the moment of darkness, when she could meet the Old Lady and start for the Sabbath. She had noticed a long conference that day between Sister Clara and the two men; and she was sure that they were themselves arranging for their departure. The suspicion was confirmed when, one after the other, they came to wish her a good night. She was more than ever determined to follow them to the Sabbath.

By nine o'clock everything was still in the garden, save for the tread of Brother Onofrio's patrol, who paced the upper terrace, chanting in the soft and low, yet stern, tones of his well-modulated voice, the exorcism that magical guardians have sung for so many ages, with its refrain: "On them will I impose my will, the Law of Light."

Iliel gave her little cough, and found herself immediately upon the path she knew so well. It only took her a few minutes to reach the rock, and there was the Old Lady waiting for her.

"I must tell you at once, my dear," she began without any preliminary, "that you must be very careful to do exactly as I say – in that country."

It was the same sing-song, with the one change of word.

"First of all, you must never speak of anything by its name – in that country. So, if you see a tree on a mountain, it will be better to say 'Look at the green on the high'; for that's how they talk – in that country. And whatever you do, you must find a false reason for doing it – in that country. If you rob a man, you must say it is to help and protect him: that's the ethics – of that country. And everything of value has no value at all – in that country. You must be perfectly commonplace if you want to be a genius – in that country. And everything you like you must pretend not to like; and anything that is there you must pretend is not there – in that country. And you must always say that you are sacrificing yourself in the cause of religion, and morality, and humanity, and liberty, and progress, when you want to cheat your neighbour – in that country."

"Good heavens!" cried Iliel, "are we going to England?"

"They call the place Stonehenge – in that country." And without another word the Old Lady dragged Iliel into the cleft of the rock. It was very, very dark inside, and she tripped over loose stones. Then the Old Lady opened a little door, and she found herself standing on a narrow window-ledge. The door shut fast behind her, almost pushing her out. Beyond the ledge was nothing but the Abyss of Stars. She was seized with an enormous vertigo. She would have fallen into that cruel emptiness, but the Old Lady's voice came: "What I said outside was nonsense, just to put the Gwalkins off the trail, my dear; there is only one rule, and that is to take things as they come – in this country."

She pushed Iliel deliberately from the window-sill; with a scream she flew through the blackness. But the chubby little old clergyman explained to her that she must go into the castle on the islet. It was only a little way to walk over the ice of the lake, but there was no sign of an entrance. The castle was fitted cunningly to the irregularities of the rock, so that one could see nothing but the masonry; and there was no trace of any door, and the windows were all very high in the wall. But as Iliel came to it she found herself inside, and she never knew how she got there. It was easy to scramble along the ladder to the golf course, but the main deck of the galleon was slippery with the oil that spurted from its thousand fountains. However, she came at last to the wardrobe where her hairbrush was hanging, and she lost no time in digging for the necessary skylarks. At last the way was clear! The pine-woods on the left; the ant-hills on the right; straight through the surf to the heathery pagoda where the chubby clergyman and the Old Lady had already arrived, and were busy worshipping the Chinese God.

Of course! It was Cyril, with Brother Onofrio and Sister Clara all the time – how stupid she had been!

But for all that the toads were a nuisance with their eternal chatter and laughter; and they wore their jewels much too conspicuously and profusely.

And then she perceived that Cyril and his two companions formed but one triangle, out of uncounted thousands; and each triangle was at a knot upon the web of an enormous spider. At each knot was such a group of three, and every one was different. There must have been millions of such gods, each with its pair of worshippers; every race and clime and period was represented. There were the gods of Mexico and of Peru, of Syria and Babylon, of Greece and Rome, of obscure swamps of Ethiopia, of deserts and mountains. And upon each thread of the

web, from knot to knot, danced incredible insects, and strange animals, and hideous reptiles. They danced, sang, and whirled frantically, so that the entire web was a mere bewilderment of motion. Her head swam dizzily. But she was now full of a curious anger; her thought was that the Old Lady had betrayed her. She found it quite impossible to approach the triangle, for one thing: she was furious that it should be Sister Clara herself who had led her into this Sabbath, for another; and she was infinitely disgusted at the whole vile revel. Now she noticed that each pair of worshippers had newborn children in their arms; and they offered these to their god, who threw them instantly towards the centre of the web. Following up those cruel meshes, she beheld the spider itself, with its six legs. Its head and body formed one black sphere, covered with moving eyes that darted rays of darkness in every direction, and mouths that sucked up its prey without remorse or cessation, and cast it out once more in the form of fresh strands of that vibrating web.

Iliel shuddered with the horror of the vision; it was to her a dread unspeakable, yet she was hypnotised and helpless. She felt in herself that one day she too must become the prey of that most dire and demoniac power of darkness.

As she gazed, she saw that even the gods and their worshippers were morsels for its mouths. Ever and anon she beheld one of the legs crooked round a triangle and draw it, god, shrine, and worshippers, into the blackness of the spider's bloated belly. Then they were thrown out violently again, in some slightly altered form, to repeat the same uncanny ritual.

With a strong shudder she broke away from that infernal contemplation. Where was the kindly earth, with all its light and beauty? In God's name, why had she left Lavinia King to explore these dreadful realms – of illusion? of imagination? of darker and deadlier reality than life? It mattered little which; the one thing needful was to turn again to humanity, to the simple sensible life that she had always lived. It was not noble, not wonderful; but it was better than this nightmare of phantoms, cruel and malignant and hideous, this phantasmagoria of damnation.

She wrenched herself away; for a moment she lost consciousness completely; then she found herself in her bed at the Villa. With feverish energy she sprang from the couch, and ran to the wardrobe to put on her travelling dress. It would be easy to drop from the wall of the terrace into the lane; in an hour she would be safe in Naples. And then she discovered that the dress would have to be altered before she could wear it. With vehemence she set instantly to work – and just as she was finishing, the door opened, and Sister Clara stood beside her.

"Come, Iliel," she said, "it is the moment to salute May Morn!"

The indignant girl recoiled in anger and disgust; but Sister Clara stood smiling gently and tenderly. Iliel looked at her, almost despite herself; and she could not but see the radiance of her whole being, a physical aura of light playing about her, and the fire of her eyes transcendent with seraph happiness.

"They are waiting for us in the garden," she said, taking Iliel by the arm, like a nurse with an invalid. And she drew over her shoulders the great lunar mantle of blue velvet with its broidered silver crescents, its talismans of the moon, and its heavy hanging tassels of seed pearls; and upon her head she set the tiara of moon-stones.

"Come, they are waiting."

So lliel suffered herself to be led once more into the garden. In the east the first rays of the sun gilded the crest of Posilippo, and tinged the pale blue of the firmament with rosy fingers. The whole company was gathered together, an ordered phalanx, to salute the Lord of Life and Light.

lliel could not join in that choir of adoration. In her heart was blackness and hate, and nausea in her mouth. What vileness lay beneath this fair semblance! Well, let it be; she would be gone.

Cyril came to her with Brother Onofrio, as the last movement of their majestic chant died away upon the echoing air. He took her in his arms. "Come! I have much to tell you." He led her to a marble seat, and made her sit down. Brother Onofrio and Sister Clara followed them, and sat upon the base of a great statue, a copy of the Marsyas and Olympas in green bronze, hard by.

"Child!" said Cyril, very gravely and gently, "look at the eastern slope of Posilippo! And look at the stars, how brightly they shine! And look at that shoal of gleaming fish, that swim so deep beneath the waters of the bay! And look at your left ear! What shapeliness! What delicate pink!"

She was too angry even to tell him not to be an idiot. She only smiled disdainfully.

He continued. "But those things are there. You cannot see them because the conditions are not right. But there are other things that your eye sees indeed, but you, not; because you have not been trained to see them for what they are. See Capri in the morning sun! How do you know it is an island, not a dream, or a cloud, or a sea-monster? Only by comparison with previous knowledge and experience. You can only see things that are already in your own mind – or things so like them that you can adjust yourself to the small percentage of difference. But you cannot observe or apprehend things that are utterly unfamiliar except by training and experience. How does the alphabet look to you when you first learn it? Don't you confuse the letters? Arabic looks 'fantastic' to you, as the Roman script does to the Arab; you can memorise one at a glance, while you plod painfully over the other, letter by letter, and probably copy it wrong after all. That's what happened to you last night. I know you were there; and, knowing you were not an initiate, I can guess pretty well what you must have seen. You saw things 'accurately', so far as you could see them; that is, you saw a projection into your own mind of something really in being. How right such vision can be, and yet how wrong! Watch my hand!" He suddenly raised his right hand. With the other he held a book between it and her eyes.

"I can't see it!" she cried petulantly.

"Look at its shadow on the wall!"

"It's the head of the devil!"

"Yet I am only making the gesture of benediction." He lowered the book. She recognised at once the correctness of his statement.

She looked at him with open mouth and eyes. He was always stupefying her by the picturesqueness of his allegories, and his trick of presenting them dramatically.

"What then?"

"This is what really happened last night – only there's no such thing as time. This is what you should have seen, and what you will see one day, if you cling to the highest in you."

He drew a note-book of white vellum from his pocket, and began to read.

MOONCHILD

The whirlwind of the Eagle and the Lion!
The Tree upon the Mountain that is Zion!
The marriage of the Starbeam and the Clod!
The mystic Sabbath of the Saints of God!
Bestride the Broomstick that is God-in-man!
Spur the rough Goat whose secret name is Pan!
Before that Rod Heaven knows itself unjust;
Beneath those hoofs the stars are puffs of dust.
Rise up, my soul! One stride, and space is spanned;
Time, like a poppy, crushed in thy left hand,
While with thy right thou reachest out to grip
The Graal of God, and tilt it to thy lip?
Lo! all the whirring shafts of Light, a web
Wherein the Tides of Being flow and ebb,
One heart-beat, pulsing the Eternal stress,
Extremes that cancel out in Nothingness.
Light thrills through Light, the spindle of desire,
Cross upon Cross of elemental Fire;
Life circles Life, the Rose all flowers above,
And in their intermarriage they are Love.
Lo! on each spear of Splendour burns a world
Revolving, whirling, crying aloud; and curled
About each cosmos, bounding in its course,
The sacred Snake, the father of its force,
Energised, energising, self-sustained,
Man-hearted, Eagle-pinioned, Lion-maned.
Exulting in its splendour as it lashes
Its Phoenix plumage to immortal ashes
Whereof one fleck, a seed of spirit spun,
Whirls itself onward, and creates a sun.
Light interfused with Light, a sparkling spasm
Of rainbow radiance, spans the cosmic chasm;
Light crystallised in Life, Life coruscating
In Light, their mood of magick consummating
The miracle of Love, and all the awe
Of Need made one with Liberty's one law;
A fourfold flower of Godhead, leaf and fruit
And seed and blossom of one radiant root,
Resolving all the being of its bloom

MOONCHILD

Into the rapture of its own perfume.
Star-clustered dew each fibre of that light
Wherein all being flashes to its flight!
All things that live, a cohort and a choir,
Laugh with the leapings of that fervid fire;
Motes in that sunlight, they are drunken of
The wine of their own energy of love.
Nothing so small, so base, so incomplete,
But here goes dancing on diviner feet;
And where Light crosses Light, all loves combine
Behold the God, the worshippers, the shrine,
Each comprehensive of its single soul
Yet each the centre and fountain of the whole;
Each one made perfect in its passionate part,
Each the circumference, and each the heart!
Always the Three in One are interwoven,
Always the One in Three sublimely cloven,
Their essence to the Central Spirit hurled
And so flung forth, an uncorrupted world,
By That which, comprehending in one whole
The universal rapture of Its soul,
Abides beyond Its own illumination,
Withdrawn from Its imperishable station,
Upholding all, an arm whose falchion flings
With every flash a new-fledged Soul of Things;
Beholding all, with eyes whose flashes flood
The veins of their own universe with blood;
Absorbing all, each myriad mouth aflame
To utter the unutterable Name
That calls all souls, the greatest and the least,
To the unimaginable marriage-feast;
And, in the self-same sacrament, is stirred
To recreate their essence with a Word;
This All, this Sire and Lord of All, abides
Behind the unbounded torrent of Its tides,
In silence of all deed, or word, or thought,
So that we name It not, or name It Naught.
This is the Truth behind the lie called God;
This blots the heavens, and indwells the clod.

This is the centre of all spheres, the flame
In men and stars, the Soul behind the name,
The spring of Life, the axle of the Wheel,
All-mover, yet the One Thing immobile.
Adore It not, for It adoreth thee,
The shadow-shape of Its eternity.
Lift up thyself! be strong to burst thy bars!
For lo! thy stature shall surpass the stars.

Cyril put away his book. "Language," said he, "has been developed from its most primitive sources by persons so passionately concentrated upon the Ideal of selling cheese without verbal infelicity that some other points have necessarily been neglected. One cannot put mystic experience into words. One can at best describe phenomena with a sort of cold and wooden accuracy, or suggest ecstasy by very vagueness. You know that line 'O windy star blown sideways up the sky!' It means nothing, if you analyse it; but it gives the idea of something, though one could never say what. What you saw, my beloved Iliel, bears about the same ratio to what I have said as what I have said does to what Sister Clara saw: or, rather, was. Moral: when Sister turns we all turn. I have now apologised, though inadequately, for inflicting my bad verses upon you; which will conclude the entertainment for this morning. Brother Onofrio will now take up the collection. He that giveth to the poor lendeth to the Lord; details of rate of interest and security on application to the bartender. The liberal soul shall be made fat; but I am Banting, as the hart banteth after the water brooks. He that watereth shall be watered also himself: I will take a cold shower before the plunge. The Mother's Meeting will be held as usual at 8.30 on Thursday evening. Those who are not yet Mothers, but who wish to become so, kindly apply to me in the Vestry at the conclusion of the service. Sister Clara, please play the people out quickly!"

Cyril babbled out this nonsense in the tones of the Sweet Young Thing type of Curate; it was his way of restoring the superficial atmosphere.

Iliel took his arm, and went smiling to breakfast; but her soul was yet ill at ease. She asked him about the identification of Sister Clara and her Old Lady.

"Yes," he said, "it was best to have her on the watch outside – on the Astral Plane – to keep you from getting into too great mischief. But you can never come to any real harm so long as you keep your vow and stay inside the circle. That's the one important point."

She was quite satisfied in her upper conscious self, which was usually her better self, because of its rationality, and its advantage of surface training, which saved her from obeying her impulses on every occasion. She was glad, she was proud, of her partnership with the adepts. Yet there was a subconscious weakness in her which hated them and envied them the more because of their superiority to her. She knew only too well that the price of their attainment had been the suppression of just such darknesses of animal instinct and savage superstition as were her chief delight. The poet speaks of "the infinite rage of fishes to have wings"; but when you explain to the

fish that it will have to give up pumping water through its gills, it is apt to compromise for a few million generations; though the word may rankle if you call it a flying-fish, when swimming-bird is evidently a properer and politer name.

She was permanently annoyed with Sister Clara; her motive for making excursions on that path had been to get rid of the idea of Cyril and his magick; and he had not even come himself to welcome her, but set this woman to disguise herself and spy upon her thoughts! It was disgusting.

Cyril had certainly done his best to put the matter in the proper light. He had even told her a story. "A charming lady, wife of a friend of Bowling's, whom her physical and mental characteristics induce me to introduce as Mrs. Dough-Nut, was once left lorn in the desert island of Manhattan, while her husband was on a spook-shikar with Lord Antony in this very Naples, which you see before you. (Slightly to the left, child!) Mrs. Dough-Nut was as virtuous as American women sometimes are, when denied opportunity to be otherwise; and the poor lady was far from attractive. But in the world of spirits, it appears, the same standards are not current as in Peacock Alley or Times Square; and she was soon supplied with a regular regiment of 'spirit lovers'. They told her what to do, and how to do it; eating, drinking, reading, music, whatever she did, all must be done under spirit control; and one day they told her that they had a great and wonderful work for her to do – the regeneration of humanity and so forth, I think it was; anyhow, something perfectly dotty. She was now quite without power to criticise her actions by reason or good sense; the voice of the 'Spirits' was for her the voice of God. So they sent her to the Bank for money, and to the Steamship office for a passage to Europe; and when she got to Liverpool they sent her to London, from London to Paris, from Paris to Genoa. And when she came to Genoa they told her which hotel to choose; and then they sent her out to buy a revolver and some cartridges; and then they told her to cock it and put the muzzle to her forehead; and then to pull the trigger. The bullet made little impression on that armour-plate of solid bone; and she escaped to tell her story. She had not even sense enough to tell it different. But that, my child, is why it is better to have a kind friend to look after you when you start a flirtation with the gay if treacherous Lotharios of the Astral World."

"I hope you don't think I'm a woman like that!"

"All women are like that."

She bit her lips; but her good sense showed her that his main principle was right. If she had only been able to stifle the formless promptings which were so alluring and so dangerous! But as she could not live wholly on the heights of aspiration, so also she could not live on the safe plains of earth-life. The voices of the swamp and the cavern called to her continuously.

And so the external reconciliation had no deep root. For a few weeks she was better and healthier in body and mind. Then she slipped back into her sulks, and went "fairy-tale-ing" as she called it, with a very determined mind to be on guard against the interference of Sister Clara. She had begun to familiarise herself with the laws of this other world, and could distinguish symbols and their meanings to some extent; she could even summon certain forms, or banish them. And she set a mighty bar between herself and Sister Clara. She kept herself to the definite creations of her own impulses, would not let herself go except upon some such chosen lines.

In her earth-life, too, she became more obviously ill-tempered; and, as to a woman of her type revenge only means one thing, she amused the garrison exceedingly by attempting flirtations. The rule of the Profess-House happened to include the virtue of chastity, which is an active and positive thing, a passion, not that mere colourless abstinence and stagnation which passes in Puritan countries by that name, breeds more wickedness than all the vice on the planet, and, at the best, is shared by clinkers.

She was clever enough to see in a few hours that she was only making herself utterly ridiculous; but this again did not tend to improve her temper, as many devout ladies, from Dido to Potiphar's wife, have been at the pains to indicate to our psychologists.

The situation grew daily more strained, with now and then an explosion which cleared the air for a while. The discipline of the Profess-House prevented the trouble from spreading; but Cyril Grey confided to Brother Onofrio that he was angrier than ever at the efficient way in which Edwin Arthwait and his merry men had been put out of business.

"I'd give my ears," said Cyril, "to see Edwin, arm in arm with Lucifuge Rofocale, coming up from the bay to destroy us all by means of the Mysterious Amulet of Rabbi Solomon, conferring health, wealth and happiness, with bag complete; also lucky moles and love-charms, price two eleven three to regular subscribers to *The Occult Review*."

But with June a great and happy change came over Iliel. She became enthralled by the prospect of the miracle that was so soon to blossom on her breast. Her sulkiness vanished; she was blithe and joyous from the day's beginning to its end. She bore fatigue and discomfort without a murmur. She made friends with Sister Clara, and talked to her for hours while she plied her needle upon those necessary and now delightful tasks of making tiny and dainty settings for the expected jewel. She clean forgot the irksomeness of her few restrictions; she recovered all the gaiety and buoyancy of youth; indeed, she had to be cautioned in the mere physical matter of activity. No longer did she indulge morbid fancies, or take unwholesome pleasure in the contemplation of evil ideas. She was at home in her heaven of romance, the heroine of the most wonderful story in the world. Her love for Cyril showed a tender and more exalted phase; she became alive to her dignity and responsibility. She acquired also a sense of Nature which she had never had before in all her life; she felt a brotherhood with every leaf and flower of the garden, told herself stories of the loves of the fishermen whose sails dotted the blue of the bay, wondered what romances were dancing on the decks of the great white liners that steamed in from America to tour the Mediterranean, laughed with joy over the antics of the children who played on the slopes below the garden, and glowed with the vigour of the sturdy peasants who bore their baskets of fish, or flowers, or their bundles of firewood, up or down the lanes which her terraces overlooked. There was one wrinkled fish-wife who was perfectly delightful: old and worn with a lifetime of toil, she was as cheerful as the day was long; bowed down as she was by her glittering burden, she never failed to stop and wave a hand, and cry "God bless you, pretty lady, and send you safe and happy day!" with the frank warmth of the Italian peasant.

The world was a fine place, after all, and Cyril Grey was the dearest boy in it, and herself the happiest woman.

CHAPTER XXI

OF THE RENEWAL OF THE GREAT ATTACK

AND HOW IT FARED

DOUGLAS had been decidedly put out by the death of his wife. After all, she had been a sort of habit; a useful drudge, when all was said. Besides, he missed, acutely, the pleasures of torturing her. His suspicions of the bona fides of Balloch were conjoined with actual annoyance.

It was at this painful moment in his career that Cremers came to the rescue. A widowed friend of hers had left a daughter in her charge: for Cremers had the great gift of inspiring confidence. This daughter was being educated in a convent in Belgium. The old woman immediately telegraphed for her, and presented her to Douglas with the compliments of the season. Nothing could have been more timely or agreeable. She was a gentle innocent child, as pretty and charming as he had ever seen. It was a great point in the game of the astute Cremers to have pleased the sorcerer; and she began insensibly to gain ascendancy over his spirit. He had at first suspected her of being an emissary of his colleague, "A. B.", who might naturally wish to destroy him. For the plan of the sorcerer who wishes to be sole and supreme is to destroy all rivals, enemies, and companions; while the magician attains supremacy in Unity by constantly uniting himself with others, and finding himself equally in every element of existence. It is the difference between hate and love. He had been careful to examine her magically, and found no trace of "A. B." in her "aura". On the contrary, he concluded that her ambition was to supplant "A. B."; and that went well with his own ideas. But first he must get her into his Fourteen, and have a permanent hold over her.

She, on the other hand, appeared singly desirous of making herself a treasure to him. She knew the one torment that gnawed continually at his liver, the hate of Cyril Grey. And she

proposed to herself to win him wholly by offering that gentleman's scalp. She sharpened her linguistic tomahawk.

One fine day in April she tackled him openly on the subject. "Say, great one, you 'n I gotta have another peek at that sperrit writing. Seems t'me that was a fool's game down there." She jerked her head towards the river. "And I don't say but that you done right about Balloch."

Douglas glanced at her sharply in his most dangerous mood. How much did she know of a certain recent manoeuvre? But she went on quite placidly.

"Now, look 'e here. We gotta get these guys. An' we gotta get them where they live. You been hitting at their strong point. Now I tell you something. That girl she live five years with Lavinia King, durn her! I see that bright daughter of Terpsichore on'y five minutes, but she didn't leave one moral hangin' on me, no, sir. Now see here, big chief, you been bearin' the water for them fish, an', natural, off they goes. For the land's sake! Look 'e here, I gotta look after this business. An' all I need is just one hook an' line, an' a pailful o' bait, an' ef I don' land her, never trus' me no more. Ain't I somebody, all ways? Didn' I down ole Blavatzsky? Sure I did. An' ain't this like earin' pie after that?"

The sorcerer deliberated with himself a while. Then he consulted his familiar demons. The omens were confusing. He thought that perhaps he had put his question ambiguously, and tried again in other words. He had begun by asking vaguely "whether Cremers would succeed in her mission", which had earned him a very positive "yes", flanked by a quite unintelligible message about "deception", "the false Dmitri" and "the wrong horse", also some apparent nonsense about Scotland and an island. This time he asked whether Cremers would succeed in luring Lisa to her destruction. This time the answer was more favourable, though tremulous. But ever since his wife's death, his demons had behaved very strangely. They seemed the prey of hesitation and even of fear. Such as it was, however, their voice now jumped with his own convictions, and he agreed to her proposal.

They spent the evening merrily in torturing a cat by blinding it, and then squirting sulphuric acid on it from a syringe; and in the morning Cremers, with Abdul Bey for bait, set out upon her journey to Naples. Arrived in that favoured spot, she bade Abdul Bey enjoy the scenery, and hold his peace. She would warn him when the hour struck. For Cremers was a highly practical old person. She was not like St. James' devils, who believe and tremble; she disbelieved, but she trembled all the same. She hated Truth, because the Truth sets men free, and therefore makes them happy; but she had too much sense to shut her eyes to it; and though she doubted the causes of magick, and scoffed at all spiritual theory, she could not deny the effects. It was no idle boast of hers that she had destroyed Madame Blavatzsky. Together with another woman, she had wormed her way into the big-hearted Theosophist's confidence, and betrayed her foully at the proper moment. She had tried the same game on another adept; but, when he found her out, and she knew it, he had merely continued his kindnesses. The alternative before her was repentance or brain fever; and she had chosen the latter.

Her disbelief in magick had left her with its correlate, a belief in death. It was the one thing she feared, besides magick itself. But she did not make the mistake of being in a hurry, on that

account. The strength of her character was very great, in its own way; and she possessed infinite reserves of patience. She played the game with no thought of the victory; and this is half the secret of playing most games of importance. To do right for its own sake is Righteousness, though if you apply this obvious truth to Art the Philistine calls you names, and your morals in question.

Cremers was a genuine artist in malice. She was not even glad when she had harmed a friend and benefactor, however irreparably; nothing could ever make her glad – but she was contented with herself on such occasions. She felt a sort of sense of duty done. She denied herself every possible pleasure, she hated happiness in the abstract in a genuinely Puritan spirit, and she objected to eat a good dinner herself as much as to consent that anyone else should eat it. Her principal motive in assisting Abdul Bey to his heart's desire was the cynical confidence that Lisa was capable of pouring him out a hell-broth at least forty per cent above proof.

The summer was well begun. The sun had turned toward the southern hemisphere once more; he had entered the Sign of the Lion, and with fierce and noble heat scarred the dry slopes of Posilippo. Iliel spent most of her time on the Terrace of the Moon at her needlework, watching the ships as they sailed by, or the peasants at their labour or their pastimes.

It was a little before sunset on the first of August. She was leaning over the wall of the Terrace. Sister Clara had gone up to the house to make ready for the adoration of the setting of the sun. Up the uneven flagstones of the lane below toiled the old fishwife with her burden, and looked up with the usual cheery greeting. At that moment the crone slipped and fell. "I'm afraid I've hurt my back," she cried, with an adjuration to some saint. "I can't get up."

Iliel, whether she understood the Italian words fully or no, could not mistake the nature of the accident. She did not hesitate; in a moment she had lowered herself from the wall. She bent down and gave her hand to the old woman.

"Say," said the woman in English, "that boy's just crazy about you; and he's the loveliest man on God's earth. Won't you say one word to him?"

Lisa's jaw dropped in amazement. "What? Who?" she stammered.

"Why, that perfectly sweet Turk, Abdul. Sure, you know him, dearie!" Cremers was watching Lisa's face; she read the answer. She gave a low whistle, and round the corner Abdul Bey came running. He took Lisa in his arms, and rained kisses passionately on her mouth.

She had no thought of resistance. The situation entranced her. The captive princess; the intrigue; the fairy prince; every syllable was a poem.

"I've longed for you every hour for months," she cried, between his kisses; "why, oh why didn't you come for me before?" She had no idea that she was not telling the truth. The past was wiped clean out of her mind by the swirl of the new impulse; and once outside the enchanted circle of the garden, her vow in tatters, there was nothing to remind her.

"I'm – here – now." The words burst, like explosions, from his lips. "Come. I've got a yacht waiting."

"Take me – oh, take me – where you will."

Cremers was on her feet, spry and business-like. "We're best out of here," she said. "Let's beat it!" Taking Lisa's arms, she and Abdul hurried her down the steps which led to the Shore-road.

Brother Onofrio's patrol witnessed the scene. He took no notice; it was not against that contingency that he was armed. But at the summons to the Adoration he reported the event to his superior.

Brother Onofrio received the news in silence, and proceeded to perform the ceremony of the Salutation.

An hour later, as supper ended, the sound of the bell rang through the House. The visitor was Simon Iff.

He found Cyril dressed in everyday clothes, no more in his green robe. The boy was smoking a cigar upon the Terrace where he had read his poem on the day after Walpurgis Night.

He did not rise to greet his master. "Tell the Praetor that you have seen Caius Marius, a fugitive seated upon the ruins of Carthage!" he exclaimed.

"Don't take it so hardly, boy!" cried the old mystic. "The man who makes no mistakes makes nothing. But it is my duty to reprove you, and we had better get it over. Your whole operation was badly conceived; in one way or another it was bound to fail. You select a woman with no moral strength – not even with that code of convention which helps so many weak creatures through their temptations. I foresaw from the first that soon or late she would throw up the Experiment."

"Your words touch me the more deeply because I also foresaw it from the first."

"Yet you went on with it."

"Oh no!" Cyril's eyes were half closed.

"What do you mean – Oh, no!" cried the other sharply. He knew his Cyril like a book.

"I never even began," murmured the boy, dreamily.

"You will be polite to explain yourself."

Simon's lips took a certain grimness of grip upon themselves.

"This telegram has consoled me in my grief," said Cyril, taking with languid grace a slip of paper from his pocket. "It came last week."

Simon Iff turned it towards the light. "Horatii," he read. "A code word, I suppose. But this is dated from Iona, from the Holy House where Himself is!" "Himself" was the word used in the Order to designate its Head.

"Yes," said Cyril, softly, "I was fortunate enough to interest Himself in the Experiment; so Sister Cybele has been there, under the charge of the Mahathera Phang!"

"You young devil!" It was the first time that Simple Simon had been startled in forty years. "So you arranged this little game to draw the enemy's fire?"

"Naturally, the safety of Sister Cybele was the first consideration."

"And 'Horatii'?"

"It's not a code word. I think it must be Roman History."

"Three Boys!"

"Rather a lot, isn't it?"

"They'll be needed," said Simon grimly. "I have been doing magick too."

"Do tell me."

"The Quest of the Golden Fleece, Cyril. I've been sowing the Dragon's Teeth; you remember? Armed men sprang to life, and killed each other."

"But I don't see any armed men."

"You will. Haven't you seen the papers?"

"I never see papers. I'm a poet, and I like my lies the way mother used to make them."

"Well, Europe's at war I have got your old commission back for you, with an appointment as Intelligence Officer on the staff of General Cripps."

"It sounds like Anarchism. From each according to his powers; to each according to his needs, you know. By the way, what's it about? Anything?"

"The people think it's about the violation of solemn treaties, and the rights of the little nations, and so on; the governments think it's about commercial expansion; but I who made it know that it is the baptism of blood of the New Aeon. How could we promulgate the Law of Liberty in a world where Freedom has been strangled by industrialism? Men have become such slaves that they submit to laws which would have made a revolution in any other country since the world began; they have registration cards harder to bear than iron fetters; they allow their tyrants to bar them from every pleasure that even their poverty allows them. There is only one way to turn the counter-jumper into a Curtius and the factory girl into a Cornelia; and I have taken it."

"How did you work it?"

"It has been a long business, But as you know. Sir Edward is a mystic. You saw that article on fishing, I suppose?"

"Oh yes; I knew that. But I didn't know it was more definite."

"It was, he did it. But he'll lose his place; he's too fair-minded; and in a year they'll clamour for fanatics. It's all right; they'll butt each other's brains out; and then the philosophers will come back, and build up a nobler type of civilisation."

"I think you accused me recently of using strong medicine."

"I was practising British hypocrisy on you. I had to see the Prime Minister that week. Excuse me if I answer a humourist according to his humour. I want to show you how necessary this step has been. Observe: the bourgeois is the real criminal, always."

"I'm with you there."

"Look at the testimony of literature. In the days of chivalry our sympathies go with the Knight-errant, who redresses wrongs; with the King, whose courage and wisdom deliver his people from their enemies. But when Kingship became tyranny, and feudalism oppression, we took our heroes from the rebels. Robin Hood, Hereward the Wake, Bonnie Prince Charlie, Rob Roy; it was always the Under Dog that appealed to the artist. Then industrialism became paramount, and we began – in Byron's time – to sympathise with brigands and corsairs. Presently these were wiped out, and today or rather, the day before yesterday, we were reduced to loving absolute scoundrels, Arsène Lupin, Raffles, Stingaree, Fantômas, and a hundred others, or the detectives who (although on the side of society) were equally occupied in making the police look like fools.

That is the whole charm of Père What's-his-name in Gaboriau, and Dupin, and Sherlock Holmes. There has never been a really sympathetic detective in fiction who was on good terms with the police! And you must remember that the artist always represents the subconscious will of the people. The literary hack who panders to the bourgeois, and makes his heroes of millionaires' sons, has never yet created a character, and never will. Well, when the People love a burglar, and hate a judge, there's something wrong with the judges."

"But what are you doing here, in a world crisis?"

"I'm over here to buy Italy. Bowling bought Belgium, you know, some time back. He was thick with Leopold, but the old man had too much sense to deal. He knew he would be the first to go smash when the war came. But Albert pocketed the good red gold without a second thought; that's partly what the trouble is over. Germany found out about it."

"And why buy Italy? To keep Austria busy, I suppose? These Wops can hardly hope to force the line, especially with the Trentino Salient on the flank."

"That's the idea. It would have been better and cheaper to buy Bulgaria. But Grey wouldn't see it. There's the eternal fear of Russia to remember. We're fighting against both sides in the Balkans! And that makes Russia half-hearted, and endangers the whole Entente. But it doesn't matter so long as enough people are killed. The survivors must have elbow-room for their souls, and the memory of heroic deeds in the lives of them and theirs to weigh against the everlasting pull of material welfare. When those men come back from a few years in the trenches, they'll make short work of the pious person that informs them of the wickedness of smoking, and eating meat, and drinking beer, and being out after eleven o'clock at night, and kissing a girl, and reading novels, and playing cards, and going to the theatre, and whistling on the Sabbath!"

"I hope you're right. You're old, which tends, I suppose, to make you optimistic. In my young ears there always rings the scream of terror of the slave when you offer to strike off his fetters."

"All Europe will be scream and stench for years to come. But the new generation will fear neither poverty nor death. They will fear weakness; they will fear dishonour."

"It is a great programme. *Qui vivra verra*. Meanwhile, I suppose I report to General Cripps."

"You will meet him, running hard, I expect, somewhere in France. It will be a fluke if Paris is saved. As you know, it always takes England three years to put her boots on. If we had listened to the men who knew – like 'Bobs' – and fixed up an army of three millions, there could have been no war – at least, not in this particular tangle of alliances. There would have been a Social Revolution, more likely, an ignoble business of greed against greed, which would have left men viler and more enslaved than ever. As it is, the masses on both sides think they are fighting for ideals; only the governments know what hypocrisy and sham it is; so the ideals will win, both in defeat and victory. Man! only three days ago France was the France of Panama, and Dreyfus, and Madame Humbert, and Madame Steinheil, and Madame Caillaux; and today she is already the France of Roland and Henri Quatre and Danton and Napoleon and Gambetta and Joan of Arc!"

"And England of the Boer wars, and the Irish massacres, and the Marconi scandals, and Tran by Croft?"

"Oh, give England time! She'll have to be worse before she's better!"

"Talking of time, I must pack up if I'm to catch the morning train for the Land of Hope and Glory."

"The train service is disorganised. I came from Toulon in a destroyer; she'll take you back there. Jack Manners is in command. Report at Toulon to the O. C.! You'd better start in half-an-hour, I'll see you safe on board. My car's at the door. Here's your commission!"

Cyril Grey thrust the document into his pocket, and the two men went up into the house.

An hour later they were aboard the destroyer; they shook hands in silence. Simon Iff went down the gangway, and Manners gave the word. As they raced northward, they passed under the lee of Abdul's yacht, where Lisa, up to the eyes in champagne, was fondling her new lover.

Her little pig-like eyes sparkled through their rolls of fat; her cheeks, the colour and consistency of ripe Camembert cheese, sagged pendulous upon a many-chinned neck which looked almost goitrous; and the whole surmounted one of those figures dear to engineers, because they afford endless food for speculation as to the means of support. The moon was now exercising her full influence, totally unchecked and unbalanced; and the woman's nature being wholly of the body, with as little brain in proportion as a rhinoceros, the effect was seen mostly on the physical plane. Her mind was a mere swamp of succulent luxury. So she sat there and swayed and wallowed over Abdul Bey. Cremers thought she looked like a snow man just beginning to melt.

With a sardonic grin, the old woman waved her hand, and went on deck. The yacht was now well out in the open sea on her way to Marseilles. Here Cremers was to be landed, so that she might return to Paris to report her success to Douglas, while the lovers went on their honeymoon. The wind blew fresh from the south-west, and Cremers, who was a good sailor, came as near as she ever could to joy as she felt the yacht begin to roll, and pictured the tepid ice-cream heroine of romance in the saloon.

Meanwhile, the destroyer, her nose burrowing into the sea like a ferret slipped into a warren, drove passionately towards Toulon. The keenness and ecstasy of Cyril's face were so intense that Manners rallied him about it.

"I thought you were one of the all-men-are-brothers crowd," he said. "Yet you're as keen as mustard to slay your cousin-German."

"Puns," replied Cyril, "are the torpedo-boat destroyers of the navy wit. Consider yourself crushed. Your matchless intelligence has not misled you as to my views. All men are brothers. As a magician, I embrace, I caress, I slobber over the cheeks of Bloody Bill. But fighting in the army is not a magical ceremony. It is the senseless, idiotic, performance of a numbskull, the act, in a word, of a gentleman; and as, to my lasting shame, I happened to be born in that class, I love to do it. Be reasonable! It's no pleasure to me, as an immortal God, to sneeze; I refuse to render myself a laughing-stock to the other Olympians by such indignity; but when my body has a cold in its head, it is proper for it to blow its nose. I do not approve, much less participate; and my body is therefore the more free to act according to its nature, and it blows its nose much harder than it would if I took a hand. That is the advantage of being a magician; all one's different parts are free to act with the utmost possible vigour according to their own natures, because the other parts do not interfere with them. You don't let your navigators into the stoke-hole, or your stokers into

the chart-house. The first art in adeptship is to get your elements sorted out and specialised and organised and disciplined. Here endeth the first lesson. I think I'll turn in."

"It's a bit beyond me, Cyril. All I know is that I'm willing to risk my life in a good cause."

"But it's a rotten bad cause! We have isolated Germany and hemmed her in for years exactly as we did a century ago with Napoleon; Wilhelm, who wanted peace, because he was getting fat on it, knew us for his real enemy. In 'ninety-nine he came within an ace of uniting Europe against us, at the time of the Fashoda Incident. But we baffled him, and since then he has been getting deeper in every moment. He tried again over the Boer War. He tried threats, he tried diplomacy, he tried everything. The Balkan War and the Agadir Incident showed him his utter helplessness. The kingdom of Albania! The war in Tripoli proved that he could no longer rely on Italy. And when Russia resorted to so shameless an assassination as that of Sarajevo – my dear good man! England has been a pirate as she always was. From Hengist and Horsa, and the Vikings, she first learnt the trick. William the Conqueror was a pirate; so was Francis Drake. Look at Morgan, whom we knighted, and all the other buccaneers! Look at our system of privateering! Ever hear of the 'Alabama'? We learnt the secret of sea-power; we can cut the alimentary canal of any nation in Europe – bar Switzerland and Russia. Hence our fear of Russia! It's the Jolly Roger you should fly, Jack Manners! We stood all Germany's expansion; we said we were her cousins – but when she, started a Navy, that was another barrel of fish!"

"I don't think I can bear this, you know!"

"Cheer up! I'm one of the pirate crew!"

"Oh, you're Captain Kidd!"

"I have already stated my opinion as to the conversational value of puns. I'm going to turn in; you get busy, and find a neutral ship to rob."

"I shall do my best to maintain the law of the sea."

"Made by the pirate to suit his game. Good God! I can't see why we shouldn't be sensible. Why must we invoke Law and Gospel every time we want to do a dirty act? My character's strong enough to let me kill all the Germans I can without persuading myself that I'm saving them from Prussian Tyranny! Goodnight!"

"The youth is unintelligible or immoral," thought Manners, as he turned his face to the spindrift; "but I bet he kills a lot of Germans!"

CHAPTER XXII

OF A CERTAIN DAWN UPON OUR OLD FRIEND THE BOULEVARD ARAGO

AND OF THE LOVES OF LISA LA GIUFFRIA AND ABDUL BEY, HOW THEY PROSPERED. OF THE CONCLUSION OF THE FALSE ALARM OF THE GREAT EXPERIMENT, AND OF A CONFERENCE BETWEEN DOUGLAS AND HIS SUBORDINATES

LORD ANTONY BOWLING was one of three men in the War Office who could speak French perfectly; despite this drawback, he had been selected to confer with the French headquarters in Paris. Here he met Cyril Grey, busy with his tailor. The young magician had once held a captaincy in a Hussar regiment, but a year of India had developed his native love of strange places and peoples. He had been tempted to resign his commission, and yielded. He had gone exploring in Central Asia, and the deadly districts beyond Assam. He could not stand gymkhanas, polo, and flirtation. Simon Iff had given him a hint now and again of what magick might effect if a war came, and the boy had profited. He had formed provisional plans.

He encountered Lord Antony by chance one evening on the Boulevard des Italiens, dined him, and on finding that all amusements, even that of watching the world from the terrace of a

café, were to end by order of the Military Governor of Paris, at eight o'clock, suggested that they should spend the evening smoking opium "*chez Zizi*", a delightful girl who lived with a brilliant young English journalist on the Boulevard M. Marcel. At midnight, serenely confident that God was in his heaven, as asserted by the late Robert Browning, they decided to finish the night at Cyril's studio. Here the young magician "reconstructed the crime" of the jumping balls of the mysterious countess, and recounted the episode of the Thing in the Garden, to the delectation of the "Merman of Mayfair". He then offered to amend Bowling's coat of arms by the introduction of twelve prawns couchant, gules, gartered azure, and the substitution of Poltergeists for the Wild Men of the ducal escutcheon.

Modestly disclaiming these heraldic glories, Lord Antony regaled his host with an ingenious account of a Swedish gentleman who materialised the most voluminous spectres from – as subsequently appeared in circumstances which can only be qualified as dramatic – the contents of a steel cylinder measuring twelve inches in length and three in diameter, which a search of the medium, stripped to the buff, had at first failed to disclose.

But neither was honestly interested in his own remarks; the subconscious excitement of the War made all conversation on any other topic sound miserably artificial. Bowling's story made them both distrait; they fell into a heavy silence, pondering methods of concealing dispatches or detecting spies. Investigation of spiritualism makes a capital training-ground for secret service work; one soon gets up to all the tricks.

Presently Cyril Grey began to preach magick.

"Germany is on a pretty good wicket," he said. "She is at war; we have only taken a holiday to go fighting. The first condition of success in magick is purity of purpose. One must let no other consideration interfere with the business in hand. But we are hypocrites in England; consequently, we compromise and fumble. When a magician does get in charge of an affair, all goes pretty well; look how Simple Simon has isolated Germany! Even there he has been thwarted by the Exchequer; five millions in the right place would have bought the Balkans. How much do you think that little economy will cost us before we're through? As for the foolishness of leaving Turkey doubtful, it's beyond all words!"

"Yes," agreed Bowling "we ought to have supported Abdul Hamid from the first. The best kind of Englishman is blood brother to the best kind of Mussulman. He is brave, just, frank, manly and proud. We should always be in alliance with Islam against the servile Hindus and so-called Christians. Where is the spirit of the Paladins and the Templars and the Knights of the Round Table? The modern Christian is the Bourgeois, whose character is based on fear and falsehood."

"There are two kinds of animals, mainly: one whose defence is obscurity, shunning death, avoidance of danger; the other whose defence is attack."

"Yes; we're all right so long as we make ourselves feared. But Victorian prudery turned our tigers into oxen; we found that it was wrong to fight, dangerous to drink beer, wicked to love; presently it was cruel to eat beef, immoral to laugh, fatal to breathe. We went in terror of the omnipresent germ. Hence we are fat, cowardly slaves. I hear that Kitchener is hard put to it to get

his first 100,000 men. Only the public schools respond. Only gentlemen and sportsmen really love England – the people that have been cursed these last few years as tyrants and libertines.

"Only the men."

"And few there are, in the crowd of canaille, old women, slackers, valetudinarians, eaters of nuts!"

"God rest the soul of Edward Seventh! I thought all would be well when Victoria died; but now –"

"This is no hour of the night to lapse into poetry! Anyhow, Germany is nearly as bad, with her Social Democratic Party."

"Do you think that?" cried Cyril, sharply, sitting up. His gesture was indecipherably intense; it seemed utterly disproportionate to Bowling's casual commonplace.

"I know it. It's one of the chief causes of the war. The Zabern Incident showed the Junkers that they were safe only for a year or two; after that the people would start out to be too proud to fight," replied Lord Antony, anticipating a transpontine chameleon.

"And so?" Cyril's voice trembled. A tense thrill ran through his body. He had become sober in an instant.

"The Court Party wanted war, to bring back the manly spirit to the nation, and incidentally to keep their place in the sun."

The boy sank with a large sigh into his seat. His tone changed to its old supercilious slurring.

"Bloody Bill was afraid for his dynasty?"

"Scared green."

"Don't talk for five minutes, there's a good chap! I've a strange feeling come over me – almost as if I were going to think!"

Lord Antony obliged with silence. The five minutes became twenty. Then Cyril spoke.

"I had better get to Cripps double quick," said he; "I'm his Intelligence Officer, and I think it my duty to inform him of the plans of the German Great General Staff!"

"Yes, you should certainly do that!" answered Lord Antony, laughing.

"Then let's stroll up the Boulevard. Dawn's breaking. We'll get a *café-brioche* at the Rotonde, and then I'll tyrannise my tailor, and get off."

They went out into the cold morning air. Three hundred yards away, outside the Santé prison, a small crowd had collected. The centre of attraction seemed to be a framework, two narrow uprights crowned with a cross-bar where a triangular piece of metal glittered in the pale twilight.

"Peace hath her victories no less renowned than war!" drawled Cyril, cynically. "Confess that I have entertained you royally! Here is a choice savoury to wind up our feast."

Lord Antony could not conceal his horror and repulsion. For he knew well enough what sight chance had prepared for them. But the fascination drew him far more surely than if his temperament had resembled that of his friend. They approached the crowd. A ring was kept about the framework by a cordon of police.

Just then the gates of the prison opened, and a little procession came out. All eyes were drawn instantly to its central figure, an old, old man whose jaw was dropped, and from whose throat

issued a hoarse howling, utterly monotonous and inhuman. His eyes were starting from his head, and their expression was one not to be described. His arms were bound tightly to his sides. Two men were half supporting him, half pushing him. Save for his horrible cry, there was no sound. There was no movement in the crowd – no whisper. Like automata the officials did their duty. In a trice the prisoner was thrown forward on to a board, thrust up toward the framework. His caterwaul suddenly ceased. A moment later a sharp order rang out in the voice of one of the prison officials. The knife fell. From the crowd burst a most dreadful sound an "Ah!" so low, so fierce, that it had no human quality. Lord Antony Bowling could never be sure whether it was after that or before it that he heard the head tumble into the basket.

"Who was it?" asked Cyril of a bystander.

"*Un anglais*," answered the man. "*Le docteur* Balloch."

Cyril started back. He had not recognised his old enemy.

But even at that moment he was accosted by one whom he would never fail to know, even dressed as he was in the uniform of French colonel – Douglas. On his arm was a child whose eyes were blear already with debauchery, who staggered, her eyes rolling, her hair dishevelled, her mouth loose and wet, laughing with indecent and profane intoxication.

"Good morning, Captain Grey; well met, well met indeed!" began Douglas, urbane in his triumph.

"I trust you passed a pleasant time in Naples."

"Very pleasant," returned Grey.

"Dr. Balloch," continued Douglas, "crossed my path. I am glad you should have seen the end of him."

"I am glad," said Cyril.

"And what end do you think I have reserved for you?" said the sorcerer, with a sudden foam of ferocity.

"Something charming, I am sure," said Cyril, silkily. "I always admired your work, you know. That translation of *The Book of the Sacred Magick of Abramelin the Mage*, in particular. You remember the passage about the wicked Antony of Prague," he went on, with sudden force and solemnity, "the marvellous things he did, and how he prospered – and how he was found by the roadside, his tongue torn out, and the dogs at feast upon his bowels! Do you know what has saved you so far? Only one bar between you and destruction – the love of your wife, whom you have murdered!" With that Cyril cried aloud three words in a strange tongue, and giving the other no chance to reply, marched rapidly away with his friend.

Douglas could not have recovered, in any case. He was as one stunned. How did this boy know of the death of his wife? Well, that might be understood; but how did he know his most secret fear, the fact that since the crime his demons had lost their courage? He shook the feeling off, and turned again to gloat over the death of Balloch.

"Who was that?" asked Bowling.

"The Grand Panjandrum himself, with the little round button on top! That's Douglas!"

"The Black Lodge man?"

"Ex-man."

"I see daylight. Balloch was condemned, you know, for a crime done twenty years ago. Douglas must have known about it and betrayed him."

"That's the regular thing."

"How does he come to be a colonel in the French Army?"

"Don't know. He was close in with one or two ministers; Becasseux, I think, in particular. There's a lot of politics in Occultism, as you know."

"I'll think that over. I might ask the minister this morning. But I tell you it's no time for trifles. Ever since all the mobilisation plans were scrapped by the failure of Liège and Namur to hold out, distraction has reigned supreme, no casual mistress, but a wife, and procuress to the Lords of Hell at that!"

"Do not quote Tennyson, even mixed, under the shadow of the Lion de Belfort! As to trifles, there are none in war. Ask the Germans if you don't believe me."

A little later, after the Rotonde Café in the Boulevard Montparnasse had refreshed them with its admirable coffee, and those brioches which remind one of boyhood's earliest kisses, they walked down to the Place de la Concorde, and parted.

Cyril went on to the Opéra, to his tailor in the Rue de la Paix. His mind was full of meditations upon the details of the great idea that had come to him, the divination of the enemy's objective. His suggestion had made Lord Antony laugh. He himself had never felt less like laughing; he was on fire with creative genius – and terrified lest his work should fall upon barren soil. Well he knew how hard it is to get Power to listen to Reason!

At the corner of the Place de l'Opéra he lifted his eyes to assure himself of a free crossing.

The mind of Abdul Bey was in turmoil. His first night upon the yacht had been mere wallowing in debauch; but he woke with a clear head, acutely alive to the complexity of his situation. He was personally triumphant; there was nothing in his private affairs to worry him. But in charge, as he was, of the Turkish Secret Service in Paris, he knew the political situation well enough. He knew that Turkey would throw in her lot with Germany, sooner or later; and he was doubtful as to the wisdom of returning to France. On the other hand, duty called him with clarion voice; and he wanted to have as many fingers as possible in the pie. After much consideration, he thought he would land at Barcelona, and get through with his American passport – for he had papers from most nations – as a distracted millionaire. His companions – both American citizens – would aid the illusion. Supposing that there was already trouble or suspicion, this subterfuge would serve; once in Paris, he could find out how the land lay, and act accordingly.

He gave orders to the captain to make for Catalonia. The voyage was uneventful, save for the brief visit of a cruiser which discovered nothing contraband; in fact, Abdul and Lisa remained drunk the whole time. Only, just off the Spanish coast, a capful of wind once again interfered with Lisa's enjoyment of the honeymoon. It had another consequence, more serious. No sooner had they landed at Barcelona, than Lisa became suddenly and terribly ill. After a week, the doctors decided upon a radical remedy-operation. The next day a girl child entered the world,

very much alive, despite the irregularity of her entrance. No ordinary child, either. She was a beautifully made baby, with deep blue eyes; and she was born with four teeth, and with hair six inches long, so fair as to be silvery white. Like a tattoo-mark, just over the heart, was a faint blue crescent.

Lisa recovered rapidly from her illness, but not too quickly for the amorous Turk; though he was surprised and annoyed to find that she had recovered her early grace and activity. The fat had gone from her in the three weeks of illness; and when she began to be able to move about, and drive in the city, she looked once more almost as she did on the night when Cyril first saw her, a gay, buxom, vigorous woman. The change cooled Abdul's ardour, and her own feelings altered with it. Her lover's sloppiness began to disgust her. As to the child, it was a source of irritation to both of them. Cremers, again, was hardly a boon companion; she would have depressed a hypochondriac going to the funeral of a beloved uncle who had left him nothing. Before Lisa had been out of bed three days, a crisis arose; she felt instinctively that Paris would be "no fun", and wanted to go to America. Abdul felt that he must lose no time in getting to Paris. Cremers, for some reason, had changed her mind about reporting to Douglas; she was homesick for West 186th Street, so she said. The explosion came at lunch, the Spanish nurse having failed to muffle the baby with due adequacy.

"Oh hell!" said Abdul Bey.

"God knows, I don't want the little beast!" said its proud mother.

"Look'e here!" remarked Cremers. "I do want it. Sure some baby!"

"Oh hell!" repeated Abdul Bey.

"Look'e here! You gimme the rocks, an' I'll take her across the pond. There's ships. Gimme three thousand bucks and expenses, and three thousand every year, and I'll fix it. You folks get off and paint Paree pink. Is it a go?"

Abdul Bey brightened immediately. Only one thought chilled him. "What about Douglas?" he said.

'I'll 'tend to that."

"It's a good scheme," muttered Lisa.

"Let's get away tonight; I'm sick of this hole." She caressed the Turk warmly.

But Paris was no longer the Paris of her dreams, no longer the Paris of idleness and luxury "where good Americans go when they die"; it was a Paris of war, of stern discipline, of patriotic enthusiasm, nothing less than a nightmare for the compatriots of the lady who didn't raise her boy to be a soldier. She blamed Abdul, who shrugged his shoulders, and reminded her that she was lucky to get dinner at all, that the Germans were likely to be in the city in a week or so. She taunted him; he let loose his ancestral feelings about women, those which lie deep-buried in all of us who are at least not utterly degenerate in soul, however loose morality may have corrupted us upon the surface. She rose in the automobile, just as they crossed the Place de l'Opéra, and broke her parasol over his head; then turned her nails loose on his eyes. He fisted her in the abdomen, and she collapsed into the seat of the car with a scream. It was this that diverted the attention of Cyril Grey from his contemplation of the designs of Germany.

The boy made a leap, and had Abdul by the throat in a moment, dragging him out of the car, and proceeding to administer summary castigation with his boot. But the police interfered; three men rode up with drawn sabres, and put an end to the affair. They arrested all parties, and Cyril Grey only escaped by the exhibition of that paper which had won him such respect months earlier on the shambles of Moret railway station.

"I have to go to my tailor: service of the minister," he remarked with a cynical smile; and was dismissed with the profoundest respect.

"After all, it was no business of mine," he muttered as he wriggled into his new tunic, to the immense admiration of the tailor, a class whose appreciation of manly beauty depends so largely upon the price of the suit. "'Tis better to have loved and lost than never to have loved at all.' The trouble comes when you can't lose 'em. Poor old Lisa! Poor old Abdul! Well, as I said, it's none of my business. My business is to divine the thoughts of the enemy, and – oh Lord! how long? – to get the powers that be to understand that I am right. Considering that they needed eight million marching men to persuade them that Bloody Bill meant war, I fear that my task may be no sinecure."

He went to the barracks, where a military automobile was waiting for him, and told the chauffeur, with bitter wit, to go out to meet General Cripps. As to Lisa and the Turk, it was twenty-four hours before they were set at liberty. The sight of Cyril, his prompt intervention in her defence, relit the flames of her half crazy passion. She rushed over to the studio to see him; it was shut up, and the concierge could give her no news. She drove wildly to the Profess-House in Montmartre. There they told her that he had gone to join the British army. Various excited enquiries in official quarters led her at last to Lord Antony Bowling. He was genuinely sympathetic: he had liked the girl at first sight; but he could hold out no hopes of arranging for her to see him.

"There's only one way for you to get to the front," said he. "Join the Red Cross. My sister's here forming a section. I'll give you a note to her, if you like."

Lisa jumped at the suggestion. She saw, more vividly than if it were actual, the obvious result. Cyril would be desperately wounded, leading the last victorious charge of the dragoons against the walls of Berlin; she would interestingly nurse him back to life, probably by means of transfusion of blood; then, raised to the peerage, Marshal Earl Grey of Cologne (where he had swum the Rhine, and, tearing the keys of the city from the trembling hands of the astonished burgomaster, had flung them back across the river to his hesitating comrades) would lead her, with the Victoria Cross in gold and diamonds on his manly bosom, to the altar at St. Margaret's, Westminster.

It was worth while learning magick to become clairvoyant like this! She dashed off, still at top speed, to enroll herself with Lady Marcia Bowling.

She gave no further thought to Abdul. He would never have attracted her, had she not perceived a difficulty in getting him.

As to that gentleman himself, if grief tore at his heart strings, he showed it that night in an unusual way. It may have been but simulation of philosophical fortitude; there is no need to

enquire. His actions are of more interest: they consisted of picking up a *cocotte* on the Boulevard des Italiens, and taking her to dinner at the Café de Paris. At the conclusion of a meal which would have certainly been prescribed as a grief-cure to any but a dyspeptic, the *maître d'hôtel* approached their table, and tendered, with a bow, an envelope. Abdul opened it – it was a summons from Douglas to appear immediately in his presence at the apartment in the Faubourg St. Germain.

The Turk had no choice but to comply. He excused himself to his fair guest, at the cost of a hundred-franc note, and drove immediately to the rendezvous.

Douglas received him with extreme heartiness.

"A thousand congratulations, dear young man, upon your brilliant victory! You have succeeded where older and more learned men failed badly. I called you here tonight to tell you that you are now eligible for a place in the Fourteen, the Ghaagaael, for a seat is vacant since this morning."

"They executed Balloch?"

Douglas nodded with a gloating smile.

"But why did you not save him, master?"

"Save him! It was I that destroyed him when he tried to betray me. Candidates take notice!"

Abdul protested his loyalty and devotion.

"The supreme test," continued Douglas, "cannot conveniently be imposed in time of war. There is too much to do just now. But – as a preliminary – how do you stand with Germany?"

Abdul shrank back, startled out of his presence of mind.

"Germany!" he stammered at last. "Why, Colonel," (he emphasised the title) "I know nothing. I have no instructions from my Government." He met the eye of his master, and read its chill contempt. "I – er – er –"

"Dare you play with me?"

The young man protested that no such thought had crossed his mind.

"In that case," pursued the sorcerer, "you won't know what that means."

Douglas took from his pocket a fifty-franc note. The Turk caught it up, his eyes grown momentarily wider with surprise.

"Examine it!" said Douglas, coldly.

The Turkish agent held it to the light. In the figures numbering the note were two small pinpricks.

"Allah!" he cried. "Then you are –"

"I am. You may as well know that my colleague in the Lodge, 'A. B.', is going to stir up trouble for the British in India. Her influence with certain classes of Hindus is very great. For your part, you may try discreetly to tamper with the Mussulman section of the French troops, the Africans. But be careful – there is more important work to your hand, no less than the destruction of the French armies in the field. Now let us see what you can do. I am going to send you to my little garden hermitage, where I occasionally appear in the character of a great ascetic; there is an old lady there, devoted to me. Have your best man there to play Yogi. In the garden – here's

the plan – is the terminal of a wire. There's another in that house where you got baptised and married – remember? Thence there's a cable up Seine to another cottage where that old Belgian mystic lives – the friend of Maeterlinck! Ha! ha! He's really von Walder, a Dresdener. And he is in charge of another cable – underground three hundred miles, thanks to Becasseux, who helped us with the road squads, to a place which by now is firmly in the hands of the Crown Prince. So all you have to do is to tell your man to sit and pretend to meditate – and tap. I shall send you plenty of information from the front. You will know my agents by a nick filed in a trouser-button. Each message will have a number, so that you will know if any go astray. All clear?"

"Admirable. I need not say how proud I am to find that we are on the same side. I was very frightened of that uniform!"

"*L'hobit ne fait pas le moine*," replied Douglas gaily. "And now, sir, let us spend the night discussing our plans in detail – and some very excellent whisky which I happen to have by me."

The spies pursued their double task, with pitiless energy, till morning was well broken. Later in the day Douglas left for Soissons. He was attached to the French army as chief of a corps of signallers – thanks, once again, to the good offices of Becasseux. His plans were perfect: they had been cut and dried for over fifteen years.

CHAPTER XXIII

OF THE ARRIVAL OF A CHINESE GOD UPON THE FIELD OF BATTLE

OF HIS SUCCESS WITH HIS SUPERIORS AND OF A SIGHT WHICH HE SAW UPON THE ROAD TO PARIS. ALSO OF THAT WHICH THEREBY CAME UNTO HIM, AND OF THE END OF ALL THOSE THINGS WHOSE EVENT BEGAT A CERTAIN BEGINNING

UNMATCHED in history is the Retreat of the British Army from Mons. It was caught unprepared; it had to fight three weeks before it was ready; it was outnumbered three to one by a triumphant enemy; it was not co-ordinated with the French armies, and they failed to support it at critical moments; yet it fought that aweful dogged fight from house to house, and field to field, through league on league of Northern France. The line was forced to lengthen constantly as the retreat continued; it was attenuated by that and by its losses to beyond any human breaking-point; but luckily for England, her soldiers are made of such metal that the thinner the wire is drawn the tougher it becomes.

However, there is a point at which "open order" is like the word "decolletée" used to describe a smart American woman's dinner dress; and General Cripps was feeling it at the moment when

his new Intelligence Officer presented himself. It was about six o'clock at night; Cripps and his staff were bivouacked in the *mairie* of a small village. They were contemplating a further retreat that night.

"Sit down, Captain Grey," said the chief kindly. "Join us at dinner – just as soon as we can get these orders out – listen and you'll pick up the outlines – we'll talk after dinner – on the road."

Cyril took a chair. To his delight, an aide-de-camp, Lord Juventius Mellor, an exquisite young dandy with a languid lisp, who, in time of peace, had been pupil and private secretary of Simon Iff, came to greet him.

"Ju, dear boy, help me out. I've got to tell Cripps something, and he'll think I'm mad. It's bluff, too; but it's true for all that – and it's the one chance in the world."

"Right O!"

"Are we retreating again?"

"All through the night. There's not a dog's chance to save Paris, and the line stretches every hour."

"Don't worry about Paris – it's as safe as Bordeaux. Safer, because the Government is at Bordeaux!"

"My poor friend, wouldn't you be better in a home?"

The British Army had no illusions about its situation. It was a thin, drab line of heroes, very thin and very drab, but there was no doubt about the heroism, and no uncertainty about what would happen to it if the Germans possessed a leader with initiative. So far the hostile legions had moved according to the rules, with all due scientific precaution. A leader of temperament and intuition might have rushed that tenuous line. Still, science was as sure as it was as slow – and the whole army knew it. They prepared to die as expensively as possible, with simplicity of manhood. They had not yet heard that Press and Pulpit had made them the laughing-stock of the world by the invention of the ridiculous story of the "Angels of Mons". Lord Juventius Mellor was something of a hero-worshipper. From Simon Iff he would have taken any statement with absolute respect, and Grey's remark had been somewhat of the Simon Iff brand. It was, therefore, almost as much an impertinence as it was an absurdity. Paris was as certain to fall as the sun to set. It was in rotten bad taste to joke about it.

"Look here!" said Cyril, "I'm serious."

"All the worse!" retorted Mellor.

"You really would be better in a home."

"You wouldn't talk like that if we were discussing magick."

"True."

"Then you are an ass. I am talking magick. If you had only ears to hear!"

"How?"

"Everything's a magical phenomenon, in the long run. But war's magick, from the word jump. Come now therefore and let us reason together, saith the Lord. I have done a divination by the Tarot, by a method which I cannot explain, for that it pertaineth to a grade so much more exalted than yours that you have never even heard the name of it; and I know the plans of the

German General Staff in detail." Cyril's tone transformed his asinine utterance into something so Sybilline, Oracular, Delphic, Cumaean, that his interlocutor almost trembled. *Verus incessu patuit Deus* – when Cyril thought it necessary to impress the uninitiate. To the majority of mankind gold looks like dross unless it be wrapped up in tinsel, and tenfold the proper price marked on it in plain figures, with the word "Sacrifice". Hence it is that the most successful merchants omit the gold altogether.

"Oh; I didn't understand."

"You'll observe that I can't explain this to Cripps; I shall have to spin some sort of a yarn."

"Yes, yes."

In point of fact the "yarn" was already spun; Cyril had not been divining by any means more occult than his innate sagacity; but Lord Juventius was one of those people who bow only before the assumption of authority supported by mystery and tomfoolery, since their reason is undeveloped. Such people make excellent secondary figures in any campaign; for their confidence in their leaders impresses the outsider, who does not know how mentally abject they are. It is said that no man is a hero to his valet. On the contrary, every man is a God to his secretary – if not, he had better get rid of the secretary!

Lord Juventius could not have followed Cyril's very astute calculations – those which he meant to lay before General Cripps; but he would have staked his life on the accuracy of a Tarot divination so obscure that he was not allowed even to hear its nature, and which in fact had not been performed. Indeed, it did not even exist, having been invented on the spur of the moment by the unscrupulous magician.

"I shall tell him that the military situation is inextricably bound up with political and dynastic considerations; I shall drop a word about *Anschauung* and *Weltpolitik*; you know!"

Lord Juventius giggled adorably.

"By the way," continued Cyril, "have you any influence – personal, I mean – with the old man?"

Lord Juventius bent forward with lowered eyelids, and sank his voice to a confidential whisper. "The day we crossed," he murmured.

"Great. But I thought –"

"Prehistoric. It's perfectly Cocker."

Such conversations lack the merit of intelligibility to the outsider; but then the outsider is particularly to be kept from understanding. Dialogues of this curious sort determine most important events in English society and "*haute politique*".

"Then see to it that I get taken seriously."

"Surely, Kurille!"

"*Precetur oculis mellitis!*"

"Kurille, Catulle!"

When Englishmen return to the use of the dead languages, it is a sign of that moral state which is said by the Psalmist to resemble the Holy Oil that flowed down upon the head of Aaron, even unto the skirts of his garments.

The orderly called the Staff to dinner. Cyril, as the guest of the evening, was on the Commander-in-Chief's right hand.

"You have been very highly recommended to me," said the old Cavalry leader, when the time came to smoke, "and I look to you to distinguish yourself accordingly. You will be under the orders of Colonel Mavor, of course; you should report to him at once."

"May I give you some information direct?" asked Cyril. "The matter hardly brooks delay, as I see it: you should know it at once, and – to be frank – I think this my best chance of your ever hearing it."

"A damned funny beginning," growled the general. "Well, get on!" The permission was not very gracious; but an irregularity is a serious thing in the British Army. General Cripps made bad worse.

"Unofficially, mind, absolutely unofficially," he added, before Cyril could begin.

This is the English expedient for listening to anything without hearing it, or saying anything without meaning it. An official conversation cannot be thus sterile; it involves notes, memoranda, dockets, recommendations, reports, the appointment of commissions, interminable deliberations, more reports, questions in Parliament, the introduction of bills, and so on. Nothing is done in the end, exactly as in the case of an unofficial conversation; so you can take your choice, sir, and be damned to you!

"Unofficially, of course, General!" agreed Cyril. "My object is merely to disclose the plans of the German General Staff."

"Thank you, Captain Grey," replied the great man, sarcastically; "this will indeed be a service. To save time, begin from Von Kluck's occupation of Paris, about four days hence."

"Impossible, General! Von Kluck will never capture Paris. Why, the man is actually of plebeian origin!"

"After dinner – but only then – such observations are in perfectly good taste. Proceed!"

"I am not joking in the least, General. Von Kluck will not be allowed to try to capture Paris."

"It is at least curious that he is marching straight upon the city!"

"Only to thin out our line, sir. Do you observe that the Germans have driven a salient to St. Mihiel?"

"I have. What of it?"

"The object, sir, I submit, is to cut off Verdun from the South."

"Yes?"

"Why Verdun? Because the Crown Prince is at the head of the army which threatens it. Paris will never be taken but by that modern Caesar!"

"Something in that, I admit. The little beast is certainly unpopular."

"They are bound to make him the national hero, at any cost."

"And where do we come in?"

"What could be clearer? Their right wing will break through somewhere, or roll us up. Verdun will be isolated. *Der Kronprinz* (God bless his noble heart!) will walk through, and goose-step all the way to Paris. It is the only chance for the Hohenzollern dynasty."

"It is military madness."

"They think they have enough in hand to risk it. But see, sir, for God's sake see the conclusion! If I'm right, Von Kluck is bound to swerve East, right across our front – and we'll smash him!"

"He couldn't risk such a crazy manoeuvre."

"Mark my word, sir, he will."

"And what do you suggest that I should do about it? Unofficially, Captain Grey, quite unofficially!"

"Get ready to lam it in, sir – quite unofficially."

"Well, sir, I congratulate you – on having talked the most amusing nonsense that I've heard since my last talk with General Buller! And now perhaps you had better report to Colonel Mavor as Intelligence Officer." The general's tone was contemptuous. "Facts are required in this army."

"Psychological facts are facts, General."

"Nonsense, sir; you are not in a debating society or at a scientific tea-party."

"That last, sir," replied Cyril coldly, "is my unavailing regret."

But Lord Juventius Mellor frustrated the effect of this impolitic speech. He fixed his languid eyes upon the red face of the veteran, and his voice came in a soft caressing whisper.

"Pardon me; do let us be unofficial for five minutes more!"

"Well, boy?"

"I think it's only fair to let General Foch enjoy the joke. I hear he has been depressed lately."

"He might not take it so easily. The French do not care to be played with when their country is at stake."

"He can only shoot poor Cyril, *mon vieux*! Just give him two days leave, so that he can run over before reporting to Mavor."

"Oh well, I dare say the Intelligence Department can get on without its champion guesser for a day or so. Trot along, Grey; but for your own sake I advise you to think up a fact or two."

Cyril saluted, and took his leave. Juventius came to see him into the car. "I'll wheedle the old ass," he whispered to his friend, "I'll get him to make such dispositions as he can without disturbing the line too much; so that if Foch should see any sense in your scheme, by any chance, we shan't be too backward in coming forward."

"Good for you. So long!"

"Ta."

Cyril drove off. It was a terrible and ominous journey to the headquarters of General Foch. The line sagged hideously here and there so that long detours were necessary. The roads were encumbered not only with every kind of military supply, all in disorder, but with fugitive soldiers and civilians, some burdened with their household goods, some wounded, a long trail of agony lumbering to the rear. The country was already patrolled by herds of masterless and savage dogs, reverted, in a month of war, to the type of the coyote and the dingo. But Cyril shouted in his joy. His confidence rose as he went; he had thought out one of General Cripps's "facts" which he felt sure would carry conviction to the mind of the French commander.

Arrived at the chateau where the general was quartered, he found no trouble in gaining

audience. The Frenchman, splendidly built, his eyes glittering with restless intelligence, concentrated all his faculties instantly on his visitor. "You have come from General Cripps?"

"Yes, my General, but on my own responsibility. I have an idea –"

Foch interrupted him.

"But you are in an English uniform!" he could not help saying with brisk Gallic surprise.

"*Cuchullus non facit monachum*," retorted Cyril Grey. "I am half-Scotch, half-Irish."

"Then pray give yourself the trouble to continue."

"I may premise that I have told my idea to General Cripps. It convinced him that I am an imbecile or a joker."

That was his "fact", his master-argument. It told heavily. The face of Foch grew instantly keen and eager with all expectation.

"Let me hear it!"

The General reached for a memorandum.

Grey laughed. In a few words he repeated his theory of the German plans. "But it is certain!" cried Foch. "One moment; excuse me; I must telephone."

He left the room. In five minutes he was back.

"Rest easy, Captain Grey," he said, "we shall be ready to catch Von Kluck as he turns. Now, will you do me the pleasure to take this note back to your chief? The British must be ready to strike at the same moment. I won't ask you to stay; but – I beg of you to come to dine with me after the victory."

It is impossible to give any idea of how the word "*victoire*" sounds in the mouth of a French soldier. It has in it the ring of a sword thrust home to the hilt, and the cry of a lover as he seizes his mistress, and the exultation of a martyr who in the moment of his murder reaches conclusively to God. Cyril went back to the British Headquarters, and handed in General Foch's request, through Colonel Mavor, officially. The events of the next week are of the very spine of history. The cruel blow was definitely parried. More still, that first great victory not only saved France for all time, but showed that the men of Bonaparte had come into their own moral sublimity again. It proved 1870 to have been but a transient weakness like our own year of shame when Van Tromp swept our ships from the seas.

General Cripps summoned Cyril Grey to his quarters.

"I'm afraid," said the old man, "that nothing can be done to recognise your services. That your crazy theory should have proved correct is only one more example – we have many such every day – of the operation of the laws of Chance. The weather forecasters themselves cannot guess wrong every time. But even if your act had merited reward, we should still have been powerless; for, as you remember, our conversation was strictly unofficial.

"Unofficially, however, you get your step and the K. C. B. Favouritism, sir, rank favouritism! Now go across to General Foch, Major – he wishes to present you to two gentlemen named respectively Joffre and Poincaré. Boot and saddle! No time to waste," he said hastily, to check any expression of gratitude. But as the two men gripped hands, their eyes were dim – they were thinking of England.

So off went Cyril on the road to Paris, where his rendezvous was fixed.

The victory had changed the aspect of the country in the rear of the armies as by stage-craft. There were no more fugitives, no more disorder. Still the long trains of wounded clogged the roads, here and there, but the infection of glory had spread like sunlight over a sky swept clear of storm. The supply trains radiated confidence. Always the young man met new guns, new wagons, new horses. At every turn of the road were fresh regiments, gaily singing on their way to the front. Cyril was enchanted at the aspect of the troops. Their elasticity and high spirits were overwhelming. Once he came upon a regiment of Turcos being transferred to another sector – every man of them with a trophy of the great battle. His intense love for all savage men, true men unspoilt by civilisation, almost mastered him: he wanted to embrace them. He saw life assurgent, the menace of the enemy thwarted, and his joy flooded his heart so that his throat caught fire, and song leaped to his lips.

And then chill caught him as he came suddenly upon a dreadful sight.

Before him on the road stood a signpost, the lance of a Spahi, thrust into the bank of a ditch; nailed to it was a placard on which was coarsely chalked the one word ESPION. A fatal curiosity drew him to the spot; as he approached, the wild dogs that were fighting around the sinister signal fled in terror from their ghastly meal.

A sword had been thrust through the belly of the corpse; the tongue had been torn out. One could recognise at a glance the work of Algerian troops – men who had lost a third of their effectives through the treacheries of the German spies. But, despite all mutilation, he recognised more than that: he recognised the carcass. This carrion had once been Douglas.

Cyril Grey did a strange thing, a thing he had not done for many years: he broke into a strong sobbing.

"I know now," he murmured, "that Simon Iff is right. The Way of the Tao! I must follow that harder path, the Path where he who would advance draws back."

He put spurs to his horse; half-an-hour later he saw the sunset glint upon the Eiffel Tower, and on the wings of one of those gallant birds that circled about it to keep watch and ward on Paris. The next morning he reported himself to the British authorities; and it was Lord Antony Bowling who presented him to the President and Commander-in-Chief.

At the banquet he found himself an Officer of the Legion of Honour; but his brilliancy and buoyancy were gone. He dined in dull decorum. His thoughts still turned to the shameful corpse in the ditch by the wayside. He excused himself early, and left the Élysée. At the gate stood an automobile. In it sat Lisa la Giuffria. She jumped out and caught him by the shoulders. She poured out the tale of her madness, and its result, and its cure, her careful tracking of his movements, her determination to recover him at any cost. He listened in silence – the silence of incurable sadness. He shook his head.

"Have you no word for me?" she cried impetuously, torn by her agony.

"Have you no gift for me?" he answered. She understood. "Oh, you are human! you are human!" she cried.

"I do not know what I am," he answered. "Yesterday I saw the end of the game – for one!"

He told her in a few words of the horror on the roadside.

"Go!" he said, "take that girl, Douglas's last victim, for your maid. Go to America; find the Child of the Moon. There may, or there may not be, other tasks for us to do; I know not – time will show."

"I will, I will," she cried, "I will go now, quickly. Kiss me first!"

Once again the tears gathered in the magician's eyes; he understood, more deeply than he had ever done, the Sorrow of the Universe. He saw how utterly incompatible are all our human ideals with the Laws of Life. He took her slowly and gently in his arms; and he kissed her. But Lisa did not respond; she understood that this was not the man whom she had loved: this was a man that she had never known, one whom she dared not love. A man set apart, an idea to adore! She knew herself unworthy, and she withdrew herself.

"I go," she said, "to seek the Child. Hail and farewell!"

"Hail and farewell!" The girl mounted unsteadily into her car. Cyril Grey, his head bowed upon his breast, plunged into the wooded pleasaunce of the Champs Élysées.

An ineffable weariness came upon him as he walked. He wondered dully if he were going to be ill. He came up against the Obelisk in the Place de la Concorde with a shock of surprise. He had not noticed that he had left the trees. The Obelisk decided him; its shape smote into his soul the meaning of the Mysteries of Egyptian Magick. It was as invigorating as a cold plunge. He strode away towards Montmartre.

The Profess-House of the Order had been converted into a hospital. But who should come to greet him if not Sister Cybele?

Beside her stood the severe figure of Simon Iff. There were two others in the background. Cyril was not surprised to see his old master, the Mahathera Phang; but the other? It was Abdul Bey.

"Come forward and shake hands," cried Simon Iff. "I have not been inactive, Cyril," added the old man. "I have had my eye on our young friend for a long time. I put my hand on him at the right moment. I showed him that spying was a dog's game, with a dog's death at the end of it. He has renounced his errors, and he is now a Probationer of our Holy Order."

The young men greeted each other, the Turk stammering out an appeal for pardon, the other laughing off his embarrassment.

"But you are ill, Cyril!" cried Sister Cybele. And in truth the boy could hardly stand.

"Action and reaction are equal and opposite," explained Simon Iff, cheerily. "You will sleep, Brother Cyril, and you will then pass seven days in meditation, in one of the high trances. I will see to the extension of your leave."

"There is a meditation," said Cyril firmly, "given by the Buddha, a meditation upon a corpse torn by wild beasts. I will take that."

Simon Iff acquiesced without comprehending. He did not know that Cyril Grey had understood that the corpse of Douglas was his own; that the perception of the identity of himself with all other living things had come to him, and raised him to a great Adeptship.

MOONCHILD

But there was one to comprehend the nature of that initiation. As Cyril walked, leaning on the arm of Sister Cybele, to the room appointed for his prescribed solitude, he beheld a great light. It shone serenely from the eyes of the Mahathera Phang.

THE BOOK
OF
THE LAW

AL
(LIBER LEGIS) THE BOOK OF THE LAW
SUB FIGURA XXXI
AS DELIVERED BY
93 – AIWASS – 418
TO
ANKHOFON-KHONSU
THE PRIEST OF THE PRINCES
WHO IS
666

THE BOOK OF THE LAW

INTRODUCTION

I THE BOOK

1. This book was dictated in Cairo between noon and 1 p.m. on three successive days, April 8th, 9th and 10th in the year 1904.

The Author called himself Aiwass, and claimed to be "the minister of Hoor-Paar-Kraat"; that is, a messenger from the forces ruling this earth at present, as will be explained later on.

How could he prove that he was, in fact, a being of a kind superior to any of the human race, and so entitled to speak with authority? Evidently he must show KNOWLEDGE and POWER such as no man has ever been known to possess.

2. He showed his KNOWLEDGE chiefly by the use of cipher or cryptogram in certain passages to set forth recondite facts, including some events which had yet to take place, such that no human being could possibly be aware of them; thus, the proof of his claim exists in the manuscript itself. It is independent of any human witness.

The study of these passages necessarily demands supreme human scholarship to interpret – it needs years of intense application. A great deal has still to be worked out. But enough has been discovered to justify his claim; the most sceptical intelligence is compelled to admit its truth.

This matter is best studied under the Master Therion, whose years of arduous research have led him to enlightenment.

On the other hand, the language of most of the Book is admirably simple, clear and vigorous. No one can read it without being stricken in the very core of his being.

3. The more than human POWER of Aiwass is shewn by the influence of his Master, and of the Book, upon actual events; and history fully supports the claim made by him. These facts are appreciable by everyone; but are better understood with the help of the Master Therion.

4. The full detailed account of the events leading up to the dictation of this Book, with facsimile reproduction of the Manuscript and an essay by the Master Therion, is published in *The Equinox of the Gods*.

II THE UNIVERSE

This Book explains the Universe.

The elements are Nuit, Space – that is, the total of possibilities of every kind – and Hadit, any point which has experience of these possibilities. (This idea is for literary convenience symbolised by the Egyptian Goddess Nuit, a woman bending over like the Arch of the Night Sky. Hadit is symbolised as a Winged Globe at the heart of Nuit.)

Every event is a uniting of some one monad with one of the experiences possible to it.

"Every man and every woman is a star", that is, an aggregate of such experiences, constantly changing with each fresh event, which affects him or her either consciously or subconsciously.

Each one of us has thus an universe of his own, but it is the same universe for each one as soon as it includes all possible experience. This implies the extension of consciousness to include all other consciousness.

In our present stage, the object that you see is never the same as the one that I see; we infer that it is the same because your experience tallies with mine on so many points that the actual differences of our observation are negligible. For instance, if a friend is walking between us, you see only his left side, I his right; but we agree that it is the same man, although we may differ not only as to what we may see of his body but as to what we know of his qualities. This conviction of identity grows stronger as we see him more often and get to know him better. Yet all the time, neither of us can know anything of him at all beyond the total impression made on our respective minds.

The above is an extremely crude attempt to explain a system which reconciles all existing schools of philosophy.

III THE LAW OF THELEMA*

This Book lays down a simple Code of Conduct.

"Do what thou wilt shall be the whole of the Law".

"Love is the law, love under will".

"There is no law beyond Do what thou wilt".

This means that each of us stars is to move on our true orbit, as marked out by the nature of our position, the law of our growth, the impulse of our past experiences. All events are equally lawful – and every one necessary, in the long run – for all of us, in theory; but in practice, only one act is lawful for each one of us at any given moment. Therefore Duty consists in determining to experience the right event from one moment of consciousness to another.

Each action or motion is an act of love, the uniting with one or another part of "Nuit"; each such act must be "under will", chosen so as to fulfil and not to thwart the true nature of the being concerned.

The technical methods of achieving this are to be studied in Magick, or acquired by personal instruction from the Master Therion and his appointed assistants.

Thelema is the Greek for Will, and has the same numerical value as *Agape*, the Greek for Love.

IV THE NEW AEON

The third chapter of the Book is difficult to understand, and may be very repugnant to many people born before the date of the book (April, 1904).

It tells us the characteristics of the Period on which we are now entered. Superficially, they appear appalling. We see some of them already with terrifying clarity. But fear not!

It explains that certain vast "stars" (or aggregates of experience) may be described as Gods. One of these is in charge of the destinies of this planet for periods of 2,000 years.* In the history of the world, as far as we know accurately, are three such Gods: Isis, the mother, when the Universe was conceived as simple nourishment drawn directly from her; this period is marked by matriarchal government.

Next, beginning 500 B.C., Osiris, the father, when the Universe was imagined as catastrophic, love, death, resurrection, as the method by which experience was built up; this corresponds to patriarchal systems.

Now, Horus, the child, in which we come to perceive events as a continual growth partaking in its elements of both these methods, and not to be overcome by circumstance. This present period involves the recognition of the individual as the unit of society.

We realise ourselves as explained in the first paragraphs of this essay. Every event, including death, is only one more accretion to our experience, freely willed by ourselves from the beginning and therefore also predestined.

This "God", Horus, has a technical tide: Heru-Ra-Ha, a combination of twin gods, Ra-Hoor-Khuit and Hoor-Paar-Kraat. The meaning of this doctrine must be studied in Magick. (He is symbolised as a Hawk-Headed God enthroned.)

He rules the present period of 2,000 years, beginning in 1904. Everywhere his government is taking root. Observe for yourselves the decay of the sense of sin, the growth of innocence and irresponsibility, the strange modifications of the reproductive instinct with a tendency to become bisexual or epicene, the childlike confidence in progress combined with nightmare fear of catastrophe, against which we are yet half unwilling to take precautions.

Consider the outcrop of dictatorships, only possible when moral growth is in its earliest stages, and the prevalence of infantile cults like Communism, Fascism, Pacifism, Health Crazes, Occultism in nearly all its forms, religions sentimentalised to the point of practical extinction.

Consider the popularity of the cinema, the wireless, the football pools and guessing competitions – all devices for soothing fractious infants, no seed of purpose in them.

Consider sport, the babyish enthusiasms and rages which it excites, whole nations disturbed by disputes between boys.

Consider war, the atrocities which occur daily and leave us unmoved and hardly worried. We are children.

How this new Aeon of Horus will develop, how the Child will grow up, these are for us to determine, growing up ourselves in the way of the Law of Thelema under the enlightened guidance of the Master Therion.

* The moment of change from one period to another is technically called The Equinox of the Gods.

V THE NEXT STEP

Democracy dodders.

Ferocious Fascism, cackling Communism, equally frauds, cavort crazily all over the globe. They are hemming us in.

They are abortive births of the Child, the New Aeon of Horus.

Liberty stirs once more in the womb of Time.

Evolution makes its changes by anti-Socialistic ways. The "abnormal" man, who foresees the trend of the times and adapts circumstance intelligently, is laughed at, persecuted, often destroyed by the herd; but he and his heirs, when the crisis comes, are survivors.

Above us today hangs a danger never yet paralleled in history. We suppress the individual in more and more ways. We think in terms of the herd. War no longer kills soldiers; it kills all indiscriminately. Every new measure of the most democratic and autocratic govenments is Communistic in essence. It is always restriction. We are all treated as imbecile children. DORA, the Shops Act, the Motoring Laws, Sunday suffocation, the Censorship – they won't trust us to cross the roads at will.

Fascism is like Communism, and dishonest into the bargain. The dictators suppress all art, literature, theatre, music, news, that does not meet their requirements; yet the world only moves by the light of genius. The herd will be destroyed in mass.

The establishment of the Law of Thelema is the only way to preserve individual liberty and to assure the future of the race.

In the words of the famous paradox of the Comte de Fénix: "The absolute rule of the state shall be a function of the absolute liberty of each individual will".

All men and women are invited to cooperate with the Master Therion in this, the Great Work. O. M.

THE BOOK OF THE LAW

THE COMMENT

Do what thou wilt shall be the whole of the Law

The study of this Book is forbidden. It is wise to destroy it after the first reading.

Whosoever disregards this does so at their own peril and risk. These are most dire.

Those who discuss the contents of this Book are to be shunned by all, as centres of pestilence.

All questions of the Law are to be decided only by appeal to my writings, each for himself.

There is no law beyond Do what thou wilt.

Love is the law, love under will.

The priest of the princes
Ankh-F-N-Khonsu

CHAPTER I

1. Had! The manifestation of Nuit.

2. The unveiling of the company of heaven.

3. Every man and every woman is a star.

4. Every number is infinite; there is no difference.

5. Help me, O warrior lord of Thebes, in my unveiling before the Children of men!

6. Be thou Hadit, my secret centre, my heart & my tongue!

7. Behold! it is revealed by Aiwass the minister of Hoor-paar-kraat.

8. The Khabs is in the Khu, not the Khu in the Khabs.

9. Worship then the Khabs, and behold my light shed over you!

10. Let my servants be few & secret: they shall rule the many & the known.

11. These are fools that men adore; both their Gods & their men are fools.

12. Come forth, O children, under the stars, & take your fill of love!

13. 1 am above you and in you. My ecstasy is in yours. My joy is to see your joy.

14. Above, the gemmed azure is
    The naked splendour of Nuit;
    She bends in ecstasy to kiss
    The secret ardours of Hadit.
    The winged globe, the starry blue,
    Are mine, O Ankh-af-na-khonsu!

15. Now ye shall know that the chosen priest & apostle of infinite space is the prince-priest the Beast; and in his woman, called the Scarlet Woman, is all power given. They shall gather my children into their fold: they shall bring the glory of the stars into the hearts of men.

16. For he is ever a sun, and she a moon. But to him is the winged secret flame, and to her the stooping starlight.

17. But ye are not so chosen.

18. Burn upon their brows, O splendrous serpent!

19. O azure-lidded woman, bend upon them!

20. The key of the rituals is in the secret word which I have given unto him.

21. With the God & the Adorer I am nothing: they do not see me. They are as upon the earth; I am Heaven, and there is no other God than me, and my lord Hadit.

22. Now, therefore, I am known to ye by my name Nuit, and to him by a secret name which I will give him when at last he knoweth me. Since I am Infinite Space, and the Infinite Stars thereof, do ye also thus. Bind nothing! Let there be no difference made among you between any one thing & any other thing; for thereby there cometh hurt.

23. But whoso availeth in this, let him be the chief of all!

24. 1 am Nuit, and my word is six and fifty.

25. Divide, add, multiply, and understand.

26. Then saith the prophet and slave of the beauteous one: Who am I, and what shall be the sign? So she answered him, bending down, a lambent flame of blue, all-touching, all penetrant, her lovely hands upon the black earth, & her lithe body arched for love, and her soft feet not hurting the little flowers: Thou knowest! And the sign shall be my ecstasy, the consciousness of the continuity of existence, the omnipresence of my body.

27. Then the priest answered & said unto the Queen of Space, kissing her lovely brows, and the dew of her light bathing his whole body in a sweet-smelling perfume of sweat: O Nuit, continuous one of Heaven, let it be ever thus; that men speak not of Thee as One but as None; and let them speak not of thee at all, since thou art continuous!

28. None, breathed the light, faint & faery, of the stars, and two.

29. For I am divided for love's sake, for the chance of union.

30. This is the creation of the world, that the pain of division is as nothing, and the joy of dissolution all.

31. For these fools of men and their woes care not thou at all! They feel little; what is, is balanced by weak joys; but ye are my chosen ones.

32. Obey my prophet! follow out the ordeals of my knowledge! seek me only! Then the joys of my love will redeem ye from all pain. This is so: I swear it by the vault of my body; by my sacred heart and tongue; by all I can give, by all I desire of ye all.

33. Then the priest fell into a deep trance or swoon, & said unto the Queen of Heaven; Write unto us the ordeals; write unto us the rituals; write unto us the law!

34. But she said: the ordeals I write not: the rituals shall be half known and half concealed: the Law is for all.

35. This that thou writest is the threefold book of Law.

36. My scribe Ankh-af-na-khonsu, the priest of the princes, shall not in one letter change this book; but lest there be folly, he shall comment thereupon by the wisdom of Ra-Hoor-Khuit.

37. Also the mantras and spells; the obeah and the wanga; the work of the wand and the work of the sword; these he shall learn and teach.

38. He must teach; but he may make severe the ordeals.

39. The word of the Law is THELEMA.

40. Who calls us Thelemites will do no wrong, if he look but close into the word. For there are therein Three Grades, the Hermit, and the Lover, and the man of Earth. Do what thou wilt shall be the whole of the Law.

41. The word of Sin is Restriction. O man! refuse not thy wife, if she will! O lover, if thou wilt, depart! There is no bond that can unite the divided but love: all else is a curse. Accursed! Accursed be it to the aeons! Hell.

42. Let it be that state of manyhood bound and loathing. So with thy all; thou hast no right but to do thy will.

43. Do that, and no other shall say nay.

44. For pure will, unassuaged of purpose, delivered from the lust of result, is every way perfect.

45. The Perfect and the Perfect are one Perfect and not two; nay, are none!

46. Nothing is a secret key of this law. Sixty-one the Jews call it; I call it eight, eighty, four hundred & eighteen.

47. But they have the half: unite by thine art so that all disappear.

48. My prophet is a fool with his one, one, one; are not they the Ox, and none by the Book?

49. Abrogate are all rituals, all ordeals, all words and signs. Ra-Hoor-Khuit hath taken his seat in the East at the Equinox of the Gods; and let Asar be with Isa, who also are one. But they are not of me. Let Asar be the adorant, Isa the sufferer; Hoor in his secret name and splendour is the Lord initiating.

50. There is a word to say about the Hierophantic task. Behold! there are three ordeals in one, and it may be given in three ways. The gross must pass through fire; let the fine be tried in intellect, and the lofty chosen ones in the highest. Thus ye have star & star, system & system; let not one know well the other!

51. There are four gates to one palace; the floor of that palace is of silver and gold; lapis lazuli & jasper are there; and all rare scents; jasmine & rose, and the emblems of death. Let him enter in turn or at once the four gates; let him stand on the floor of the palace. Will he not sink? Amn. Ho! warrior, if thy servant sink? But there are means and means. Be goodly therefore: dress ye all in fine apparel; eat rich foods and drink sweet wines and wines that foam! Also, take your fill and will of love as ye will, when, where and with whom ye will! But always unto me.

52. If this be not aright; if ye confound the space-marks, saying: They are one; or saying, They are many; if the ritual be not ever unto me: then expect the direful judgments of Ra-Hoor-Khuit!

53. This shall regenerate the world, the little world my sister, my heart & my tongue, unto whom I send this kiss. Also, O scribe and prophet, though thou be of the princes, it shall not assuage thee nor absolve thee. But ecstasy be thine and joy of earth: ever To me! To me!

54. Change not as much as the style of a letter; for behold! thou, O prophet, shalt not behold all these mysteries hidden therein.

55. The child of thy bowels, he shall behold them.

56. Expect him not from the East, nor from the West; for from no expected house cometh that child. Aum! All words are sacred and all prophets true; save only that they understand a little; solve the first half of the equation, leave the second unattacked. But thou hast all in the clear light, and some, though not all, in the dark.

57. Invoke me under my stars! Love is the law, love under will. Nor let the fools mistake love; for there are love and love. There is the dove, and there is the serpent. Choose ye well! He, my prophet, hath chosen, knowing the law of the fortress, and the great mystery of the House of God.

All these old letters of my Book are aright; but [Tzaddi] is not the Star. This also is secret: my prophet shall reveal it to the wise.

58. I give unimaginable joys on earth: certainty, not faith, while in life, upon death; peace unutterable, rest, ecstasy; nor do I demand aught in sacrifice.

59. My incense is of resinous woods & gums; and there is no blood therein: because of my hair the trees of Eternity.

60. My number is 11, as all their numbers who are of us. The Five Pointed Star, with a Circle in the Middle, & the circle is Red. My colour is black to the blind, but the blue & gold are seen of the seeing. Also I have a secret glory for them that love me.

61. But to love me is better than all things: if under the night stars in the desert thou presently burnest mine incense before me, invoking me with a pure heart, and the Serpent flame therein, thou shalt come a little to lie in my bosom. For one kiss wilt thou then be willing to give all; but whoso gives one particle of dust shall lose all in that hour. Ye shall gather goods and store of women and spices; ye shall wear rich jewels; ye shall exceed the nations of the earth in splendour & pride; but always in the love of me, and so shall ye come to my joy. I charge you earnestly to come before me in a single robe, and covered with a rich headdress. I love you! I yearn to you! Pale or purple, veiled or voluptuous, I who am all pleasure and purple, and drunkenness of the innermost sense, desire you. Put on the wings, and arouse the coiled splendour within you: come unto me!

62. At all my meetings with you shall the priestess say – and her eyes shall burn with desire as she stands bare and rejoicing in my secret temple – To me! To me! calling forth the flame of the hearts of all in her love-chant.

63. Sing the rapturous love-song unto me! Burn to me perfumes! Wear to me jewels! Drink to me, for I love you! I love you!

64. I am the blue-lidded daughter of Sunset; I am the naked brilliance of the voluptuous night-sky.

65. To me! To me!

66. The Manifestation of Nuit is at an end.

CHAPTER II

1. Nu! the hiding of Hadit.

2. Come! all ye, and learn the secret that hath not yet been revealed. I, Hadit, am the complement of Nu, my bride. I am not extended, and Khabs is the name of my House.

3. In the sphere I am everywhere the centre, as she, the circumference, is nowhere found.

4. Yet she shall be known & I never.

5. Behold! the rituals of the old time are black. Let the evil ones be cast away; let the good ones be purged by the prophet! Then shall this Knowledge go aright.

6. I am the flame that burns in every heart of man, and in the core of every star. I am Life, and the giver of Life, yet therefore is the knowledge of me the knowledge of death.

7. I am the Magician and the Exorcist. I am the axle of the wheel, and the cube in the circle. "Come unto me" is a foolish word: for it is I that go.

8. Who worshipped Heru-pa-kraath have worshipped me; ill, for I am the worshipper.

9. Remember all ye that existence is pure joy; that all the sorrows are but as shadows; they pass & are done; but there is that which remains.

10. O prophet! thou hast ill will to learn this writing.

11. I see thee hate the hand & the pen; but I am stronger.

12. Because of me in Thee which thou knewest not.

13. For why? Because thou wast the knower, and me.

14. Now let there be a veiling of this shrine: now let the light devour men and eat them up with blindness!

15. For I am perfect, being Not; and my number is nine by the fools; but with the just I am eight, and one in eight: Which is vital, for I am none indeed. The Empress and the King are not of me; for there is a further secret.

16. I am The Empress & the Hierophant. Thus eleven, as my bride is eleven.

17. Hear me, ye people of sighing!
   The sorrows of pain and regret
   Are left to the dead and the dying,
   The folk that not know me as yet.

18. These are dead, these fellows; they feel not. We are not for the poor and sad: the lords of the earth are our kinsfolk.

19. Is a God to live in a dog? No! but the highest are of us. They shall rejoice, our chosen: who sorroweth is not of us.

20. Beauty and strength, leaping laughter and delicious languor, force and fire, are of us.

21. We have nothing with the outcast and the unfit: let them die in their misery. For they feel not. Compassion is the vice of kings: stamp down the wretched & the weak: this is the law of the strong: this is our law and the joy of the world. Think not, O king, upon that lie: That Thou Must Die: verily thou shalt not die, but live. Now let it be understood: If the body of the King dissolve, he shall remain in pure ecstasy for ever. Nuit! Hadit! Ra-Hoor-Khuit! The Sun, Strength & Sight, Light; these are for the servants of the Star & the Snake.

22. I am the Snake that giveth Knowledge & Delight and bright glory, and stir the hearts of men with drunkenness. To worship me take wine and strange drugs whereof I will tell my prophet, & be drunk thereof! They shall not harm ye at all. It is a lie, this folly against self. The exposure of innocence is a lie. Be strong, O man! lust, enjoy all things of sense and rapture: fear not that any God shall deny thee for this.

23. I am alone: there is no God where I am.

24. Behold! these be grave mysteries; for there are also of my friends who be hermits. Now think not to find them in the forest or on the mountain; but in beds of purple, caressed by magnificent beasts of women with large limbs, and fire and light in their eyes, and masses of flaming hair about them; there shall ye find them. Ye shall see them at rule, at victorious armies, at all the joy; and there shall be in them a joy a million times greater than this. Beware lest any force another, King against King! Love one another with burning hearts; on the low men trample in the fierce lust of your pride, in the day of your wrath.

25. Ye are against the people, O my chosen!

26. I am the secret Serpent coiled about to spring: in my coiling there is joy. If I lift up my head, I and my Nuit are one. If I droop down mine head, and shoot forth venom, then is rapture of the earth, and I and the earth are one.

27. There is great danger in me; for who doth not understand these runes shall make a great miss. He shall fall down into the pit called Because, and there he shall perish with the dogs of Reason.

28. Now a curse upon Because and his kin!

29. May Because be accursed for ever!

30. If Will stops and cries Why, invoking Because, then Will stops & does nought.

31. If Power asks why, then is Power weakness.

32. Also reason is a lie; for there is a factor infinite & unknown; & all their words are skew-wise.

33. Enough of Because! Be he damned for a dog!

34. But ye, O my people, rise up & awake!

35. Let the rituals be rightly performed with joy & beauty!

36. There are rituals of the elements and feasts of the times.

37. A feast for the first night of the Prophet and his Bride!

38. A feast for the three days of the writing of the Book of the Law.

39. A feast for Tahuti and the child of the Prophet – secret, O Prophet!

40. A feast for the Supreme Ritual, and a feast for the Equinox of the Gods.

41. A feast for fire and a feast for water; a feast for life and a greater feast for death!

42. A feast every day in your hearts in the joy of my rapture!

43. A feast every night unto Nu, and the pleasure of uttermost delight!

44. Aye! feast! rejoice! there is no dread hereafter. There is the dissolution, and eternal ecstasy in the kisses of Nu.

45. There is death for the dogs.

46. Dost thou fail? Art thou sorry? Is fear in thine heart?

47. Where I am these are not.

48. Pity not the fallen! I never knew them. I am not for them. I console not: I hate the consoled & the consoler.

49. I am unique & conqueror. I am not of the slaves that perish. Be they damned & dead! Amen. (This is of the 4: there is a fifth who is invisible, & therein am I as a babe in an egg.)

50. Blue am I and gold in the light of my bride: but the red gleam is in my eyes; & my spangles are purple & green.

51. Purple beyond purple: it is the light higher than eyesight.

52. There is a veil: that veil is black. It is the veil of the modest woman; it is the veil of sorrow, & the pall of death: this is none of me. Tear down that lying spectre of the centuries: veil not your vices in virtuous words: these vices are my service; ye do well, & I will reward you here and hereafter.

53. Fear not, O prophet, when these words are said, thou shalt not be sorry. Thou art emphatically my chosen; and blessed are the eyes that thou shalt look upon with gladness. But I will hide thee in a mask of sorrow: they that see thee shall fear thou art fallen: but I lift thee up.

54. Nor shall they who cry aloud their folly that thou meanest nought avail; thou shall reveal it: thou availest: they are the slaves of because: They are not of me. The stops as thou wilt; the letters? Change them not in style or value!

55. Thou shalt obtain the order & value of the English Alphabet; thou shalt find new symbols to attribute them unto.

56. Begone! ye mockers; even though ye laugh in my honour ye shall laugh not long: then when ye are sad know that I have forsaken you.

57. He that is righteous shall be righteous still; he that is filthy shall be filthy still.

58. Yea! deem not of change: ye shall be as ye are, & not other. Therefore the kings of the earth shall be Kings for ever: the slaves shall serve. There is none that shall be cast down or lifted up: all is ever as it was. Yet there are masked ones my servants: it may be that yonder beggar is a King. A King may choose his garment as he will: there is no certain test: but a beggar cannot hide his poverty.

59. Beware therefore! Love all, lest perchance is a King concealed! Say you so? Fool! If he be a King, thou canst not hurt him.

60. Therefore strike hard & low, and to hell with them, master!

61. There is a light before thine eyes, O prophet, a light undesired, most desirable.

62. I am uplifted in thine heart; and the kisses of the stars rain hard upon thy body.

63. Thou art exhaust in the voluptuous fullness of the inspiration; the expiration is sweeter than death, more rapid and laughterful than a caress of Hell's own worm.

64. Oh! thou art overcome: we are upon thee; our delight is all over thee: hail! hail: prophet of Nu! prophet of Had! prophet of Ra-Hoor-Khu! Now rejoice! now come in our splendour & rapture! Come in our passionate peace, & write sweet words for the Kings.

65. I am the Master: thou art the Holy Chosen One.

66. Write, & find ecstasy in writing! Work, & be our bed in working! Thrill with the joy of life & death! Ah! thy death shall be lovely: whoso seeth it shall be glad. Thy death shall be the seal of the promise of our age long love. Come! lift up thine heart & rejoice! We are one; we are none.

67. Hold! Hold! Bear up in thy rapture; fall not in swoon of the excellent kisses!

68. Harder! Hold up thyself! Lift thine head! breathe not so deep – die!

69. Ah! Ah! What do I feel? Is the word exhausted?

70. There is help & hope in other spells. Wisdom says: be strong! Then canst thou bear more joy. Be not animal; refine thy rapture! If thou drink, drink by the eight and ninety rules of art: if thou love, exceed by delicacy; and if thou do aught joyous, let there be subtlety therein!

71. But exceed! exceed!

72. Strive ever to more! and if thou art truly mine – and doubt it not, an if thou art ever joyous! – death is the crown of all.

73. Ah! Ah! Death! Death! thou shalt long for death. Death is forbidden, O man, unto thee.

74. The length of thy longing shall be the strength of its glory. He that lives long & desires death much is ever the King among the Kings.

75. Aye! listen to the numbers & the words:

76. 4 6 3 8 A B K 2 4 A L G M O R 3 Y X 24 89 R P S T O V A L. What meaneth this, O prophet? Thou knowest not; nor shalt thou know ever. There cometh one to follow thee: he shall expound it. But remember, O chose none, to be me; to follow the love of Nu in the star-lit heaven; to look forth upon men, to tell them this glad word.

77. O be thou proud and mighty among men!

78. Lift up thyself! for there is none like unto thee among men or among Gods! Lift up thyself, O my prophet, thy stature shall surpass the stars. They shall worship thy name, foursquare, mystic, wonderful, the number of the man; and the name of thy house 418.

79. The end of the hiding of Hadit; and blessing & worship to the prophet of the lovely Star!

CHAPTER III

1. Abrahadabra; the reward of Ra-Hoor-Khut.

2. There is division hither homeward; there is a word not known. Spelling is defunct; all is not aught. Beware! Hold! Raise the spell of Ra-Hoor-Khuit!

3. Now let it be first understood that I am a god of War and of Vengeance. I shall deal hardly with them.

4. Choose ye an island!

5. Fortify it!

6. Dung it about with enginery of war!

7. I will give you a war-engine.

8. With it ye shall smite the peoples; and none shall stand before you.

9. Lurk! Withdraw! Upon them! this is the Law of the Battle of Conquest: thus shall my worship be about my secret house.

10. Get the stele of revealing itself; set it in thy secret temple – and that temple is already aright disposed – & it shall be your Kiblah for ever. It shall not fade, but miraculous colour shall come back to it day after day. Close it in locked glass for a proof to the world.

11. This shall be your only proof. I forbid argument. Conquer! That is enough. I will make easy to you the abstruction from the ill-ordered house in the Victorious City. Thou shalt thyself convey it with worship, O prophet, though thou likest it not. Thou shalt have danger & trouble. Ra-Hoor-Khu is with thee. Worship me with fire & blood; worship me with swords & with spears. Let the woman be girt with a sword before me: let blood flow to my name. Trample down the Heathen; be upon them, O warrior, I will give you of their flesh to eat!

12. Sacrifice cattle, little and big: after a child.

13. But not now.

14. Ye shall see that hour, O blessed Beast, and thou the Scarlet Concubine of his desire!

15. Ye shall be sad thereof.

16. Deem not too eagerly to catch the promises; fear not to undergo the curses. Ye, even ye, know not this meaning all.

17. Fear not at all; fear neither men nor Fates, nor gods, nor anything. Money fear not, nor laughter of the folk folly, nor any other power in heaven or upon the earth or under the earth. Nu is your refuge as Hadit your light; and I am the strength, force, vigour, of your arms.

18. Mercy let be off; damn them who pity! Kill and torture; spare not; be upon them!

19. That stele they shall call the Abomination of Desolation; count well its name, & it shall be to you as 718.

20. Why? Because of the fall of Because, that he is not there again.

21. Set up my image in the East: thou shalt buy thee an image which I will show thee, especial, not unlike the one thou knowest. And it shall be suddenly easy for thee to do this.

22. The other images group around me to support me: let all be worshipped, for they shall cluster to exalt me. I am the visible object of worship; the others are secret; for the Beast & his Bride are they: and for the winners of the Ordeal x. What is this? Thou shalt know.

23. For perfume mix meal & honey & thick leavings of red wine: then oil of Abramelin and olive oil, and afterward soften & smooth down with rich fresh blood.

24. The best blood is of the moon, monthly: then the fresh blood of a child, or dropping from the host of heaven: then of enemies; then of the priest or of the worshippers: last of some beast, no matter what.

25. This burn: of this make cakes & eat unto me. This hath also another use; let it be laid before me, and kept thick with perfumes of your orison: it shall become full of beetles as it were and creeping things sacred unto me.

26. These slay, naming your enemies; & they shall fall before you.

27. Also these shall breed lust & power of lust in you at the eating thereof.

28. Also ye shall be strong in war.

29. Moreover, be they long kept, it is better; for they swell with my force. All before me.

30. My altar is of open brass work: burn thereon in silver or gold!

31. There cometh a rich man from the West who shall pour his gold upon thee.

32. From gold forge steel!

33. Be ready to fly or to smite!

34. But your holy place shall be untouched throughout the centuries: though with fire and sword it be burnt down & shattered, yet an invisible house there standeth, and shall stand until the fall of the Great Equinox; when Hrumachis shall arise and the double-wanded one assume my throne and place. Another prophet shall arise, and bring fresh fever from the skies; another woman shall awake the lust & worship of the Snake; another soul of God and beast shall mingle in the globed priest; another sacrifice shall stain the tomb; another king shall reign; and blessing no longer be poured To the Hawk-headed mystical Lord!

35. The half of the word of Heru-ra-ha, called Hoor-pa-kraat and Ra-Hoor-Khut.

36. Then said the prophet unto the God:

37. I adore thee in the song –

    I am the Lord of Thebes, and I
    The inspired forth-speaker of Mentu;
    For me unveils the veiled sky,

The self-slain Ankh-af-na-khonsu
Whose words are truth. I invoke, I greet
Thy presence, O Ra-Hoor-Khuit!

Unity uttermost showed!
I adore the might of Thy breath,
Supreme and terrible God,
Who makest the gods and death
To tremble before Thee:–
I, I adore thee!

Appear on the throne of Ra!
Open the ways of the Khu!
Lighten the ways of the Ka!
The ways of the Khabs run through
To stir me or still me!
Aum! let it fill me!

38. So that thy light is in me; & its red flame is as a sword in my hand to push thy order. There is a secret door that I shall make to establish thy way in all the quarters, (these are the adorations, as thou hast written), as it is said:

The light is mine; its rays consume
Me: I have made a secret door
Into the House of Ra and Turn,
Of Khephra and of Ahathoor.
I am thy Theban, O Mentu,
The prophet Ankh-af-na-khonsu!

By Bes-na-Maut my breast I beat;
By wise Ta-Nech I weave my spell.
Show thy star-splendour, O Nuit!
Bid me within thine House to dwell,
O winged snake of light, Hadit!
Abide with me, Ra-Hoor-Khuit!

39. All this and a book to say how thou didst come hither and a reproduction of this ink and paper for ever – for in it is the word secret & not only in the English – and thy comment upon this *Book of the Law* shall be printed beautifully in red ink and black upon beautiful paper made by hand; and to each man and woman that thou meetest, were it but to dine or to drink at

them, it is the Law to give. Then they shall chance to abide in this bliss or no; it is no odds. Do this quickly!

40. But the work of the comment? That is easy; and Hadit burning in thy heart shall make swift and secure thy pen.

41. Establish at thy Kaaba a clerk-house: all must be done well and with business way.

42. The ordeals thou shalt oversee thyself, save only the blind ones. Refuse none, but thou shalt know & destroy the traitors. I am Ra-Hoor-Khuit; and I am powerful to protect my servant. Success is thy proof: argue not; convert not; talk not over much! Them that seek to entrap thee, to overthrow thee, them attack without pity or quarter; & destroy them utterly. Swift as a trodden serpent turn and strike! Be thou yet deadlier than he! Drag down their souls to awful torment: laugh at their fear: spit upon them!

43. Let the Scarlet Woman beware! If pity and compassion and tenderness visit her heart; if she leave my work to toy with old sweetnesses; then shall my vengeance be known. I will slay me her child: I will alienate her heart: I will cast her out from men: as a shrinking and despised harlot shall she crawl through dusk wet streets, and die cold and an-hungered.

44. But let her raise herself in pride! Let her follow me in my way! Let her work the work of wickedness! Let her kill her heart! Let her be loud and adulterous! Let her be covered with jewels, and rich garments, and let her be shameless before all men!

45. Then will I lift her to pinnacles of power: then will I breed from her a child mightier than all the kings of the earth. I will fill her with joy: with my force shall she see & strike at the worship of Nu: she shall achieve Hadit.

46. I am the warrior Lord of the Forties: the Eighties cower before me, & are abased. I will bring you to victory & joy: I will be at your arms in battle & ye shall delight to slay. Success is your proof; courage is your armour; go on, go on, in my strength; & ye shall turn not back for any!

47. This book shall be translated into all tongues: but always with the original in the writing of the Beast; for in the chance shape of the letters and their position to one another: in these are mysteries that no Beast shall divine. Let him not seek to try: but one cometh after him, whence I say not, who shall discover the Key of it all. Then this line drawn is a key: then this circle squared in its failure is a key also. And Abrahadabra. It shall be his child & that strangely. Let him not seek after this; for thereby alone can he fall from it.

48. Now this mystery of the letters is done, and I want to go on to the holier place.

49. I am in a secret fourfold word, the blasphemy against all gods of men.

50. Curse them! Curse them! Curse them!

51. With my Hawk's head I peck at the eyes of Jesus as he hangs upon the cross.

52. I flap my wings in the face of Mohammed & blind him.

53. With my claws I tear out the flesh of the Indian and the Buddhist, Mongol and Din.

54. Bahlasti! Ompehda! I spit on your crapulous creeds.

55. Let Mary inviolate be torn upon wheels: for her sake let all chaste women be utterly despised among you!

56. Also for beauty's sake and love's!

57. Despise also all cowards; professional soldiers who dare not fight, but play; all fools despise!

58. But the keen and the proud, the royal and the lofty; ye are brothers!

59. As brothers fight ye!

60. There is no law beyond Do what thou wilt.

61. There is an end of the word of the God enthroned in Ra's seat, lightening the girders of the soul.

62. To Me do ye reverence! to me come ye through tribulation of ordeal, which is bliss.

63. The fool readeth this Book of the Law, and its comment; & he understandeth it not.

64. Let him come through the first ordeal, & it will be to him as silver.

65. Through the second, gold.

66. Through the third, stones of precious water.

67. Through the fourth, ultimate sparks of the intimate fire.

68. Yet to all it shall seem beautiful. Its enemies who say not so, are mere liars.

69. There is success.

70. I am the Hawk-Headed Lord of Silence & of Strength; my nemyss shrouds the night-blue sky.

71. Hail! ye twin warriors about the pillars of the world! for your time is nigh at hand.

72. I am the Lord of the Double Wand of Power; the wand of the Force of Coph Nia – but my left hand is empty, for I have crushed an Universe; & nought remains.

73. Paste the sheets from right to left and from top to bottom: then behold!

74. There is a splendour in my name hidden and glorious, as the sun of midnight is ever the son.

75. The ending of the words is the Word Abrahadabra.

The Book of the Law is
Written and Concealed.
Aum. Ha.

THE BOOK OF THE LAW

THE COMMENT.

Do what thou wilt shall be the whole of the Law.

The study of this Book is forbidden. It is wise to destroy this copy after the first reading.
Whosoever disregards this does so at his own risk and peril. These are most dire.
Those who discuss the contents of this Book are to be shunned by all, as centres of pestilence.
All questions of the Law are to be decided only by appeal to my writings, each for himself.
There is no law beyond Do what thou wilt.

Love is the law, love under will.
The priest of the princes,
Ankh-f-n-khonsu

FURTHER READING

BOOKS BY ALEISTER CROWLEY

Novels:
The Diary of a Drug Fiend (1922)
Moonchild (1929)

Poetry:
White Stains (1898)
Songs of the Spirit (1898)
The Sword of Song (1904)
Oracles: The Biography of an Art (1905)
The Winged Beetle (1910)
Konx om Pax: Essays in Light (1907): A collection containing both essays and poetry.

Magical works:
The Book of the Law or *Liber AL vel Legis* (1904)
The Vision and the Voice (1909)
The Book of Thoth (1944)
777 and Other Qabalistic Writings (1909)
Magick in Theory and Practice (1929)
The Holy Books of Thelema: originally published in various years, starting from the early 1900s.
The Confessions of Aleister Crowley (1929)

FURTHER READING

BOOKS BY OTHER AUTHORS

Aleister Crowley and Western Esotericism edited by Henrik Bogdan and Martin P. Starr (Oxford University Press, 2012)

Aleister Crowley: The Beast in Berlin: Art, Sex, and Magick in the Weimar Republic by Tobias Churton (Inner Traditions, 2014)

Understanding Aleister Crowley's Thoth Tarot by Lon Milo DuQuette (Red Wheel/Weiser, 2003)

Perdurabo: The Life of Aleister Crowley by Richard Kaczynski (North Atlantic Books, 2010)

The Weiser Concise Guide to Aleister Crowley by Richard Kaczynski and James Wasserman (Weiser Books, 2009)

The Magical World of Aleister Crowley by Francis King (Foulsham, 1977)

Aleister Crowley: Magick, Rock and Roll, and the Wickedest Man in the World by Gary Lachman (TarcherPerigee, 2014)

Aleister Crowley: Thelemic Magick by Mogg Morgan (Mandrake, 2022)

Do What Thou Wilt: A Life of Aleister Crowley by Lawrence Sutin (St. Martin's Griffin, 2002)